Political Attitudes in Venezuela

T0367220

The Texas Pan American Series

Political Attitudes in Venezuela
Societal Cleavages and Political Opinion

Enrique A. Baloyra and John D. Martz

University of Texas Press, Austin

The Texas Pan American Series is published with
the assistance of a revolving publication fund established
by the Pan American Sulphur Company.

Library of Congress Cataloging in Publication Data
Baloyra, Enrique A   1942–
    Political attitudes in Venezuela.
    (The Texas Pan American series)
    Includes index.
    1. Public opinion—Venezuela.   2. Venezuela—Social conditions.
I. Martz, John D., joint author.   II. Title.
HN370.Z9P82   301.15′43′309187   78–14241
ISBN: 978-0-292-73980-2

Copyright © 1979 by the University of Texas Press

Printed in the United States of America

"If I have learned anything from Latin America it is the following: that unreason is inefficacious; that, by and large, American behavioral science is inefficacious; and that tyranny and dictatorship are inefficient and inefficacious. . . ."

Kalman Silvert, "Coming Home" (1976)

We dedicate this book to
his memory.

Contents

Illustrations

Preface

It has been five years since we went to Venezuela in the fall of 1973 to collect data for this study. Our effort involved simultaneous gathering of two types of information: campaign-activity data to fill a rather large empirical and theoretical gap in the discipline and public opinion data in order to formulate a preliminary statement about the relationship between major societal cleavages and political opinion and behavior. This book concerns the latter, and constitutes what we believe to be an important first step toward the clarification of other analytical problems which were in dire need of preliminary spadework.

Our association with DATOS, C.A. of Venezuela proved to be pleasant, harmonious, and fruitful. We owe a large debt of gratitude to Andrew Templeton's foresight and personal trust, given the difficult circumstances in which he had to meet our desire to conduct a major national study during a general election. His ability to understand the nature of our research and transmit it to his associates as well as the dedication of the latter have played no small part in bringing our study to a successful conclusion. Nelson Villasmil provided a screen through which we filtered our instrument, benefiting from his opportune suggestions and criticism concerning all aspects of the questionnaire. Domingo Acevedo's familiarity with Venezuelan communities, long professional experience with DATOS, and enormous patience produced an excellent sample. Ivar Stabilito, Pedro Rodríguez, and José Vicente Alemán saw to it that we obtained the best possible field results while the interviews were being conducted, and their sustained effort resulted in an unusually high rate of supervised interviews.

Juan del Aguila and Carlos Suárez made it possible for us to have a preliminary version of the data file inputted by early January of 1974, having completed coding of the 1,521 interviews one week after the last batch arrived in Chapel Hill in December of 1973. Thus we had an operational file of our data less than sixty days after the last interview was completed. Once we were "in the system," Bill Reynolds, Kenneth Hardy, Karl Hoffman, and Peter Galderisi of the Institute for Research in Social Science generously offered their expertise and talents, answering those questions and problems that always arise after hours and require both empathy and intellectual ability. They did not serve us the usual pap of cotton-dry programmer's jargon but tried to understand the substantive implications of utilizing one procedure or another, of making one decision or another. George Rabinowitz added his own efforts whenever they were requested and maintained our lifeline of departmental computer funds, no matter how often we went back to ask for more. We are grateful to our department for this support. We owe a very large debt to Ms. Marie Clegg of the Department of Political Science, for her retyping of chapters four, five, and seven of the second version of this manuscript, especially since this was done during Christmas of 1976. Vonda Hogan and Bonita Samuels were responsible for typing the third. Rowena Morrison incorporated the last set of corrections to the text. We are very grateful to them.

In Venezuela we benefited from the comments and criticism by Pedro Pablo Yánez and Alejandro Grajal of the Centro de Estudios del Futuro, and by Gene Bigler and José Antonio Gil of the Instituto de Estudios Superiores de Administración. In Chapel Hill the comments and criticism of Federico Gil, George Rabinowitz, Dave Kovenock, Angell Beza, Jim Prothro, Frank Munger, Alan Stern, Paul Kress, Jeff Obler, Henry Landsberger, and Martin Zechman helped us understand the nature of what we were trying to do. Max Castro, Rose Spalding, and Juan del Aguila also contributed their valuable criticism. We owe a large debt of gratitude to Barbara Burnham, Social Science Editor at the University of Texas Press, for her patience and dedication in seeing our manuscript through. We are also indebted to Kathy Lewis and Holly Carver, of Texas Press, for their invaluable editorial assistance.

We have collected and analyzed our data during a period of considerable change in domestic and world politics—during a stage in which many old assumptions of a political and intellectual nature are being challenged and reevaluated. We mention some of these issues as they affect the study of Latin American politics in chapter 1, as well as in other relevant passages later. It was not our intention to use any of these as a moral shield or theoretical justification for going to a foreign country to collect data about its citizens' ideas on a range of sensitive issues. At least from the standpoint of questionnaire construction, we departed from what could be construed— perhaps unfairly and simplistically—as a "behavioralist perspective." However, we have carefully refrained from interpreting our results in a manner that leaves no room for alternative conceptualizations that may not dwell within the camp of positivistic social science. Even though we are utilizing the instruments and artifacts of survey research, the most idoneous and appropriate technique required to obtain the type of data that we wanted, we are not wedded to any particular school of thought concerning the multitude of issues covered by the data.

In appendix A, we devote considerable space to establishing some "basic credibility" concerning the design and execution of our study. Since we have findings that will challenge some current assumptions about contemporary Venezuelan politics, it is important that our techniques be discussed in such detailed fashion. Latin Americanists have shown considerable skepticism toward any study of opinion conducted in the region which cannot vouch for itself in terms of authenticity and accuracy; we hope to shut the door on such skepticism, as well as on the possibility of interpreting some of our findings in terms of sampling inadequacies.

In a general sense, we show that most Venezuelans think of themselves as middle class, that a plurality are on the right, and that they are very critical of the government and strongly anticommunist and very much wedded to developmentalist policies. On the other hand, we also point out that most Venezuelans believe in the legitimacy of political opposition, in the need for party competition, and that they oppose coups. These, we emphasize, are some dimensions of Venezuelan public opinion and are not the result of sampling error. Then there are the usual findings that most studies of public opinion produce: large segments of the public are incapable and inefficacious; they are concerned with "pedestrian issues" such as inflation and unemployment; and almost half of them would not vote if not required by law to do so. We have devoted little time to trying to figure out if the percentages behind these modal opinions are "too little" or "too much." Neither have we organized the book in this fashion; that is, we have not followed an approach centering on areas of opinion.

Instead, we have chosen to select a series of substantive aspects for discussion and refer these to the more obvious ways in which Venezuelans group themselves politically. We believe that this approach offers a comprehensive and comprehensible perspective which others may utilize to improve their understanding of Venezuelan politics. It also provides an initial set of generalizations and inferences that may be checked and verified in future research. One of the basic problems which we confronted was the fact that there was no general statement describing the major cleavages of Venezuelan political opinion and behavior. To be sure, much has been said and written about the dominance of the political parties, the changes brought about by social change, and the role of regionalism and religion. But there was very little hard evidence available to substantiate these. We hope that the present volume has remedied this situation. We will not take refuge behind Philip Converse's observation concerning the greater reliability of the inferences produced by survey data to claim that our findings are better, but his point is nonetheless important to bear in mind. Up to the publication of this study, knowledge about Venezuelan politics has come by way of personal observation or works based on ecological data; as our findings will show, there are some important discrepancies between those and our own conclusions.

The need for this preliminary work is perhaps best dramatized in chapter 2, where we try to explore the meaning of class images and social stratification in Venezuela. Then in chapter 3 we put these classes and strata under the light of some extant propositions concerning social and political inequality. In chapter 4 we attempt to assess the relative importance of regionalism, a factor which is unfailingly identified as one of the more important influences in Venezuelan politics, comparing it with urbanization and trying to determine the interaction between the two. Religion is also examined as another cultural factor with community linkages. Chapter 5 is something of a methodological extravaganza, with its extended discussion of the procedures utilized to arrive at our typology of individual ideology; we find this element to be considerably more important than has been believed by some students of Venezuelan society, as was the case with social class and social stratification. It is in these cases that our knowledge about Venezuelan elites, institutional groups, and parties must be complemented and refined with the perspectives taken from the "lower floor" level of the electorate. Otherwise we run the risk of ascribing attributes to the general population which only characterize those individuals who are more likely to be the contact points between foreign scholars and the Venezuelan community. We are aware that mass-elite differences are a matter of old wine in old bottles and do not reemphasize this in our discussion. Once again, however, we warn those familiar with Venezuela to remember this very basic fact.

Chapter 6 takes us to old and familiar territory: the question of partisanship. We try to improve on some of the more customary measures of partisanship utilized in the context of North American social science by producing more stringent operational measures of this phenomenon. We also introduce the notion of "political self-image" which, in our view, has not been utilized before and offers attractive possibilities of a theoretical and empirical nature for future research. Chapter 7 is an attempt to recast and summarize our discussion, pointing to the more striking aspects of the evidence and trying to assess the relative importance of the different cleavages discussed.

A word is in order about what we did not do in the book—about the unfinished related agenda that would have to include participation, electoral and campaign behavior, evaluation of the democratic regime, and a series of substantive issues which it is possible to explore from the perspective of our data. We have already addressed some of these topics elsewhere, while others will be examined very shortly and may see the light of day before this manuscript is published. Given the wealth of our data, we chose to proceed first with the more fundamental steps. With that perspective, we would hope to be evaluated on how well we did what has been undertaken in these pages, rather than by what someone else might have done.

Finally, we want to acknowledge the support of the National Science Foundation, which made this project possible through two generous grants (GS-38050 and SOC 75-17518-AOF), and to thank the panel of evaluators who recommended that our project be funded. We hope that this fulfills, at least in a modest way, their expectations.

Enrique A. Baloyra, Chapel Hill, North Carolina
John D. Martz, University Park, Pennsylvania
September 1978

1

Political Attitudes in Venezuela:
Problems and Prospects

Introduction

Current trends in the study of Latin American politics share a number of common features. One is the rejection of any single analytical formulation that departs from the very narrow concern represented by a central focus on the success or failure of a particular type of political regime in this or in any other area of the world. Another is the rejection of the leading premises of orthodox development theory, as these have been applied to the Latin American case. Since this study deals with Venezuela, a country that presently combines democratic reformism with dependent capitalism, it is imperative to preface our discussion with a brief examination of such recent disciplinary developments so that our avowed goals and objectives may be more appropriately evaluated. Our central concern is with Venezuela, a dependent, capitalist democracy. Research focus was placed on the reaction of the public to contemporary political institutions, which are democratic.

The Emphasis on Dependence

One of the outstanding features of recent research and writing about Latin America has been the increasing emphasis on the issue of dependence, accompanied by utilization of political economy as a major analytic framework. A broad spectrum of scholarly opinion is included, running from the pragmatism of a Celso Furtado to the advocacy position of an André Gunder Frank. As such, the dependency thesis is by no means the exclusive preserve of "critical Marxism," although as theory it is more congruent with the latter than with "sociologism."[1] We believe that this new orientation blends with a broad range of ideological postures and disciplinary preferences to suggest that contemporary scholars of different persuasions may utilize the theory of dependence as a guiding theoretical framework. Moreover, the emphasis on dependence has helped to clarify the evident difficulty of Latin America following the capitalist model of democratic political development.

The dependency thesis has shed light on the trajectory of the political economy of Latin America and its gradual transition from Iberian imperialism to Anglo-American dominance.[2] According to most authors, economic dependence is characterized by unfavorable terms of trade, increasing foreign indebtedness, and denationalization of capital.[3] Efforts to elaborate a similar framework of the political aspects of these phenomena have been less successful.[4] In short, the dependency thesis has established itself as one of the leading approaches, and has also helped to clarify the nature of capitalist development in Latin America.[5]

Venezuela's is a dependent capitalist economy, but successive reformist regimes have increased governmental control of the oil industry, offering an interesting example of democratic reformism committed to the reduction of dependence. Venezuelan society offers the full gamut of incongruent modules of development, from affluent consumerism to abject poverty. Following the nationalization of major multinational firms, the Venezuelan state has increased its ability to manipulate social and economic change. It therefore becomes extremely interesting to monitor the developmental policies and strategies pursued by these reformist regimes in trying to make Venezuela a nation in the social sense.

Venezuela is admittedly atypical, capable of making significant and critical choices among extant strategies of economic growth and political institutionalization. This cannot be said of many Latin American countries; but of greater interest and significance is the eventual outcome which the Venezuelan case may offer us in the near future. That is to say, Venezuela can choose among alternative developmental strategies; this implies that the country's political economy affords the opportunity for almost any kind of regime to consolidate itself. Authoritarian alternatives may be rejected and the present democratic regime may become firmly institutionalized, but the important point is that Venezuela can afford the type of regime most congruent with its political preferences and values.

Most Venezuelans expect a very active state to promote growth and redistribution. Recording their reactions to the performance of the regime, delimiting the contours of the political cleavages created by the ongoing changes, measuring popular expectations about the nature of such changes, and composing the political profiles of contemporary Venezuelans constitutes a research agenda of considerable intellectual and political relevance. One may anticipate a series of results congruent with knowledge of the Venezuelan polity and society, but must necessarily approach this agenda in an open-ended fashion, guided by the conviction that the sociohistorical and economic processes forging that polity and society are significantly different from those experienced by North American and Western European societies.

A Search for Roots

The socioeconomic emphasis of the dependency thesis, with its focus on external sources of constraint, contrasts markedly with the postulates and assumptions utilized by a second group of scholars who have turned their attention to predominantly internal factors related to cultural, ideological, and psychological predispositions of the Latin Americans. With the reformist model on the wane, a number of scholars have been trying to fill the theoretical vacuum with a series of models based on the "true" heritage of Latin America. It would be inaccurate to force these scholars into a single category, but all have engaged in a reductionism derived from cultural considerations. Compared to the theorists of dependence they seem a relatively homogeneous group, but with less definitional precision. A summary of their major assumptions and propositions would include the following:

(1) despite appearances to the contrary, the liberal principle has never been adopted by the Latin Americans; the failure to adopt this principle reflects the fact that the Latin Americans did not reject their Hispanic heritage;[6]

(2) the conservative principles of Thomistic Catholicism provide the moral and legal justification for the political systems of Latin America;[7]

(3) Thomistic Catholicism is more congruent with a monistic, authoritarian, and corporatist type of political regime;[8]

(4) together, the colonial heritage and the Thomistic tradition provided the foundations of a political culture which is incongruent with democratic institutions;[9] and

(5) increasingly, Latin American societies have been reverting to their origins—especially those dominated by conservative military juntas.[10]

It is ironic that the reformist concern about democracy in Latin America previously considered the area deviant because it failed to conform to some developmental model, while today any democratic regime which surfaces in the area must be considered deviant because it is *not* authoritarian, monistic, and corporatist. It is also possible to criticize certain of these arguments by way of contradictory evidence presented by other scholars, whether on grounds of inadequate definitional clarity,[11] inability to specify the institutional continuity presumed by the model,[12] or methodological shortcomings inherent to the techniques utilized by the different authors.[13] But we agree with Dahl that it is not surprising that ". . . because of their concern with rigor and their dissatisfaction with the 'softness' of historical description, generalization, and explanation, most social scientists have turned away from the historical movement of ideas. As a result, their own theories, however 'rigorous' they may be, leave out an important explanatory variable. . . ."[14]

Our criticism stems more from those factors that might make the Venezuelan case congruent with the arguments of the cultural revisionists. After all, it is difficult to envision a country where the prospects for a democratic regime would seem slighter in terms of heritage and political tradition. Indeed, Venezuela boasts a record of nineteenth-century caudillism that is second to none in Latin America. The interesting question, however, is not why democracy failed at that time, but rather, how Venezuelans were able to organize any kind of political regime whatever in the midst of such unbridled turmoil. We leave this issue to the historians but, where contemporary societies are concerned, find ourselves frankly appalled by the paucity of survey findings concerning the political beliefs, values, attitudes, and orientations of Latin Americans. Recognizing the uses and limitations of survey research, one cannot but castigate those who continue to produce works about Latin American "political culture" without the merest shred of empirical evidence.[15] Admittedly, survey research is not feasible for many contemporary Latin American societies. Nonetheless, one of the most powerful statements about the quality of knowledge concerning Latin American political culture is the sheer fact that few are in a position to proffer any definitive statements. Levine states the situation in precise terms: "The study of culture, in Latin America as elsewhere, is burdened with a series of unexamined premises and assumptions. These intellectual predispositions have important consequences for the range of phenomena understood by the term 'culture,' the perceived relation between cultural patterns, social class, and institutional organization, and for the methods deemed appropriate for cultural analysis. . . ."[16]

Rather than placing heavy reliance on the concept of political culture, we prefer more measurable concepts such as attitudes, values, beliefs, orientations, and opinions. Two important if unrelated grounds dictated our choice. First, we were unable to imitate the procedure utilized by Donald J. Devine in his analysis of American political culture.[17] Given the absence of longitudinal data, inferences could not be drawn about political culture; although the results of a study conducted over a decade ago in Venezuela were available, its design and sampling techniques were not directly comparable to ours.[18] Reference will be made to its findings throughout our discussion, but without overgeneralizations. Second, we have been persuaded by the admonition of a fervent advocate of political culture who complained recently that the concept was in need of less vulgarization and more refinement.[19]

In summary we are dealing with several paradoxes: a democratic regime where history suggests authoritarianism, participatory politics in a country without full citizenship, and the ability to make choices resulting from a protracted struggle to control the most successful cartel in this century after reason and prudence indicated a more moderate approach. Thus, can one really say that a society becomes democratic in spite of itself? Can such a formulation receive any theoretical or practical credibility? Our data cannot answer all of these, but they point the argument in the direction of a more appropriate set of questions.

Analytic Perspectives

The nature of our evidence requires additional consideration of issues that have received limited attention in the literature of Latin American politics. These do not merely involve the usual questions of validity and reliability, which are discussed in considerable detail in appendix A, but also a host of theoretical and analytical issues which complicate some of the more familiar problems of cross-cultural opinion research. Our comments here are directed primarily to those especially familiar with the literature of public opinion and voting behavior in the United States. These readers will note the substantial reliance on measures of political attitudes and political behavior evolved through three decades of survey research in the United States.[20] This stems from a desire to increase the comparability of our data and from the decision to confront the related issues of validity and reliability by departing from a core of thoroughly utilized items that could be adapted to the Venezuelan context through a series of modified versions of our measuring instrument. These readers will nonetheless find ours a limited application of the conceptual paradigms which have inspired these measurements. They will also notice that our main concern is less with the verification of such paradigms in the Venezuelan context than with a maximal effort to illuminate the dynamics of political opinion in Venezuela.

Several reasons underlie this decision. First, contextual differences irreducible to cross-cultural variation present problems of theory construction that must be entertained with considerable care. While an extensive bibliographic search of the literature of public opinion reveals a series of interesting propositions and relevant analytical indicators, *the nature of the Venezuelan political context has been the most relevant criterion utilized* in selecting the topics to be discussed and the hypotheses to be tested in this volume.

Consider the question of political participation. Verba and Nie's seminal study of political participation in the United States begins by pondering

> . . . why the participant population (of the United States) comes disproportionately from the upper-status groups of society. We will do this by proposing and testing a simple model of the process by which citizens come to participate—a model we call our *standard socioeconomic* model of participation. According to this model, the social status of an individual . . . determines to a large extent how much he participates. It does this through the intervening effects of a variety of "civic attitudes" conducive to participation: attitudes such as a sense of efficacy, of psychological involvement in politics, and a feeling of obligation to participate. . . .[21]

In Venezuela, neither this nor any other model adequately explains voting participation, because popular compliance with a system of compulsory suffrage is such that practically everyone votes. One therefore does not find many significant differences between the participation rates of major population groups such as socioeconomic classes or political generations. In addition, these high rates of voting participation coexist with markedly high levels of support for the institution of elections *and* very low levels of political efficacy.[22] What does one make of the standard socioeconomic model in such a context?

We do not imply that Verba and Nie are simplistic or that their contribution bears limited value for comparative research. They perceived their model as merely a "base line" from which to look for deviations due to position in the life cycle, race, party affiliation, the nature of the community of residence, and political beliefs.[23] Furthermore, their study has provided considerable theoretical inspiration in our testing other aspects of participation in Venezuela.[24] Where they emphasize class we have stressed the tremendous importance of parties in Venezuela; the question of race was not pertinent, and we devoted greater attention to the community dimension.

However, the Venezuelan version of the standard socioeconomic model cannot be our central analytical focus, for other issues must first be resolved. These stem primarily from the existing state of the art of public opinion research in Venezuela. Lack of extensive previous empirical evidence prevents us from exploring a series of suggestive and relevant hypotheses in this book. In short, we do not have the benefit of a wealth of evidence produced by decades of survey work in Venezuela, which would allow us to concentrate on very specific aspects of opinion formation. There are no reliable or commonly accepted benchmarks which might be acknowledged in efforts to verify the conclusions of previous research. Notwithstanding a number of sophisticated analyses of Venezuelan politics, there is nothing comparable to, say, *The American Voter*.[25]

It would be presumptuous to claim that ours is such a study. But our situation is, nevertheless, similar to that confronting Campbell and his associates when they set out to examine the reaction of the American public to the presidential campaign of 1956. We therefore feel an obligation to lay a foundation, *to provide a framework of evidence concerning the most relevant aspects of the political attitudes and political behavior of the Venezuelan public*. This will not prohibit the testing of hypotheses, but gives our analytical effort the character of a preliminary inquiry. For example, in chapter 3, we incorporate some of the concerns implicit in Verba and Nie's orientation, but discussion of their model is presented within the context of the relationship between class and politics in Venezuela.

In fulfilling our agenda and seeking a base line from which to construct our analysis and develop theoretical coherence, we pose a very broad and general question. Basically, our respondents were urged to think about "what are you in Venezuelan politics?" This was approached from several different perspectives, including the socioeconomic, ideological, cultural, and partisan. These are by no means the only filters through which people perceive politics in Venezuela, nor the only factors relevant to the process of politicization. But they respond to universal concerns of political inquiry and practical politics. Classes, ideologies, and parties are basic concerns of political sociology and provide a convenient point of departure.

We approach the analysis of these different base lines by examining their importance and relationship to one another. Lacking comparable data for most of Latin America, our initial expectations were relatively bland and amorphous, shaped to some extent by findings concerning the mass publics of contemporary democratic societies. Thus far, the accumulation of such evidence has resulted in a profile of the "average" or "typical" citizen or member of the public which puts in doubt the relevance of ideological referents,[26] the internal consistency of the attitudes held by the public,[27] and commitment to the formal requirements of a democracy.[28] We have neither the desire nor necessity to enter the thicket of ongoing controversies concerning stability and change in the American electorate,[29] the question of "voter rationality,"[30] or the salience of ideological sources of opinion constraint.[31] These issues are mentioned only when relevant in the Venezuelan context. However, our reaction to the substantive implications of these findings and skepticism concerning their universality constitute another justification for conducting our analysis of Venezuelan opinion in a fashion some might find unorthodox.

Differences in context are less relevant in this connection than our reaction to thoughtful criticism of the vision of the "average person" provided by contemporary social science. Obviously, we could argue that if North Americans can take their democracy for granted, many Venezuelans still recall how it was when their country was not democratic—some may shudder while others are nostalgic. Most can readily compare their condition to that of their brethren living under bureaucratic authoritarianism. They may have greater reason for worry and therefore become more ideological or coherent. However, our greatest concern is not with obvious differences in context, but with the political implications of an uncritical utilization of the profile of the average person produced by contemporary social science.

This preoccupation has been stated cogently by the Mexican sociologist Pablo González Casanova:

> The loss of a moral sense in the social sciences in relation to the given social system takes them closer to the natural sciences in style and to a politically conservative position with relation to society. Thus the struggle between two styles in sociology, quantitative and qualitative, has a political root and is never based on propositions that are purely scientific . . . the sciences of man cannot avoid being political sciences no matter how closely they approach the sciences of nature in the quantitative manipulation of social facts. . . .[32]

Although rejecting the contention that quantitative analysis has inherent conservative biases, we are most wary of the broken image of the ordinary citizen often produced by such analysis. We feel uncomfortable with conclusions concerning the political behavior of "marginals" which rely too heavily on cultural reductionism. Neither are we satisfied with explanations of "low levels of political efficacy" or "high levels of cynicism" of average citizens on the bases of inadequate levels of political information, limited education, or lack of civic attitudes. These explanations permeate much of the literature concerning marginal groups, although they are now being challenged by ongoing research on urban[33] and peasant[34] groups in Latin America.

Our analysis emphasizes the evaluative nature of the interaction between ordinary citizens and political actors, such as bureaucrats, party politicians, and political groups, and treats extant attitudes of the mass public toward the latter as consequences of previous individual or group interactions with them. While psychological and cultural factors also have an impact on processes of attitude formation, we feel that greater emphasis should be directed toward political factors. Therefore, our treatment of trust in government and political efficacy, to mention only two important aspects of opinion, deviates considerably from that found elsewhere in the literature. We do not make assumptions concerning correct responses to questions measuring the political experiences of individuals. If government involves the "authoritative allocation of values," political criticism cannot simply be a matter of misinformation; those who criticize a regime and its institutions deserve more than treatment as deviant cases. Indeed, ". . . every human being is *in possession* of a world of his own, and . . . nobody can interpret this world better (or more 'expertly') than he can himself . . . 'cognitive respect,' means then, that one takes with utmost seriousness the way in which others define reality. It does *not* mean that one makes no moral distinctions among those definitions. . . ."[35]

To be sure, our methodology does violate those insights to a degree, but we have been sensitized by the comments of contemporary critics who lament, ". . . in a world of experts, what becomes of the imaginative energies of ordinary people? Where everything— *everything*—has been staked out as somebody's specialized field of knowledge, what is the thinking of ordinary people worth? Precisely zero. For what do they know about anything that some expert does not know better?"[36] Awareness of the problem may not be enough, but our effort to recover the insight of ordinary Venezuelans from their survey responses is genuine, as our utilization of additional materials concerning their political experiences would suggest. At the same time, we agree with the contention that "What the abbreviated survey approach is admirably suited to assess . . . is the character of the interaction between citizen and government, that is,

9

the functioning of public opinion in the kind of communication system that democratic institutions become in practice, if not necessarily in theory." [37]

An Encapsulated Review

This study, then, concerns the political beliefs, attitudes, and orientations of the mass public in a dependent nation, governed by a reformist democratic regime which has been in power almost twenty years. The presentation of the data and discussion of evidence follow a path suggested by two kinds of guidelines. First, we try to respond to a series of questions that any political scientist should ask about Venezuela if in possession of our data. These include partisanship and its concomitants, the relationship between social class and political attitudes, the special problem of ideology, differences among political generations, and the public's evaluation of the regime. At the same time, we entertain certain questions which have provoked the curiosity of scholars explicitly interested in Venezuela; among these are the attitudes of the Venezuelan public toward military intervention, differences between the loyalists of the AD (Social Democratic) and COPEI (Social Christian) parties, regionalism as a source of attitudinal cleavages, and the extent to which a right-left continuum is discernible in the orientations of the mass public.

An additional aspect of the agenda is to utilize our findings in evaluating some of the assumptions and propositions offered by the cultural revisionists and the dependency theorists. Having selected a case of considerable intellectual and political significance, one which is representative of controversies raging in the literature, we seek to shed light on two additional questions. First, how successful have the Venezuelan reformers been in making converts to the democratic alternative among the mass public? This is an important consideration because, although regime stability is not necessarily dependent on a majority consensus on values that are congruent with the regime, no one has previously considered the degree to which the mass public has internalized democratic values in Latin America. The literature is awash with conjecture, speculation, and impressionistic observations, but concrete evidence has never been provided. Second, given the availability of resources necessary for a society to remove the more undesirable aspects of dependence, what kinds of regimes are most likely to be favored by the mass public? Thus, assuming that an adequate level of resources is available to support any type of regime, which are more likely to emerge, and what may this imply about the political preferences of that society?

These introductory remarks attempt to locate our study within ongoing disciplinary trends. Our fellow Latin Americanists, ever distrustful of survey studies in "their region," should realize that in seizing the opportunity to conduct a national sample survey in one of the few democratic regimes left in the region, we are trying to increase our understanding of the context of political opinion. Those of our colleagues unfamiliar with Latin America and well-versed in survey work may find our treatment unorthodox and our reticence in using their paradigms disappointing. Given the difficulty of satisfying the competing demands of these infrequently matched varieties of scholarship, we hope that our agenda will have some relevance for both, and that our motives and intention now stand explicitly illuminated for the reader.

2

The Social Context
of Political Opinion

Introduction

We do not perceive the liberal and radical traditions as the only ones
relevant for Venezuelan politics, nor as the only two schools with
which a Venezuelanist might affiliate.[1] But certainly they comprise
the two most relevant approaches to the study of Venezuelan politics
at the present time; although one may borrow elements from each,
they constitute mutually exclusive propositions. We do not believe
that a synthesis is possible without sacrificing one set of assumptions to satisfy the other. Neither do we believe that the "truth" lies
somewhere in the middle. However, we do find a similarity of procedure between liberals and radicals in that what one neglects by
default the other adopts as a central concern. The liberal interpretation takes the predominance of parties for granted, does not entertain the concept of classes to any great extent, and tends to treat
dependency-related phenomena as symptoms of underdevelopment.[2] The radical view diminishes the importance of parties, insists
on the ultimate relevance of class conflict, and treats underdevelopment as an inevitable result of *dependencia*.[3]

The Political Role of Classes

Differences between liberal and radical views of Venezuelan politics reflect similar controversies of contemporary social science.
Venezuela is scarcely the only country that presents difficulty in the
analysis of the political role of social classes. In fact, the relationship between class and party has been elusive and difficult to probe
in social science research on Latin America, at least in part as a
result of the frequent collapse of democratic regimes in the area. But
there is a long-standing debate which has divided Latin Americanists on this question, beginning with basic disagreement over the
class structure which prevails in the area,[4] the relationship of the
different classes to the means of production and the state apparatus,[5]
and the more recent queries about whether Latin American societies
are really pluralist or fragmented.[6]

As is the case with European scholarship, the middle classes have come to occupy the central focus of the discussion, receiving the closest scrutiny and attention from liberal scholars.[7] Moreover, one major difference between European and Latin American political sociology is precisely this: the relative clarity with which the linkages between classes and parties have been elucidated in both areas.[8] To say that Latin Americanists are behind their European and North American colleagues in this regard is not to imply that there is a consensus outside Latin America; the obvious differences between Ralf Dahrendorf[9] and Raymond Aron,[10] on the one hand, and Ralph Miliband[11] and Herbert Marcuse,[12] on the other, quickly dissipate such a false impression. There is at least tacit agreement on the importance of the question, however. By contrast, many Latin Americanists have simply given up on this point, abandoning the field to the cultural revisionists.[13] More recently, radical Latin Americanists have turned to a more intense examination of the problems of the working class.[14]

Venezuela is not a postindustrial society, and Latin America's political economy could not be more different from Europe's—thus the uncritical utilization of pluralist theory, developmental theory, or dogmatic Marxism is likely to run counter to the fact that, in Latin America,

> . . . the historical development of dependent capitalism has generated a class structure that is heterogeneous with regard to life styles associated with a certain level of development of the productive forces, but not heterogeneous with respect to the means of control of production. The insistence on seeing these class differences through lenses ground to focus on quite different situations, such as those that exist in the dominant center countries, has induced theorist and practitioner alike to make mistakes with serious political consequences. . . .[15]

The conceptual scaffold erected around the question of class cleavages by political sociologists elsewhere can lend conceptual solidity to our own inquiry. To be sure, classes in Europe have not been warped by *dependencia* and they tend to reflect, to a greater extent than do classes in Latin America, the distribution of control of the means of production. Yet this is no reason to prevent our use of Dahrendorf's extremely thoughtful discussion on how "quasi groups" may be politicized into "conflict groups,"[16] or to preempt a careful utilization of the concept of cleavage as a guide for inquiry into the dynamics of political conflict in Venezuela;[17] neither does it prevent us from following the research agenda utilized in Richard Centers' pioneering if largely forgotten discussion of classes in the United States.[18] Whatever its nature, Venezuelan pluralism is not anchored on an industrial or postindustrial order but, as Ralph Miliband has suggested, the fact that people are not class conscious at all times does not mean that there are no classes.[19] Furthermore, the fact that industrialization was not the main agent for the formation of social classes in Venezuela does not mean an absence of classes there.

Social classes do not seem to constitute important conflict groups in Venezuelan politics at the present time, at least in a classical Marxist sense. As with many other relevant subgroups created by the cleavages of Venezuelan society, however, it is important to examine the political potential of class cleavages in order to understand better the dimensions of political conflict in Venezuela. Analysis of the relationship between socioeconomic cleavages and political attitudes must be undertaken despite the failure to recognize that political parties are not necessarily an epiphenomenon of dependent capitalism and the fact that the inability to provide a clear statement about the relationship between social classes and political parties in Latin America is likely to stay with us for the foreseeable future. The results of our inquiry will not bridge the gap between liberal and radical propositions, but may contribute to their further refinement. We cannot conceive a dialectico-historical miracle which might reconcile the two perspectives, yet believe that the evidence presented here will be relevant for both. Thus, we present the data first "before reaching any conclusion concerning the degree of class consciousness encountered or absent."[20]

Social Class and Social Status

There are three possible ways to measure socioeconomic cleavages. The first examines the manner in which individuals and groups identify themselves with different classes and is a procedure routinely utilized by survey researchers. Butler and Stokes' treatment of the question of class and party in England provides an excellent illustration of the measurement of these "class images."[21] The second employs what sociologists call "socioeconomic status" and customarily involves the overlapping of individual characteristics such as income, education, and occupation which, as a result of their uneven distribution, create inequalities in society. Utilization of this concept may involve causal assumptions about the pattern of temporal relationships between these three characteristics, as posited by Blau and Duncan in their seminal study,[22] or a simultaneous utilization of the three without any explicit assumptions about the hierarchy of causality among them.[23] We began our inquiry following the latter alternative, making no initial assumptions about their relative importance, although we were able to determine which of the three is more relevant in Venezuela. A third and final approach deals with the concept of "class status," which, according to Silva Michelena, is more inclusive than the previous two and involves class identification and socioeconomic status as well as decisional control over the means of production.[24] We measured class status with the index introduced in appendix C, while recognizing that the index deviates from Silva's operational usage somewhat.[25]

We will present and discuss three measures of socioeconomic cleavages, describe their mutual interaction, and determine their overlapping with other societal cleavages. This will provide a fairly comprehensive definition which will permit inferences about the basic points of cleavage separating different Venezuelan socioeconomic groups. At every juncture we will try to assess the costs and benefits behind different classifications and typological alternatives, concentrating our discussion on the more important categories. Then we will turn to the more relevant differences found among the attitudes, orientations, and value preferences that are characteristic of these groups in Venezuela.

Class Identification

We utilized an open-ended question to measure the pattern of class identification, rather than a series of precoded categories into which our respondents had to fit themselves.[26] We asked them, "Today much is said and written about *social classes*—which social classes do you belong to?" The pattern of responses was somewhat surprising. First of all, the number of "middle class" identifiers appeared inordinately large; 57 per cent placed themselves in that category. This suggested that this middle class is either too heterogeneous, too incongruent with the socioeconomic stratification of the country, or both. Second, only 4 per cent could be considered "working class," having identified themselves as *clase obrera, clase trabajadora, trabajadores,* or *proletariado*. Third, a substantial minority could not think of themselves in terms more appropriate than "poor." Including the 1 per cent who claimed to be "upper class," and the 6 per cent who said they were "lower class," we obtained a positive identification with some social class for 1,416 of our respondents, roughly 93 per cent of the sample.

We were expecting results somewhat similar to these, although not of the same proportions. Naturally, we wanted to probe further concerning the social location of these classes, bearing in mind Centers' caveat that classes are ". . . psycho-social groupings, something that is essentially subjective in character, dependent upon class consciousness . . . a class is not more nor less than what people collectively think it is. . . . Thus conceived, it becomes readily apparent that classes demand social definitions. . . ."[27]

We started the search for such a social definition of these classes by comparing the patterns of responses by each of these classes to the rest of our instrument, assuming that a very close similarity between the patterns of responses of two or more classes implied that they were really one. We had to delete the "upper class" and "working class" categories since they were too small for meaningful statistical manipulation. This left 1,339 cases. The cross-tabulations producing these comparisons revealed a great deal of similarity between the lower class and the poor, suggesting that their differences were small enough to justify combining them without introducing much distortion. These decisions led us to a dichotomous typology of Venezuelan social classes: the poor and the middle class, representing 35 and 65 per cent of the remaining cases, respectively. For several reasons, the typology appeared attractive and worthy of further elaboration.

First of all, although it is probably an exaggeration to regard these two classes as natural antagonists, some authors have pondered the implications of the basic inability to serve their respective interests given shrinking fiscal and economic resources.[28] At the very least, it can be said that although the interests of the poor are not always explicit, the cleavage between the poor and the middle class can be activated—politicized—as has already occurred in some cases.[29] Second, the dichotomy may not include all the classes and individuals—deletion of the upper and working classes left us with 88 per cent of the sample—but focuses attention on two classes that are receiving considerable attention in the literature.[30] Moreover, from the standpoint of political sociology, these two would seem to include what are normally construed as nonelite sectors, and to emphasize them is to delve into the area of mass politics. Although we will refrain for the moment from terming these classes "marginal" and "affluent," it is transparent that this dichotomous classification allows us to examine some propositions extant in the literature. The different approaches—reformist, developmental, and Marxist—offer divergent assumptions about the role of these classes and the pattern of social, economic, and political interactions between the two. This is true even though they are not related in a dominance-subordination sense and we cannot, in all probability, account for conflict between the two without bringing into consideration their interactions with the upper class.

Evidence from a study conducted during the late sixties in Venezuela offers some support for the validity of a dichotomous conceptualization of class at the level of the mass public. The study relied on in-depth interviews which included aspects of class definitions and social distinctions elaborated by respondents.

A poorly housed artisan:

I would not be able to tell if there are different social strata in the country. I believe I belong to the *gente humilde* or *proletaria*.
I consider a person *humilde* when that person lives normally in poverty, tightly. It is deprivation of some things what makes you humble. My class is different from the others because of this.
Before, I belonged to a different class, when I lived with my dad I belonged to the middle class. I do not know the word bourgeoisie and a proletarian is a person of the working, laboring class.

A middle-class man:

I believe there are distinct social strata in our country; the dispossessed, the middle and that of the more powerful with more capital. There is a hierarchy among the classes [and] I believe I belong in the middle level. My class is not marked by social distinctions, those who form the class have a profession and a more or less decent salary, regular education, they have habits and good manners derived from this milieu. University professionals, merchants, technicians belong to my class and, in order to reach this level, they had to come from the stratum or be in close contact with it. I believe that my class has productive and commanding functions in society. In my view, a bourgeois is someone who lives in superior comfort because he exploits man and a proletarian is a salaried person who works for a living serving the upper classes.

A middle-class woman:

> I believe there are distinct social strata in our society, the upper, the middle and the lower, and that they are ordered but I do not know which is that order, although I believe this is the way it should be. I believe I belong to the middle class, which is the most *fregada* [handicapped] because we want to pretend that we are what we are not and want to keep up with the upper and cannot. I do not know who else belongs in the class. Upper-class people have a lot of money, middle-class people a little, and lower-class people none. The function of my class is to help the upper class climb higher. I believe a bourgeois is someone who more or less has money and a proletarian someone who does not have anything. Formerly I did not belong to a different class, but I do believe that I belong to a class different from that of my ancestors because in the past there were not the very marked distinctions of today, and the middle and upper classes were identified very closely.

And, finally, a bourgeois:

> I consider there are different strata in our society. They would be the opulent, the middle and the so-called lower, that I would denominate working. They are in a hierarchy of power and acquisitive capacity. I believe I belong to the middle class, which is constituted by those of us who work daily to support our families and must face the social requirements that our positions demand from us. People with a regular education belong in this class and also professional people even though their purchasing power may not be too high. It is different from the other classes especially in the economic sense. I do not believe the class has one special function in Venezuelan society but it is the class that, anywhere in the world, works and has responsibilities. . . . To me a bourgeois is a parasitic person who does not work, lives off its rents and does not worry about [what's going on in] the world, and the proletarian is . . . more or less similar [!][31]

These descriptions may give the impression of considerable confusion and disorientation among the respondents, suggesting that they had been asked to do something not normally undertaken—namely, to think about class differences. However, further reflection and study of the responses indicates that, although they utilized different terms to identify persons who are not middle class, respondents understood and agreed upon some of the basic characteristics of the latter, as well as the more relevant differences between middle, lower, and upper classes. Not having pursued these semantic differences in our own investigation, we cannot utilize the profiles in full, but they lend greater validity to our dichotomous conceptualization of classes in Venezuela.

The comments of Silva Michelena help justify our next analytic step. He believes that ". . . income, education, and occupational prestige may be used for drawing the basic profile of describing the hierarchies of societies in the same stages of development as Venezuela. . . . [Moreover] the overarching process of change in Venezuela is urbanization; therefore, the extent to which a group has assimilated urban ways of life serves to define its position in the social hierarchy. . . ."[32] We may utilize these three variables, which are related to status, to gain insight into the social location of the poor and the middle class, by looking at the proportions of persons from different educational, income, and occupational groups who identify with one of these two classes. These data appear in the first two columns of table II-1, which presents the percentages of middle-class identifiers in the different categories. Examining the distributions it is immediately evident that identification with the middle class starts relatively low in the social structure —judged by majorities of respondents identifying themselves as such. Furthermore, the cleavage points between the two classes are relatively sharp. Identification with the poor is more frequent among those with little or no formal education, and also among persons who are heads or members of households with monthly incomes below 500 *bolívares* (then some $115) derived from predominantly rural and manual occupations: peasants and farmhands, domestic workers and servants, laborers and peons. A majority of the respondents in all other categories perceive themselves as middle class.

Additional evidence found in the literature tends to confirm the basic lines of socioeconomic cleavage separating the poor and the middle class. Pernaut utilized estimates of the Central Office of Coordination and Planning (CORDIPLAN) to put the proportion of "poor" at 44 per cent—the proportion of people earning less than Bs. 500 per month.[33] Blank estimated the "marginal urban" at 40 per cent and the "peasant" at 30 per cent of the population respectively.[34] Both of these groups lived on incomes of less than Bs. 600 per month and, although he was careful not to use their combined

Table II-I. Social Location and Socioeconomic Composition of the Poor and the Middle Class

Categories	Location[a] % middle	Composition[b] Poor	Middle	Sample[c]
Monthly income[d] (N = 1,287)				
Below Bs. 100	27.2	16.8	3.3	8.0
Bs. 100 to 500	45.0	49.1	21.3	30.9
Bs. 500 to 1,000	69.0	24.4	28.9	27.4
Bs. 1,000 to 2,000	86.3	8.1	27.0	20.4
Bs. 2,000 to 3,000	96.8	.7	10.9	7.4
More than Bs. 3,000	94.7	.9	8.6	5.9
Educational level attained (N = 1,339) None	24.7	28.0	4.9	13.0
Some elementary	47.8	38.7	19.1	25.9
Elementary	71.6	18.4	24.9	22.6
Some secondary	82.1	9.8	24.2	19.2
Vocational school[e]	80.3	3.0	6.5	5.3
Secondary	96.9	.6	10.9	7.3
College (at least one year)	92.1	1.5	9.4	6.6
Occupation[d] (N = 1,227) Peasants and farmhands	36.0	12.7	3.9	7.0
Domestic workers	39.5	6.0	2.1	3.5
Laborers and peons	43.7	11.3	4.8	7.1
Service workers	54.1	24.5	15.7	18.8
Artisans[f]	57.4	19.9	14.6	16.5
Retailers	75.0	7.6	12.5	10.8

Table II-1. Social Location and Socioeconomic Composition of the Poor and the Middle Class (*Continued*)

Categories	Location[a] % middle	Composition[b] Poor	Composition[b] Middle	Sample[c]
Clerical workers	77.5	7.2	13.5	11.2
Hacendados	76.7	1.6	2.9	2.4
Low prestige professionals[g]	81.7	3.9	9.6	7.6
Skilled workers and technicians	83.3	3.5	9.4	7.3
High prestige professionals[h]	92.9	1.2	8.2	5.7
Large proprietors	92.0	.5	2.9	2.5

[a] Percentage of respondents in the category who identify as middle class (column percentages).
[b] Percentage of the respondents included in the class contributed by the category (row percentages).
[c] Row percentages.
[d] Heads of household.
[e] Alumni and graduates of commercial, trade, and technical schools and academies, and of the Instituto Pedagógico Nacional.
[f] Furniture makers, blacksmiths, carpenters, electricians, welders, and kindred workers who operate their own shops.
[g] Schoolteachers, journalists, nurses, social workers, sales agents, and salespeople on commission.
[h] Engineers, architects, physicians, lawyers, planners, university professors, economists, psychologists, and accountants.

total of 70 per cent as an indicator of the proportion of the poor, Blank pointed out that these two were the lowest status groups in the VENELITE study.[35]

The Instituto Venezolano de Acción Comunitaria (IVAC) studied some of the Caracas *barrios* and put the average weekly income of a *barrio* family at Bs. 212; the proportion of families which fell below their poverty estimate of Bs. 299 per week was 65 per cent.[36] Talton F. Ray estimated the proportion of *barrio* families in the "general class" at between 75 and 90—depending upon the city— while referring to their lack of formal education and their permanent unemployment or underemployment.[37] Silva Michelena and his associates found that the following proportions of their three low-status rural groups earned less than Bs. 400 per month: traditional peasants, 67.2 per cent; peasants receiving benefits from the Agrarian Institute, 73.8 per cent; and agricultural workers, 74.5 per cent.[38] Our own estimates, based on recomputations of the data of the 1971 "Encuesta de Hogares," put the average weekly salary of employed urban workers at Bs. 184, with 62 per cent of those included in the computation of this average falling below that value.[39]

Although concurring with Centers' admonition that ". . . class lines of cleavage may or may not conform to what seem to social scientists to be logical lines of cleavage in the objective or stratification sense . . . ,"[40] we find a sizable discrepancy between class identification and social reality. In short, individual class images differ considerably from what one would anticipate from a reading of the literature. Surely, income is not class. Neither are education nor occupation, for that matter, but although available estimates suggest that anywhere from 44 to 75 per cent of the Venezuelan people are living in conditions of poverty, only 35 per cent *say* they are poor. In other words, more Venezuelans are poor statistically than those who identify themselves as poor.

Table II-1 offers evidence on the socioeconomic composition of these two classes. The second and third columns of the table present data on the relative contribution of the different categories of income, education, and occupation to the two classes. Under the last column of the table we have also provided the sample distribution of the three variables, in order to see if the respondents with a particular characteristic fall into one of the two classes with more than average frequency. For instance, although those earning less than Bs. 500 per month constitute some 40 per cent of the sample, they comprise about two-thirds of the poor; the same is true of those with little or no formal education. Occupational characteristics are somewhat more difficult to determine, given the composition of the labor force. Although the three groups with lowest occupational prestige are shown to be especially prone to identify with the poor—see the first three rows under "Occupation"—they do not constitute the majority of this class; the class includes such urban occupations as service workers and artisans, which are more numerous than the rural.

By contrast, almost 60 per cent of the middle class comes from intermediate categories of income, education, and occupation. Most members of the class earn between 500 and 2,000 *bolívares* per month, have completed at least elementary school, and are in manual or white-collar occupations of relatively low prestige. Obviously, this does not mean that persons of higher status do not belong in this middle class, but they are not a majority of the class. In fact, their numerical contribution to the class is little more than average when compared to the sample; this is especially true of the top occupational categories.

In conclusion, class identification patterns place nine out of every ten Venezuelans in one of two classes: the poor or the middle class. The ratio is almost two-to-one in favor of the latter, which seems relatively more heterogeneous in a socioeconomic sense. To a certain extent, both classes recruit members from practically every level of the social structure. However, the overlapping of social characteristics between poor and middle class should not be taken as an indication of a lack of cleavage between them. Our data show that the two classes are separated by relatively clear cut differences, although their internal composition is relatively heterogeneous. We present a summary of these differences in table II-2, where composite profiles of the two classes have been recorded. They include measures of class status and socioeconomic status which will be discussed in full below. These profiles show that the two classes *are* different. It could be argued, on the bases of comparable evidence and our own observation of Venezuelan society, that there are more socioeconomic cleavages than suggested by this characterization. Urban-rural differences are crucial for finer distinctions among the poor; educational differences are probably paramount in establishing further analytical discrimination within the middle class; income would produce still further differences between the intermediate and the higher echelons of the middle class; finally, a combination of the top categories of income, education, and occupation would produce a final distinction between the middle and upper classes in terms of supervision and managerial control over persons with lower status, characteristics associated with peak social groupings. However,

Table II-2. A Profile of the Poor and the Middle Class in Venezuela

The Poor	The Middle Class

Modal characteristics

The Poor	The Middle Class
N = 468, or 31% of sample	N = 871, or 57% of sample
Income: between Bs. 100 and Bs. 500 per month (49% of class in this category).	*Income*: between Bs. 500 and Bs. 2,000 per month (56% of class in this category).
Education: some elementary education (39%) or none (28%).	*Education*: primary education (25%) or some secondary education (24%).
Occupation: most peasants and farmhands (12%), most domestic workers (6%), service workers (25%), artisans (20%), laborers and peons (11%).	*Occupation*: service workers (16%), artisans (15%), retailers (13%), and clerical workers (14%).
Class status: very low, class E (58%).	*Class status*: low, class D (48%) or class C (35%).
Socioeconomic status: low (51%).	*Socioeconomic status*: moderate (38%) and high (27%).

Statistical profile[a]

The Poor	The Middle Class
Income = 2.294 (.925)	Income = 3.466 (1.268)
Education = 1.291 (1.233)	Education = 2.788 (1.662)
Occupation = 4.539 (2.394)	Occupation = 6.555 (2.816)
Class status = 1.457 (.567)	Class status = 2.171 (.700)
Socioeconomic status = 1.869 (.739)	Socioeconomic status = 2.850 (.880)

Note: Each pair of means of a characteristic described above and presented in the statistical profile includes those which differ from each other by statistically significant amounts (probability less than .001).

[a] The first value given for each characteristic represents the mean value of the characteristic for the class; the next value appearing in parentheses is the standard deviation.

since our operational measure of class identification is dichotomous, it seems more appropriate to utilize these refinements with our indicators of socioeconomic status and class status.

Social Stratification

> Unlike social class, social stratification . . . is merely a descriptive term for the existence of high and low in society . . . it is theoretically possible to have as many kinds of stratification as one can discover objective criteria for defining. It is a valuable and useful concept *because of this very objectivity*, and it is unfortunate that the word class, which involves something subjective, has so often been identified with it. . . . Stratification is assumed to be a permanent characteristic of any organized social group. . . .[41]

We utilized income, educational level, and occupation to construct an index of socioeconomic status as the operational tool to measure stratification. The rationale behind the index of class status is discussed in appendix C (Estimation of Social Class Status), and its frequency distribution appears in the questionnaire in appendix B ("Página del Supervisor: Perfil de la Persona Entrevistada: Clase Social"). The index of socioeconomic status was derived from standardized (Z) scores of the income, education, and occupation of the number of cases (1,339) for which we had complete information for all three variables. This four-point index allowed us to classify our respondents as follows: (1) *very low status*, 17.4 per cent; (2) *low status*, 38.4 per cent; (3) *moderate status*, 27.9 per cent; and (4) *high status*, 17.4 per cent.[42]

The two indices discriminate four different strata, although as might be expected, the frequencies associated with them are not identical. The number of respondents included in the top and bottom categories of the two distributions are very different; the index of class status includes more persons in its bottom category, while the same is true of the top category of the other index. The frequencies of the intermediate categories of "low" and "moderate" status are relatively even for both. As was the case with the "upper class," which had to be deleted from the discussion of class identification, the top category of class status, "the rich," lacks sufficient respondents to warrant its inclusion in the rest of the analysis. Furthermore, persons in this category of class status were the most difficult

Table II-3. Composition of Socioeconomic Strata and Class Strata

	Socioeconomic status				Class strata		
	Very low	Low	Moder-ate	High	Class E	Class D	Class C
Monthly income	(N = 1,339)				(N = 1,414)		
Below Bs. 100	36.7	4.1	.3	—	20.9	4.1	.6
Bs. 100 to 500	60.6	49.6	9.6	.4	53.5	30.8	5.7
Bs. 500 to 1,000	2.8	41.2	37.7	3.9	22.2	36.7	19.9
Bs. 1,000 to 2,000	—	4.9	41.7	36.9	3.0	24.3	34.5
More than Bs. 2,000	—	.2	10.7	58.8	.4	4.1	39.2
Educational level	(N = 1,339)				(N = 1,417)		
None	54.1	13.4	.8	—	30.1	10.4	1.5
Some elementary	38.1	40.7	12.6	2.1	38.1	27.4	9.1
Elementary	7.3	31.9	28.9	9.0	19.5	25.5	22.8
Some secondary	.5	11.5	36.6	22.7	9.6	20.9	26.1
Vocational school	—	1.9	8.6	10.7	1.6	6.1	7.9
Secondary	—	.4	7.8	25.3	.6	5.0	16.7
College (at least one year)	—	.2	4.8	30.0	.4	4.6	15.8
Occupation	(N = 1,339)				(N = 1,349)		
Peasants and farmhands	35.3	4.5	.3	—	16.6	4.9	.7
Domestic workers	15.6	2.9	—	—	6.4	3.7	—

Table II-3. Composition of Socioeconomic Strata and Class Strata (*Continued*)

	Socioeconomic status				Class strata		
	Very low	Low	Moder-ate	High	Class E	Class D	Class C
Laborers and peons	23.4	9.9	1.1	—	15.5	5.3	2.0
Service workers	16.1	34.2	11.0	2.1	22.7	22.2	10.1
Artisans	8.3	27.0	17.4	3.0	21.0	18.0	10.1
Retailers	1.4	12.1	13.4	8.6	7.3	10.5	14.4
Clerical workers	—	5.6	23.8	11.2	3.8	12.7	17.3
Hacendados	—	1.6	5.3	2.6	1.1	2.9	3.9
Low prestige professionals	—	1.2	13.1	16.3	1.8	7.8	12.7
Skilled workers and technicians	—	1.0	12.3	18.0	3.5	8.5	9.5
High prestige professionals	—	—	1.6	28.3	.2	2.7	15.0
Large proprietors	—	—	.8	9.9	.2	.8	4.2
Class identifications		(N = 1,181)				(N = 1,296)	
Poor	75.1	47.7	17.0	4.7	65.3	31.1	5.6
Middle class	24.9	52.3	83.0	95.3	34.7	68.9	94.4

to interview—more so than any other category or class—and although their responses are valid in other respects, their inclusion in our analysis of stratification is problematic. Given their high ratio of interview refusals, some doubt is cast on the extent to which those individuals whom we managed to interview from classes A and B are representative of these classes.[43] Concerning the index of class status it is useful to note that two of its categories were identified as "middle class" (class C, moderate status) and "working class" (class D, low status) in the training manual utilized in this study. The remaining category, class E (very low status), includes *rancho* dwellers as well as rural poor so it should not be considered "lumpen" or "peasant," although this category incorporates persons of very marginal standing in the society. In short, we can operationalize three levels of class status and four levels of socioeconomic status.

Cross-tabulations and comparisons between the larger categories of the two indices revealed that there was little justification for combining them and scant analytical benefit in doing so. For instance, the "low" and "moderate" categories of the index of socioeconomic status seemed to be fairly heterogeneous; the same was true of class status categories C and D. Given a certain similarity in their attitudes and orientations, persons with "very low" and "low" socioeconomic status could have been combined in a single category, but their socioeconomic differences were substantial, and such a combination would have ignored those differences.[44] On the other hand, the socioeconomic heterogeneity of the middle class, already discussed, diminishes if observed from the standpoint of class stratification.

Questions about the types of persons included in these different clusters of status are answered in part by data presented in table II-3 on the income, educational, and occupational correlates of socioeconomic status and class status. Due to the fact that the index of socioeconomic status is based on precisely these attributes, it produces finer discriminations.[45] This explains why there are more empty cells on this section of the table; incidentally, cell frequencies of less than 2 per cent can be treated as measurement error, so there is an even greater number of empty cells than first appears. In short, the index of socioeconomic status concentrates people of similar characteristics into fewer categories.

The index of class status, on the other hand, provides a useful profile of a "working class" group (class D, low status) missing from our previous discussion of class. This objective measure unveils a working class composed of artisans (18 per cent), service workers (22 per cent), clerical workers (13 per cent), and retailers (11 per cent); these four occupational groups account for 64 per cent of those included in the status category. The occupational heterogeneity of this working class is not the result of a careless utilization of the criteria described in appendix C. Instead, it is a reflection of an occupational structure in which employment in the manufacturing sector accounts for only 15 per cent of total employment; moreover, a large proportion of these workers are concentrated in small artisan shops employing a fairly reduced number of workers.[46] Thus one may have some difficulty in finding a working class in Venezuela which is homogeneous in an occupational sense. In short, our data are consonant with the well-documented fact that most manual workers in Venezuela are not involved in a situation of mass production in factories or industrial establishments employing a large number of individuals.

We also find in table II-3 that the group of individuals with a "middle-class" status (class C, moderate status) does not represent the same middle class created by class identification patterns. Most people with a middle-class status earn between Bs. 1,000 and Bs. 3,000 per month (56 per cent), are clerical workers, retailers, or professional (59 per cent in all), and are relatively well educated. Thus, utilization of the criterion of class status produces a cluster of individuals far more affluent than the "middle class."

A final comment involves the patterns of class identifications of the status groups. First, most persons in the different categories of socioeconomic or class status tend to identify overwhelmingly with one of the two classes, with the exception of those of low socioeconomic status. Persons with this status—nearly 40 per cent of the population—are almost as likely to identify with one of the two classes as with the other. The immediate implication is that prediction of their class identification would be extremely difficult because it involves persons with almost identical socioeconomic characteristics going their separate ways in this respect. All other status groups fall predominantly into one of the two classes: three-to-one poor among those of very low socioeconomic status, five-to-one middle class and more than twenty-to-one middle class for moderate and high socioeconomic status, respectively. Class status groups show similar trends; two-to-one poor for those in class E (poor), two-to-one middle class for those in class D (working class), and about seventeen-to-one middle class for those in class C (middle class).

Patterns of Class Consciousness

One may logically ask which of these different measures of socio-economic cleavages is more useful theoretically and more relevant empirically. Admittedly, the three measures discussed thus far are conceptually and operationally different. *Class images* are measured from interviewee responses to an open-ended question; *socioeconomic status* is operationalized with a composite index of income, education, and occupation; and *class status* is measured with an index derived from objective criteria applied by our interviewers. Class images would be more useful in testing hypotheses concerning group consciousness and its impact on processes of attitude formation; the measures of status would be more relevant in determining the overlap between socioeconomic and political inequality. All are pertinent for any attempts at mapping the distribution of political preferences and normative orientations. Finally, all provide some insight into the social and economic aspects of the role of the individual in the political process and are in this sense complementary.

Thus far we have refrained from second-guessing our respondents' identification with classes that are relatively incongruent with their individual status. However, since we will combine the two measures of status to create an index of stratification and will not utilize them in the remainder of the analysis, it is useful to determine the interrelatedness of the three measures. This will be done through multiple regression analyses of the three measures.[47] This serves two additional purposes: first, to measure the salience of income, education, and occupation on the formation of class images, as well as on the perception of class status; and second, to identify the patterns of class identification of different types of respondents.

Our regression results indicate that the three measures are not identical, nor do they give the same importance to income, educational, and occupational characteristics. For instance, the magnitude of the beta weights obtained for class status suggests that our interviewers somehow emphasized income (beta = .50) to a far greater extent than education (.21) and occupation (.12) when assigning a class status to their interviewees. The latter seemed to have been influenced by their income (beta of .30) and education (.23) to a greater degree than by occupation (.07). The similar magnitudes of the beta coefficients of income (.39), occupation (.39), and education (.38) obtained for the index of socioeconomic status merely confirm the efficacy of our weighting procedure in constructing this index. On the other hand, if socioeconomic status and class status are utilized to predict class images, the former turns out to be somewhat more relevant, as shown by the magnitude of the beta coefficients (.31 versus .38, respectively).[48] Even though these two measures explain only 29 per cent of the variance of class images, utilization of the regression equation derived in this particular solution results in the correct prediction of the class images of 77 per cent of our respondents.[49]

Obviously, the strength of the relationships between the three measures is reduced by their operational and conceptual distinctiveness, but is sufficient to allow for prediction of class images within a tolerable margin of error. Thus the pattern of class identification of the Venezuelan public is complex but does not defy explanation in terms of status characteristics. Lags in status crystallization, expectations of vertical mobility, and the very nature of the Venezuelan occupational structure may stand behind the 23 per cent of the cases that cannot be accounted for. Furthermore, the correlation between class status and socioeconomic status ($r = .66$) suggests a degree of complementarity that justifies their combined utilization at a later stage in the analysis. The fact that class images and class status correlate more strongly with income (r's of .46 and .68, respectively) than with other individual characteristics associated with status suggests that income is the most relevant of these characteristics in Venezuela. By contrast, occupation seems a rather distant influence (r's between occupation and class images and class status .34 and .50, respectively), perhaps resulting from measurement error produced by our attempt to reduce occupational groups to a few major categories.[50] However, additional evidence on the problem of group consciousness in general suggests otherwise.

Surveys of industrialized societies routinely include questions about group identification patterns of the mass public.[51] Responses to this type of question produce what are treated as operational measures of the reference groups of the public, even though the array of groups identified in this fashion resists operational treatment as ordinal measurement unless the categories are reordered in terms of some type of criterion. This practice responds to sound argumentation supported by historical evidence,[52] as well as by decades of research on group dynamics. Indeed, pluralist politics and the theory of polyarchy are predicated on the salience of group identifications related to the dominant cleavages of the society. Interaction between cleavages and group memberships may be cumulative or overlapping, depending on whether or not one finds basically the same individuals in different clusters of ethnic, racial, regional, religious, and ideological, as well as socioeconomic groups.[53]

One vital concern of our agenda is precisely this—the identification of the most relevant lines of cleavage in Venezuelan politics. Our open-ended question of class images was intended to probe the socioeconomic aspect of "what are you in Venezuelan politics?" We incorporated a version of the question of reference groups which was sufficiently distant from the former in the interview protocol and very different in its actual wording. The question attempted to determine which of eight different groups—a total of twenty-two were utilized in the pretest—included people who most resembled the respondent. That is, we asked our respondents to tell us which of the eight was *their* group.[54] Six were chosen with much greater frequency than the rest: "peasants" (7 per cent), "workers" (22 per cent), "students" (12 per cent), "housewives" (21 per cent), "middle-class people" (14 per cent), and "common people" (17 per cent).

Except for peasants and housewives, the majority of persons included in these groups proffered middle-class images. Cross-tabulations of these categories with occupation suggested that the groups were not very homogeneous in this sense. However, we found statistically significant differences between the socioeconomic status and class status of the different groups. This suggested that even though the predominant patterns of group identification are not sufficiently specific with respect to class, they reflect differences in status—group identifications seem to overlap socioeconomic inequality. In short, we could utilize these groups to compare the patterns of class identification of individuals with different status characteristics, and thus avoid the theoretical and operational problems of a similar analysis conducted in terms of occupation. As Verba and Nie have suggested, the key variable in group consciousness is consciousness itself;[55] what measure, then, could produce finer and more relevant discriminations of the phenomenon of class consciousness than a related but different measure of consciousness? In addition, these authors treat the "group consciousness model" as a competing explanatory framework of their "standard socioeconomic model."[56] The implication (which will be more relevant in testing hypotheses at a later point) is that group consciousness may be one of the factors which causes individuals to deviate from the norm—that is, to act or hold attitudes and evaluations that are not consonant with their socioeconomic status.

We should preface discussion of the patterns of class identification of the different groups with the evidence presented in table II-4. As one reads these data from left to right (that is, from the lowest to the highest groups according to their socioeconomic

Table II-4. Group Consciousness and Class Consciousness

	Peasants	Workers	Housewives	Common people	Middle class people	Students
Middle class	34%	56%	49%	68%	89%	81%
Frequency	32	154	139	156	176	139

Pearson r's: group consciousness and class consciousness = .31
group consciousness and socioeconomic status = .41
both significant at .01 level.

33

status), it becomes apparent that increases in the proportion of middle class respondents are not monotonic. Assuming that socioeconomic status and class status are the more relevant predictors of the class images of the individual, as our previous discussion suggests, one finds that "workers" and "middle-class people" identify with the middle class in greater proportions than their status characteristics would project. Perhaps this is one reason why group consciousness has an almost imperceptible impact on the formation of class images once the impact of socioeconomic status and class status are accounted for in a multiple regression solution (standardized beta for group consciousness on class image, controlling for socioeconomic status and class status, is .10). Whether this is actually the case or not, it is clear that of all groups to be discussed, *workers and middle-class people are more prone to exaggerate their social standing.* By implication, they are probably overrepresented among the 23 per cent of individuals for which prediction of their class images is in error.

We utilized stepwise multiple regression analyses to generate the path analytic models of class identification presented in figure 1. The graphic representation of the paths follows the standard usage described in the literature, although we have not decomposed the total (direct and indirect) causal effect of the independent variables in the three-variable models.[57] Neither do we identify disturbance terms[58] other than those of the class images. The figure includes eight different models, identified alphabetically; one for each of the six groups and, for purposes of comparison and reference, the model obtained for the sample, as well as a model of the dependents, that is, the respondents who are not heads of households.

Our first comments concern the adequacy of model A. We find that this model is equivalent, and therefore valid, for the groups represented by the models B (dependents), F (common people), and H (students). These are practically carbon copies of model A. The similarity between models A, B, and H is reassuring, for we feared that they would be very dissimilar as a result of the fact that income and occupation referred to the head of the household, whether or not this was the respondent. More importantly, this similarity suggests that there are no major within-family gaps in the patterns of class identification, although, if observed from the standpoint of group consciousness, housewives (model E) deviate considerably from the general model. However, some housewives are self-supporting in Venezuela, 15 per cent of those women identifying as such in our sample. Our initial inferences, then, are that *dependency status within the family, as such, does not seem to affect*

Figure 1. Patterns of Class Identification of Different Groups

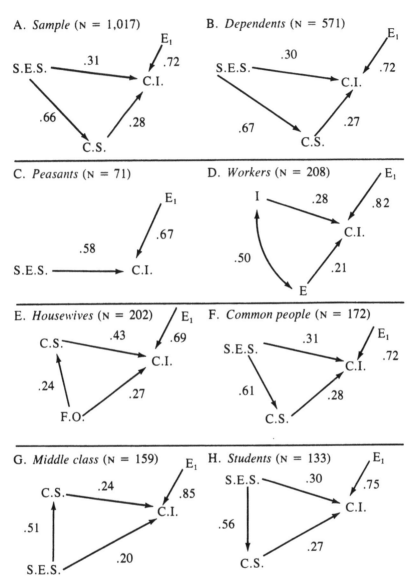

Note: All arrows in the figures represent paths measured by standardized (beta) coefficients; all are significant at the .01 level. Disturbance terms for the dependent variable (E_1) are expressed as the percentage of unexplained variance. Abbreviations to identify the variables should be read as follows: C.I. = class image, S.E.S. = socioeconomic status, C.S. = class status, F.O. = father's occupation, E = education, and I = income.

the pattern of class identification and that the *groups of lower socio-economic status deviate considerably from the general pattern.*

The magnitude of the disturbance terms of the different models provides some initial indication about the solidarity and cohesion of the different groups—the higher the magnitude the lower the strength of this internal characteristic of the group. However, this must be qualified to avoid erroneous inferences. For example, models D (workers) and G (middle class) have very high values for their disturbance terms. It could be assumed that solidarity and cohesion are very weak for both, but this inference would only be appropriate with regard to workers. In fact, the magnitude of the disturbance of model G is the result of the lack of variation of the dependent variable class image, since almost 9 out of 10 individuals who identify with the middle-class group have middle-class images. Whatever the reasons—and we could advance a similar set of socio-economic concerns and a great deal of interaction among individuals with these characteristics—middle-class images and middle-class consciousness reinforce one another. We must conclude that the middle class has at least the potential for great solidarity and seems already to enjoy substantial cohesion. However, in view of the skewness of the dependent variable, model G cannot be taken seriously and thus will not receive further attention.

On the other hand, the magnitude of the disturbance of model D is directly attributable to the sharp cleavage of class images within this group, as can be seen from table II-4; in this sense, only the housewives are a more divided group. Apparently, solidarity and cohesion are weak within this working-class group because respondents with very similar status characteristics have quite divergent class images. Since only 29 identified themselves as "working class" both in terms of class image and reference group, it is obvious that, whatever the reasons—and we find some in the class descriptions obtained by Abouhamad through her in-depth interviews[59]—working-class images and working-class consciousness do not reinforce one another in Venezuela. In other words, the working-class group does not crystallize into a working class because, in Venezuela, if you do not identify with the middle class, chances are you will identify yourself as "poor" or "lower," not working class.

Even though an individual may have the working class as reference group, he or she is not likely to have a working-class (class) consciousness. Given the generalized orientation to consumption in Venezuelan society, people may come to the conclusion that whoever can afford the affluent consumerism of urban Venezuela is middle class, while those who cannot are poor. Notice that income and education are the relevant predictors in model D. The cleavage in class images is expressed in terms of income (*tiene o no tiene reales*) and educational differences (*es doctor, es bachiller o no es nada*). Obviously, those above the cutoff point can afford varying degrees of middle-class consumption, those below cannot. Logically, if both kinds of class images coexist within the group in fairly similar proportions, what is the basic difference? One between poverty and affluence, it would appear. However, this basic difference seems highly subjective and relatively unencumbered by the recognition of specific cutoff points of income and education. If that were the case, the predictive power of the model would be much greater. Since this is not the case, we must conclude that income and education influence but do not really determine the class orientations within this group.

Model C (peasants) seems the most parsimonious and the simplest. The magnitude of the disturbance term for this model is the lowest of all, in addition to which this low value is obtained with only one causal predictor, socioeconomic status. Given their relatively low status, peasants seem to have class images relatively congruent with this low status. Furthermore, the class cleavage within the group is marked by the summary measure of status, not its separate individual characteristics. It would be difficult to estimate whether peasants enjoy greater cohesion and solidarity than middle-class people; they seem a much more homogeneous group than the latter. However, given the congruence between their class images and their status characteristics we can assume that inability to identify themselves as middle class, since they do not share in urban consumerism, does not weaken the interaction between peasant consciousness and poor or lower-class images. In other words, peasants who identify with the middle class would do so in terms of their status, not some idiosyncratic factor, as with the workers.

Finally, the model of class identifications of the housewives (E) stands in marked contrast with the rest, from both qualitative and quantitative standpoints. Its predictive power is relatively good, but the model is based on ascriptive characteristics. Once the class status of the respondent is accounted for, the effect of socioeconomic status is no longer significant. The only other factor with a meaningful effect on the dependent variable is father's occupation. Thus the model tells us very little about specific characteristics of the individuals which affect the pattern of class images within the group. On the other hand, since most women who identified themselves as housewives have relatively low status, their class cleavages are related more closely to status differentials, a further obstacle to group solidarity and cohesion regardless of the relatively low magnitude of the disturbance term. In other words, here we may have two groups instead of one.

In conclusion, the pattern of class consciousness in Venezuela is influenced more by socioeconomic status and class status. The overlap between class consciousness and group consciousness helps reinforce the solidarity and cohesion of the middle-class group and peasant group, while it severely undermines that of the working class and the housewives. Exaggeration of their social standing by some middle-class and working-class individuals, defined in terms of group consciousness, tends to reduce the predictive power of a model of class consciousness based on status characteristics. The terms may not be very familiar, but *class and group consciousness exist in Venezuela and the two are related to socioeconomic inequality*. Since we are speaking of inequality, this is the appropriate moment to introduce our final measure of socioeconomic inequality, which concerns the location of the individual in the social structure.

A Typology of Social Stratification

Given their complementarity, we feel it is justifiable to combine our measures of socioeconomic status and class status into an index of stratification. The correspondence between individual and aggregate levels of measurement here is so direct that we would encounter little difficulty in defending the operational reliability of the measure. However, status is an individual characteristic, while stratification refers to a property of the society, so there is an important qualitative difference between the two levels. The twelve strata that could be produced by combining the three categories of class status and the four of socioeconomic status were reduced to six by collapsing similar cases and deleting the numerically trivial or conceptually incongruent. These six types, which from a purely sociological standpoint could be reduced to four, are presented in table II-5. The table presents the particular combination of socioeconomic and class status categories utilized to create each stratum; the size of the stratum in absolute and relative terms; class and group images found in the stratum; and extended definitions of the *modal* attributes of income, education, and occupation which are most characteristic. The typology includes 1,226 of our respondents, or 80.6 per cent of our sample.

Examination and comparison of the strata depicted in table II-5 allow us to draw some conclusions about the nature of the strata themselves. First, they are predominantly urban, with only stratum I (the lowest) offering what appears to be a combination of elements typical of the rural poor in Venezuela: no formal education, predominantly agricultural occupations, and incomes below subsistence levels. Further confirmation rests in the fact that 54 per cent of the persons included in stratum I reside in rural areas.[60] Although we do not report place of residence in the table, it is clear that stratum I falls under the first major line of cleavage with profound socioeconomic implications: the *rural-urban cleavage*. On the other hand, stratum I is probably larger than the 14 per cent we estimated in our results, because this is precisely the stratum that we chose to underrepresent in our sample.[61]

Strata II and III appear so similar that they could be considered subcategories of the same stratum of manual workers. Although statistically significant, the differences between the two are very small; moreover, there is pronounced continuity in terms of occupation. However, a major difference rests in their respective patterns of class identification; stratum II is predominantly "poor" while III is largely "middle class." This constitutes a major substantive difference in terms of class consciousness; all others are matters of degree largely overshadowed by this second major line of cleavage, that is, by differences between manual and white-collar occupations. Thus the more interesting distinctions between strata III and IV become different occupational compositions, with higher levels of prestige for the occupations included in the latter. There are some manual or blue-collar workers in stratum IV, to be sure, but they are highly specialized and constitute only a minority. There is also the dramatic increase in the proportion of middle-class identifiers, one presumably related to occupational differences. It is not implausible to argue that stratum IV's higher levels of occupational prestige are supported by and a result of higher educational levels, which lead to higher levels of income as well.

Similarities between strata IV and V appear greater than those reported between II and III. Only two discrepancies are found relating to income and to proportion of middle-class identifiers. In addition, there is virtually no blue-collar representation in stratum V. This is, consequently, the first stratum which is predominantly white collar in composition. However, as was the case with strata II and III, sufficient differences were detectable between the political attitudes and orientations of strata IV and V to preserve their separate identity.

A more important distinction, the last major line of cleavage that

Table II-5. A Model of Social Stratification in Venezuela

Stratum I: N = 218 (14% of sample)
S.E.S.:   very low
C.S.:   poor and working class
C.I.:   75% poor
Income: 61% in Bs. 100–500/month
Education: 54% without formal education
Occupation: Peasants and farmhands (35%), domestic workers (16%), and laborers and peons (24%)
G.I.:   peasants (22%), workers (32%), and housewives (29%)

Stratum II: N = 223 (15% of sample)
S.E.S.:   low
C.S.:   poor
C.I.:   63% poor
Income: 59% in Bs. 100–500/month
Education: 42% with some elementary and 31% with elementary
Occupation: service workers (31%) and artisans (32%)
G.I.:   workers (33%) and housewives (27%)

Stratum III: N = 257 (17% of sample)
S.E.S.:   low
C.S.:   working class
C.I.:   59% middle class
Income: 48% in Bs. 500–1,000/month
Education: 41% with some elementary and 32% with elementary
Occupation: service workers (38%) and artisans (24%)
G.I.:   workers (25%), housewives (26%), and common people (20%)

Stratum IV: N = 202 (13% of sample)
S.E.S.:   moderate
C.S.:   working class
C.I.:   80% middle class
Income: 44% in Bs. 1,000–2,000/month
Education: 29% with elementary and 34% with some secondary

Table II-5. A Model of Social Stratification in Venezuela (*Continued*)

	Occupation: clerical workers (23%), artisans (18%), low prestige professionals (13%), and retailers (11%)
	G.I.: housewives (20%), common people (20%), and middle class (19%)

Stratum V: N = 128 (8% of sample)
S.E.S.: moderate
C.S.: middle class
C.I.: 92% middle class
Income: 66% in Bs. 1,000–3,000/month
Education: 31% with elementary and 38% with some secondary
Occupation: retailers (17%), clerical workers (26%), and low prestige professionals (14%)
G.I.: common people (19%), middle class (30%), and students (14%)

Stratum VI: N = 198 (13% of sample)
S.E.S.: high
C.S.: middle class
C.I.: 95% middle class
Income: 68% in Bs. 1,000–3,000/month
Education: 26% with secondary and 29% with at least some college
Occupation: low prestige professionals (28%), skilled workers and technicians (19%), and high prestige professionals (28%)
G.I.: common people (24%), middle class (19%), and students (35%)

Note: S.E.S. = socioeconomic status
C.S. = class status
C.I. = class image
G.I. = group identification.

we are able to measure with our data, underlies the more significant difference between strata V and VI: educational level attained. Distinctions in income and occupational prestige are also found between the two strata but they are really a result, at least in part, of the former. As table II-5 indicates, about 55 per cent of the persons included in stratum VI have at least completed a secondary education—the *bachillerato*—with a smaller but significant proportion of that percentage advancing to college. Thus, this is the stratum characterized by more advanced educational achievement, and an absence of that characteristic represents a major obstacle to the vertical mobility of anyone beneath this line of cleavage.

The final important line, which we cannot measure, deals with decisional control over production or work activities as a result of ownership or managerial responsibilities. Thus far, the overwhelming majority of the persons classified are employees or independent operators of modest means, and this final distinction segregates those who can set production quotas and work schedules and make hire-and-fire decisions. The fact that many persons performing these functions in contemporary Venezuela are foreigners eliminated them from our sample. This, together with deletion of "upper-class" individuals and classes A (the rich) and B (the affluent) from our analysis of stratification, deprives us of the opportunity to describe the stratum in detail.

The empirical relevance and operational validity of our typology of stratification can be defended with the evidence presented in figure 2, which suggests that the strata in effect differ in their more basic characteristics. The standardized (Z) scores presented in the figure were computed from means obtained for each of the strata, in a "multiple range" (one-way analysis of variance) comparison of the five characteristics. The comparisons were made following a criterion of "least significant differences" (LSD), under the assumptions of homogeneous variances and a "fixed effects" model.[62] The scores indicate the position of the strata in each of the five dimensions, as well as the statistically significant differences between them. Brackets identify cases in which any pair of strata do not differ in one of these characteristics.[63]

There are only three such cases in figure 2. They include a lack of significant differences in educational level and socioeconomic status of the groups of strata IV and V, which, as we indicated above, are the most similar. In addition, we find a reversal in the ranking of these strata relative to occupational prestige. The remaining case concerns the similarity in occupational prestige of the individuals included in strata II and III.

Social Context of Political Opinion

Figure 2. Standardized Differences between the Strata

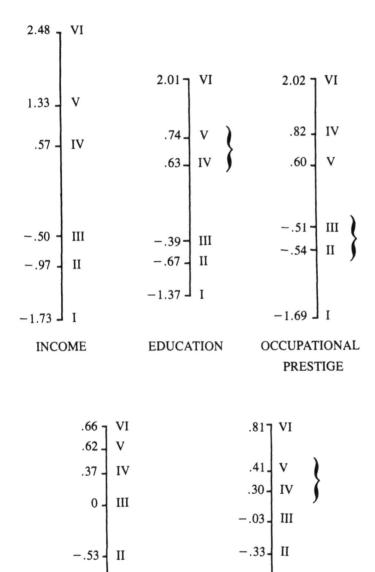

We must also report that, contrary to our expectation, self-employment did not constitute a major line of cleavage separating the upper strata from the rest. We were trying to utilize self-employment to add to the differences between strata, especially IV and V, which we were planning to identify as "salaried middle class" and "independent middle class," respectively. In this, we hoped to replicate the procedure and findings of Richard Hamilton, who utilized such distinctions in his analysis of the North American case.[64] In fact, quite the opposite occurs and, surprising as it may sound, self-employment and social stratification are *negatively* related among the individuals included in our typology (Pearson's r = −.16 with .001 significance). The only case in which self-employment coincides with a major line of cleavage is the urban-rural cleavage that separates strata I and II; stratum I is the only one in which most individuals (50 per cent) are self-employed. On the other hand, the higher strata (V and VI) have the lowest proportions of self-employed individuals. It would appear that self-employment was a symptom of the individual's ability to resist the onslaught of industrialization; Venezuela is, after all, a country in which a considerable proportion of blue-collar workers and artisans have not been displaced by industrialization and where small grocers and shopkeepers have managed to stay in business despite the chain stores and the *automercado*. It is not a matter of modern and traditional occupations, but rather a question of the extent to which dependent capitalism can reasonably be expected to create an occupational structure congruent with the system of social stratification.

The fact that occupation and phenomena related to it have introduced considerable operational and theoretical difficulty into our analysis should not be allowed to pass without final comment. In Venezuela, occupational differences seem most important at the two extremes of the social structure and, as previously noted, coincide with the rural-urban cleavage at the very bottom and the managerial-employee distinction at the top. But it means relatively little at intermediate levels, for almost all occupations are included there. Thus, the salience and function of occupational role in relation to group and class consciousness is very modest and overshadowed by income, which reflects individual, not group success. This clearly represents a serious obstacle to the processes of group and class consciousness, for individuals of similar position in the social structure are engaged in such a wide array of roles that their best way of self-identification is as "middle class," whether in a group or class sense. This suggests that, in retrospect, the 65 per cent of our respondents who consider themselves "middle class" are not as disoriented as they may appear. They seem to lack more specific points of reference with which to identify themselves.

For the sake of simplification, although at the risk of some distortion, we will identify the strata as follows: the *agricultural poor* (I); the *manual strata*, which consist of *manual poor* (II) and *manual middle class* (III); the *white-collar strata*, which are composed of *lower* (IV) and *upper* (V) *white collar*; and the *professional stratum* (VI). These labels reflect the main vertical cleavages of the society as well as the modal characteristics of the strata, yet are not mutually exclusive, because occupations and classes are not concentrated in a single stratum. Moreover, the allusion to occupation is intended to underline this characteristic of Venezuelan stratification. These labels may not appear highly congruent or sophisticated but accurately reflect the character of the social aggregates they purport to identify. In addition, they seem more relevant to contemporary Venezuela than the three-tier structure of *gente cualquiera*, *gente decente*, and *clase media* described by Dupouy in 1949.[65]

3

The Social Context
of Political Experience

Introduction

An astute student of the relationship between class and politics has
called attention to ". . . a persistent problem which appears in the
discussion of class: how to assess the differences that do appear.
Most studies show some percentage difference in the political
choices and in the attitudes on issues. It then becomes a question of
whether to express astonishment over the enormity of the differences or satisfaction that they are so small. . . ."[1] In addition,
there is the problem of how to account for cases in which one class
does not fit the political profile assigned it by paradigmatic thinking
on the political role of classes in complex societies.[2] Lipset argued
that North American workers are less tolerant and less likely to support democratic rules of procedure and that their life experiences
produce rigid and intolerant approaches to politics.[3] By contrast, in
Latin America, neither the cohesion within the lower and middle
classes nor the alliance between these two classes has developed in
the manner predicted by the liberal interpretation.[4]

In short, contemporary social science has produced a very complex, if broken, vision of the political role of classes. Whether it is
the persistent leftist character of working-class politics in France,[5]
working-class Tory deference to the conservative establishment in
England,[6] coalitions between middle classes and military in Latin
America,[7] or the suspected authoritarian leanings of lower and
working classes,[8] it is extremely difficult to set reasonable standards
of reference in the analysis of the political behavior of classes.

Our analysis will concentrate on comparisons between classes
(lower versus middle), strata (manual versus white collar), and
groups (workers versus middle-class people) in terms of their evaluation of the regime and its institutions, policy orientation, ideological orientation, participatory behavior, and partisanship.

Evaluating the Regime

Evidence about the authoritarian propensities of different classes
and strata has centered on opinion about the application of funda-

mental rules of the regime to unpopular groups, as these seek to organize and participate in the political process.[9] Our data do not allow us to make such specific determinations of the bounds of political tolerance in Venezuela, but do permit analysis of differences between social groupings in level of support for operational rules of the democratic regime and, in particular, opinion about the institution of elections, opposition criticism, and party competition; also relevant is public reaction to military coups d'etat, the most frequent mechanism of illegal or extraconstitutional removal of political regimes in Latin America.

Comparisons of the classes, strata, and reference groups in terms of these four areas of regime evaluation lead to two unequivocal inferences. First, the high level of consensus found in Venezuela on these matters is reproduced within the classes, strata, and groups. Second, whatever differences do appear are merely ones of degree and do not seem to follow the direction predicted in the literature. More specifically, if attention is focused on the differences between manual and white-collar *strata*, and between worker and middle-class *groups*, one fails to observe differences of major consequence. Neither can one identify more authoritarian predispositions from any of the social aggregates presented in table III-1. The table shows at a glance that all of these are very close to modal opinion concerning the four aspects. Support for the institution of elections is very high, as one would imagine, given the long struggle to legitimize suffrage in Venezuela. Opposition to military coups and to one-party rule is also high, and support for opposition criticism is highest. In none of these do we find differences that would suggest any of the classes, strata, or reference groups is deviant as compared to the rest. Thus, neither class and group consciousness nor location in the social structure are important when individuals adopt a position concerning some of the more basic operational ingredients of the democratic regime in Venezuela.

Of additional interest is the fact that differences within each major type of cleavage do not substantiate the claims of those who believe in the more authoritarian outlook of the working class. In terms of their social position and group identification, individuals who can be classified as "working class" or at least "blue collar" seem to have *higher* levels of support for rules of democratic procedure than their white-collar and middle-class counterparts. Obviously, the differences are small and, in many cases, not statistically significant, but they do not confirm the suspicions of Lipset and others. Furthermore, some of the differences between strata and groups concerning opinion about one-party rule are not significant, because when all

Table III-1. Support for Operational Norms of the Democratic Regime by Major Socioeconomic Cleavages

	Classes		Strata		Reference Groups		Complete sample
	Poor	Middle	Manual[a]	White collar[b]	Working class	Middle class	
Scale Highly supportive of elections	74*	73*	75	70	72	69	74
Scale Opposed to military coups	75	70	73*	70*	71	67	73
(8) Opposition to one-party rule	66	67	71*	67*	65*	73*	66
(9) Supportive of opposition criticism	73	79	74	81	79*	76*	77

Note: All table values are row percentages. Numerals in parentheses identify questionnaire items. The scales of support for elections and opinion about military coups are described in appendix F.

[a] Includes "manual poor" and "manual middle class."

[b] Includes "lower white collar" and "upper white collar."

* Not significant at .05.

the groups and strata are included in the comparison, manual versus white collar and workers versus middle class distinctions are overshadowed by similarities between the remaining categories. In other words, the modest differences that do appear are diluted by the similarities between the other strata and groups. Even though polarization of opinion could be more drastic between the classes, since there are only two classes, opinion differences in this respect are of little importance.

Dealy's hypothesis that Latin America lives in a "monistic tradition" as surely as the United States lives within a liberal tradition also seems to be contradicted by our evidence. He contends that a consensus model informs the modus operandi of political behavior in monistic democracies.[10] To be sure, our data suggest high levels of consensus on party competition, the need for opposition criticism, support for elections, and opposition to coups d'etat. This represents a popular consensus on the need for political diversity, and not unity as Dealy contends.

In conclusion, the link between levels of support for the operational norms of the democratic regime and socioeconomic inequality is very tenuous in Venezuela. There are no major differences between classes, strata, and reference groups of unequal status to suggest that any of these is more democratic or authoritarian than the rest. Obviously, this does not foreclose the possibility of differences in other authoritarian propensities, but it fails to substantiate their existence in the context of basic operational norms of the democratic regime that are mutually exclusive with the operation of monistic authoritarianism.

Evaluating Political Institutions

It is necessary to distinguish the regime itself from its policy outputs and outcomes, from the administration in power, and from different institutional actors that function under the regime's operational norms. It is useful to separate and distinguish "diffuse support" for the regime from "specific support" for those institutions found in it.[11] There is really no reason to expect a high degree of correspondence between the two, especially in a competitive political system like the Venezuelan, in which government turnover has become a legitimate outcome of the political process. In addition, it is important to determine the social location of criticism in order to better understand the nature of the regime.[12] Following Easton's familiar definition of politics as "the authoritative allocation of values,"[13] we treat criticism and discontent as natural consequences of the political process, and not as symptoms of disorientation, misinformation, or inadequate political socialization.

We adopt the view that evaluation of political institutions is a result of previous individual and group experience in dealing with the actor or institution subject to such evaluation; the more critical or adverse the evaluation, the more negative these experiences are likely to have been. At issue here is whether any kind of differences related to social inequality in the patterns of evaluation of political institutions in Venezuela can be detected, for we assume that such differences would reveal the experience of the different classes, strata, and groups in their dealings with the government and other relevant actors.

Our first measure of evaluation of political institutions is a Guttman scale based on opinion about the policy performance of the administrations covering the period 1958 through 1973, including the two Social Democratic administrations of Acción Democrática (1959–1969) and the Social Christian administration of Rafael Caldera (1969–1974). The four items included in the scale were prefaced by the comment "Let us begin with your opinion about governments in general, about the governments which have ruled the country during the last fifteen years. . . ." The scaled items measured opinion about the national impact of the policies implemented by those governments; whether these had served the interests of the people or of very powerful groups; opinion about the adequacy of public resources expenditures; and views concerning the honesty of government officials. Twenty-nine per cent of our respondents scored in the top level of criticism of this evaluative scale, while an additional 27 per cent responded negatively on three of the four, thus placing in the next highest category of criticism. We are obviously dealing with highly critical opinion in this area.

It was possible to differentiate opinion about the policy performance of the regime from that concerning the policy performance of the incumbent administration by asking questions about the latter. We standardized responses to these questions, which included opinion about the Social Christian administration's policy impact on the economic situation of the respondent's family, impact on the respondent's reference group, plus opinion about the manner in which the government had handled issues considered of major importance. Measured along these lines, public dissatisfaction with administration policies stood at about 52 per cent, the proportion of respondents scoring above the mean population average of zero on this measure.

High levels of criticism were also found in the public's evaluation of the role and performance of Venezuelan professional politicians. Four items scaled with the Guttman criteria summarize this aspect and bear considerable interest in terms of political and theoretical significance. First of all, party politicians are important brokers of the Venezuelan democratic regime and serve as crucial points of contact between the masses and the regime. Venezuelan politics is, to a great extent, partisan, and whatever happens to politicians is of great consequence to the system. Moreover, the authoritarian alternative is frequently offered in intellectual and political circles of the Western Hemisphere as the only way out of the inefficiency and disorder that partisan politics has produced in Latin America.

In Venezuela, the authoritarian alternative was represented by a number of minor right-wing parties in the election of 1973, and most notably by former treasury secretary Pedro Tinoco, Jr., who presented his position in unmistakable *desarrollista* terms.[14] Even though this option lacked popular appeal at that time, such a challenge cannot be ignored because, as Blank has suggested, the Venezuelan establishment is populist,[15] and the advocates of bureaucratic authoritarianism argue that theirs is the one inevitable solution capable of coping with problems of internal order, economic growth, and social development, offering "a means to the depoliticization of society, hence to a renewal of ordered performance of functions in the body politic, hence also the enlightened rule of technical and administrative expertise."[16] Tinoco's cosmeticized version of the *nuevo ideal nacional* of former dictator Marcos Pérez Jiménez received only minuscule electoral support, but the 49 per cent of the public highly critical of politicians cannot be taken lightly, especially when this comes together with high levels of dissatisfaction over the policies of the regime.

Furthermore, popular discontent and criticism increase when it comes to evaluating the role of political parties in the political process, for while a majority of the people (70 per cent) believe this role is important, even higher proportions agree that there are just too many parties (96 per cent), and that they are instruments of very powerful minorities (81 per cent); there is also the dominant view that parties only concern themselves with winning elections (70 per cent).

Does the evidence reviewed thus far suggest that Venezuela is, to paraphrase Newton, ready to oust the functional and political elites of a populist phase in favor of the "new military"?[17] More specifically, which social sectors would appear most eager to support such a move, based on their levels of discontent with regime and administration policies, parties, and politicians? What would be the bases of such predispositions? Would they stem from ideological propaganda, psychological disorientation, faulty communication, inadequate democratic socialization, or inexperience in dealing with a democratic regime? If our assumption is correct, and criticism is a result of individual and group experiences in dealing with political actors, of evaluating what those actors have done to benefit individuals and the community with whom they identify, we should be able to describe the social context of the regime from these patterns of evaluation.

The Social Context of Criticism

There is a tendency in the contemporary literature to treat the political criticism or cynicism of lower-status citizens as a result of "lags" of one sort or another. One such element concerns the extent and quality of political information available to these citizens who, given their intermittent political involvement, low educational levels, and lack of sustained interest in the political process, are supposed to rely on very faulty information.[18] It is important for us to show that this is not valid for Venezuela in the light of subsequent information to be presented concerning differences in kinds and degrees of criticism of major socioeconomic groups.

We operationalized level of political information in terms of the number of questionnaire responses to which an individual did not have to reply "don't know." We classified our respondents as adequately or inadequately informed, depending on whether they were above or below the sample average of "don't know" responses. This deviates from standard practice but seems more valid in the Venezuelan context.[19] Using this approach we produced the data presented in figure 3, which suggest that major social groupings do not differ in the amount of political information available to them through the channels of political communication. None of the comparisons produced significant differences in the levels of political information of the classes, strata, and groups, which seem to fluctuate relatively close to the population mean of 67 per cent with adequate levels of information. However, it must be emphasized that the best informed of all seems to be the working-class group, at 73 per cent, since they will appear to be the more critical as well. More importantly, we can assume that differences in levels of criticism to be discussed cannot be reduced to differences in levels of

Figure 3. Level of Political Information and Major Socioeconomic
Cleavages

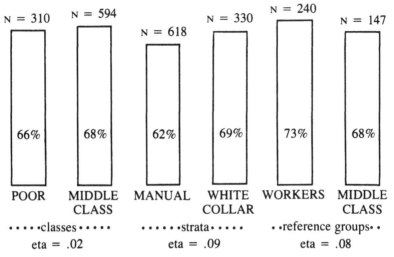

N = 310   N = 594   N = 618   N = 330   N = 240   N = 147

66%   68%   62%   69%   73%   68%

POOR   MIDDLE   MANUAL   WHITE   WORKERS   MIDDLE
        CLASS   COLLAR   CLASS

• • • • •classes• • • • •   • • • • • •strata• • • •   • •reference groups• •
    eta = .02   eta = .09   eta = .08

Note: Level of political information is measured by the percentage of
respondents within each category who are below the population average
in their total number of "don't know" responses to our questionnaire.
None of the etas are significant at alpha of .05.

information. Instead, we contend that whatever differences do appear stem from experience.

Comparisons of the levels of criticism of regime policies of major
social groupings are presented in figure 4, without any statistically
significant differences appearing between the classes and between
the strata. Very minimal differences are detectable between levels of
criticism of regime policies by the poor and the middle class, while
those between manual and white-collar strata are virtually negligi-
ble. Differences do emerge between workers and middle-class people, with the former showing the highest level of criticism, at 62 per
cent. However, it is obvious that criticism of regime policies appears uniformly high regardless of class or group identification, or
position in the social strata. It is also apparent that identification
with the middle-class group produces a clustering of individuals
who are less critical of regime policies than their white-collar and
middle-class counterparts (47 per cent versus 56 and 54 per cent,
respectively). If our assumption is correct, the data indicate that the
middle-class group seems to have received more benefits from the
regime than the middle class and the white-collar strata, but not to
the extent of making it unique in this sense. It would seem that this
mode of criticism is so widespread that it lacks an identifiable social

Figure 4. Level of Criticism of Regime Policies and Major Socioeconomic Cleavages

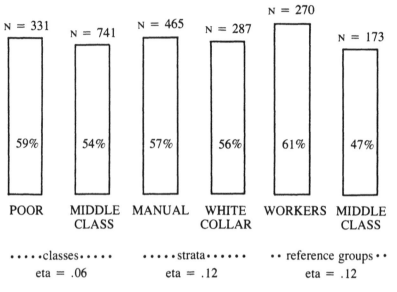

Note: Level of criticism is measured by the percentage of respondents within each category scoring in the two highest values of the scale. Only the eta for the comparison of reference groups is significant at the .05 level.

expression. In other words, dissatisfaction with the policy outcomes of the regime is so extensive that one cannot find a class, stratum, or group which seems to have been the target of favoritism or neglect. Most have clearly found reason to complain about the policy performance of the regime.

Party politicians are probably the more visible agents of the democratic regime in Venezuela, and it is very significant that criticism of their present role in the political process is distributed among the major lines of socioeconomic cleavage in a pattern very similar to that just discussed. The evidence presented in figure 5 suggests a marked similarity between the two kinds of criticism. Workers and the poor appear most dissatisfied and the middle class least so, while differences between the strata fail to reach statistical significance. Given the clientelistic nature of the major political parties and the fact that persons of lower socioeconomic status would appear more dependent on a patron state and its agents to improve their social condition, the reality that it is precisely these types of persons who are most dissatisfied with regime policies and party politicians suggests adverse experiences in dealing with both. To be sure, all functional groups seek the favor of the Venezuelan state, but it is the lower sectors of the society who lack the direct access to the execu-

Figure 5. Level of Criticism of Politicians and Major Socioeconomic
Cleavages

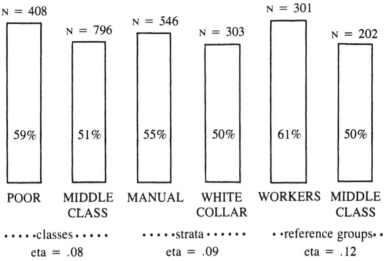

N = 408

N = 796

N = 546

N = 303

N = 301

N = 202

| 59% | 51% | 55% | 50% | 61% | 50% |

POOR   MIDDLE   MANUAL   WHITE   WORKERS   MIDDLE
       CLASS   COLLAR   CLASS

• • • • •classes• • • • •   • • • • •strata• • • • • •   • •reference groups• •
eta = .08   eta = .09   eta = .12

Note: Level of criticism is measured by the percentage of respondents
within each category scoring in the two highest values of the scale. With
the exception of the comparison involving the strata, all etas are
significant at the .05 level.

tive and bureaucracy enjoyed by the better-organized groups of the
upper strata. Thus, discontent is fairly generalized but seems more
deeply rooted among the poor and the workers.

Additional insight is provided and a sharper polarization of opinion found in connection with evaluation of the policy performance
of the Caldera administration. The differences appear in figure 6
and suggest a fairly robust connection between this kind of criticism
and social inequality. Classes, strata, and groups differ considerably
and significantly in their evaluation of the policy impact of the administration of Dr. Caldera. The covariations between social inequality and the former, measured by the eta coefficients presented
in the figure, show that satisfaction with administration policies
increases with the social status of the individual and that of his or
her reference group. There are clear differences between poor and
middle-class, manual and white-collar strata, and workers and middle-class people in this regard, and always in the same direction. In
short, the Caldera administration is perceived to have been more
beneficial by groups and individuals of higher social status, whether
one looks at class or group identification or position in the social
structure.

Differences in the way the classes, strata, and groups evaluate

Figure 6. Level of Satisfaction with Caldera's Policies and Major Socioeconomic Cleavages

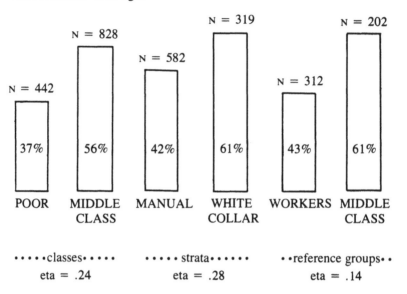

Note: Level of satisfaction is measured by the percentage of respondents within each category scoring above the population mean. All etas are significant at .01.

the policy performance of the Caldera administration may be spurious. In other words, the relationship between the two may merely reflect the relationship between partisan preferences and social inequality. In order to determine the extent to which the differences presented in figure 6 are authentic, we can control for the partisan factor by using sympathy toward Dr. Caldera as an intervening variable. This variable correlates very strongly with sympathy toward the Social Christian party (COPEI) and also (negatively) with sympathy toward the Social Democratic (AD) party. Thus it represents a useful summary measure of attitude toward the leader of the administration in power as this is influenced by partisan considerations. More specifically, since the upper strata are more sympathetic toward COPEI and the lower toward AD, we need to remove the effect of these partisan predispositions in order to observe the residual effect that may be directly attributable to social inequality.

Figure 7 summarizes the results of this statistical manipulation.[20] The continuous line represents the plot of the relationship between evaluation of administration policies and stratification, while the broken line plots this once the effect of the partisan factor has been removed. The slopes of both lines show that criticism of Caldera decreased with increasing individual status. There is a clear cut-

Figure 7. Evaluation of Policy Performance of the Caldera Administration by the Strata

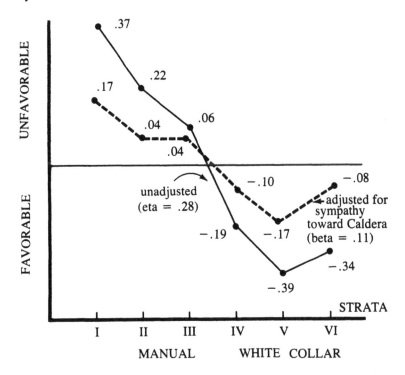

Note: The magnitudes presented in the figures are units above or below the population mean of zero. The value of eta measures the simple correlation between level of criticism and stratification. Beta refers to the first-order partial between the two controlling for sympathy toward Caldera. Both measures are significant at the .01 level.

off point which coincides with the manual–white collar cleavage and separates predominantly critical from predominantly favorable evaluations. Both of these features, slopes and inflection points, are observable whether we look at the adjusted or unadjusted curves. This suggests that the differences are real, although they are decidedly influenced by the partisan factors. When the deviations from the population mean are adjusted to control for sympathy toward Caldera, their magnitudes are reduced considerably. However, this reduction, which can be appraised by comparing the magnitude of the eta and beta coefficients for the unadjusted (.28) and adjusted scores (.11), falls short of making the relationship disappear altogether.

To summarize, the evidence presented thus far suggests that socioeconomic differences do not constitute a major influence on the public's support for the operational norms of the democratic regime or on the evaluation of its policy outcomes. Support for the operational norms of the regime is relatively high among all classes, strata, and groups, while criticism of regime policies and party politicians follows a similar pattern. Evaluation of the policy performance of the Caldera administration was the only aspect of political evaluation to evidence deep cleavages of opinion along socioeconomic lines. This, which could be attributed to the distribution of partisan preferences, has been shown as a pattern reflecting real differences between strata. Given the limitations of the evidence reviewed we cannot claim that the arguments concerning monistic constraints,[21] lower-class authoritarianism,[22] and a neat pattern of attitudinal differences between the strata[23] are totally groundless in the Venezuelan context. However, our evidence suggests that these may not be as relevant as one could imagine. Finally, it is important to stress that, concerning the "high" and "low" in Venezuelan society, we are not dealing with two kinds of publics, one well-informed and affluent, the other largely ignorant and disoriented due to its low socioeconomic status.

Social Inequality and Policy Preferences

Considerable doubt has been cast on the issue content of the political evaluations of the mass public, as well as its ability to understand complex issues and maintain a sustained interest in them.[24] In Venezuela, it has been said that persons of the lower strata have a tendency to project their own personal problems and consider them issues of national scope, therefore looking for the state to come up with solutions to every imaginable problem.[25] In short, the most common distinction found in the literature concerning the issue orientation and policy preferences of the classes and strata assumes an increased sophistication that comes with higher educational levels of the upper strata.

Our first caveat holds that, in Venezuela, there is a solid consensus on the need for a very active state, and socioeconomic differences do not appear to disturb this. No class or stratum deviates much from the 84 per cent of the population who identify the public sector as the more idoneous agent for the solution of contemporary national problems. When it comes to personal problems, the picture is little different: the poor (67 per cent) and the middle class (62 per cent) are very close to the 63 per cent of the total population who identify actors of the public sector as capable of solving their personal problems. The contrast between the manual and white-collar strata is more pronounced (69 versus 55 per cent), but the majority of individuals included in the latter concur with this appraisal. Thus, the belief that the state has a primary responsibility for the solution of personal and national problems is not associated with social stratification.

This being the case, what kinds of differences exist between the types of problems identified? In the fall of 1973, the national economy was the source of greatest concern, with inflation and unemployment the aspects more frequently identified as requiring immediate action from the government; differences between classes and strata were a matter of degree, not of the specific nature of the issues identified.[26] Greater differences appeared in the area of personal problems, with economic topics continuing to be mentioned most frequently. There seemed to be a common concern with pocketbook issues that cut across socioeconomic distinctions. Other issues attracting some attention included urban crime, housing, the quality of education, medical care, and the scarcity of agricultural commodities resulting from endemic bottlenecks and aggravated by a drought earlier in the year. But none of these generated the level of concern and preoccupation produced by inflation and unemployment. Therefore, our second observation is that the issues identified and the agent for their resolution turned out to be rather similar for all classes and strata.

Given such uniformity, what were the particular courses of action or policy alternatives endorsed by the major social groupings in order to cope with these problems? We offered our respondents a choice among three grand strategies of overall policy priorities, including: (a) continued emphasis on economic development, (b) strengthening the democratic regime, or (c) redistributing wealth.[27] Classes and strata differed, to a limited extent, in the size of the majorities of individuals who favored the developmental alternative of *más desarrollo*. The poor and the manual strata appeared to endorse this alternative somewhat less enthusiastically but, nevertheless, it was the most popular alternative for them (53 per cent and 59 per cent, respectively). The middle-class and the white-collar strata offered identical levels of majority support (66 per cent) for this alternative.

We had expected the manual strata and the poor to endorse the redistributive alternative somewhat more wholeheartedly. After all, it is reasonable to believe that persons who identify themselves as poor have a greater sense of economic deprivation and would have more to gain from such policies. On the other hand, assuming that the upper strata have a more secure economic position and could turn their attention to other issues of more "civic" content—such as the demand for greater efficiency and less corruption in government, and a greater concern with "quality of life" issues—we were surprised to find that they did not feel so secure in an economic sense.

In summary, we found that the issues perceived, the agents identified for their solution, and the course of action to be pursued did not provoke any significant cleavage of opinions among the Venezuelan classes and strata. Neither were the lower classes and strata more adamant about redistribution, nor were the upper less concerned with economic issues. Most seemed to favor the kind of gradualist approach that has characterized the economic policies of the regime, although it is possible that examination of additional evidence would reveal more profound and conflictual differences. To be sure, we are not saying that class conflict does not exist in Venezuela. The explanation of this uniformity of opinion must be sought in the presence of a very powerful state, endowed with abundant resources that have been utilized to subsidize, directly or indirectly, prices and wages. The consensus reveals a general awareness of the very large role played by the state in the economy, and it is obvious that all Venezuelan classes and strata are turning to the state to take care of their more pressing problems, which happen to be economic. Evidence from case studies suggests a pattern of relationships between organized interests and government agencies which fits Lowi's description of interest group liberalism and belies apparent differences between strata in their dependence on government regulation.[28]

Social Inequality, Ideology, and Authoritarianism

Political ideology is one of those topics that refuses to die out or fade away, despite long responsorial psalms intoned by Daniel Bell[29] and others who have managed to deemphasize but not erase the subject from the literature. A number of authors have continued to examine the topic, whether explicitly[30] or through the related notions of "belief systems"[31] and "values."[32] In general, one finds substantial skepticism in the literature concerning the relevance of ideological referents and ideological thinking among the mass public. However, even those who subscribe to such interpretations recognize that there are situations in which ideological tendency provides a more lasting orientation to politics than party labels, especially in situations where the latter are in a state of flux.

Although we will present a more comprehensive discussion of ideology in chapter 5, we can discuss the ideological orientations of the major social groupings here in terms of individual self-placements on the left-right continuum. The work of J. A. Laponce offers a reliable measure of this kind of orientation, predicated on the assumption that "the spatial location of the left-right continuum is a simple and powerful means of reaching an individual's political position in terms of both party preference and ideology. . . ."[33] Our operational measure evolves from the question: "It is also said, in a political sense, that *fulano* or *mengano* are on the right, the center, or the left in Venezuelan politics. Where are you in Venezuelan politics: on the left, the center, or the right?"

We found that 16 per cent of the public did not perceive themselves anywhere on the continuum, while 21 per cent located themselves on the left, 21 per cent in the center, and 31 per cent on the right. Eleven per cent responded "do not know." If this is adjusted to delete the latter and those who did not place themselves anywhere, the distribution of ideological orientations becomes: left, 28 per cent, center, 30 per cent, and right, 42 per cent.

Thus the right seems the modal position of the Venezuelan public, with the center and left trailing behind but not too distant from one another. How reliable is this finding? A study of Caracas *barrio* residents suggested that between 1963 and 1967, the climate of opinion shifted from the left to the right.[34] In contrast, a CENDES-MIT study of predominantly urban elite groups put the proportion of rightists at 37 per cent, leftists at 28 per cent, and centrists at 35 per cent.[35] However, what is the meaning of left and right in Venezuela? Judging from the results of our pretest instrument, using a predominantly urban sample of 250 respondents, those differences entail opposition between rich and poor, or between democratic and revolutionary politics.[36] In addition, the Oficina de Estudios Económicos of the Ministry of Education argued, in a secondary analysis of survey data about Caracas *barrios*, that the term "left" had come to signify something undesirable for the lower classes, associated with violent attempts to overthrow the government, although there was no allusion to the percentages involved.[37] The study argued that, for those groups, the term "right" was being applied with increasing frequency to the government, that is, the target of leftist revolutionary violence.[38]

The evidence presented in table III-2 confirms the existence of a relationship between ideological preference and socioeconomic status. The lower the status of the class, stratum, or reference group, the greater the frequency of a rightist orientation. The opposite does not hold, for although preference for the right declines with increasing status, a preference for the left is not substituted. Instead, a centrist orientation becomes more frequent. Only the student group and the professional stratum escape this rightist predominance, with only the former favoring the left most frequently. In short, there is a rightist predominance that seems more pronounced among the lower strata of the society, and there is a smooth decline in such an orientation as one moves up through the strata.

Additional commentary concerning these data is necessary for further evaluation of extant views on the authoritarian leanings of the classes. In terms of the literature of Latin American politics, the authoritarian threat is perceived as a predominantly rightist phenomenon, returning these societies to their corporatist tradition.[39] The Venezuelan lower strata's preference for the right is less an endorsement of corporatism than a reaction against the left for trying to destroy a popularly elected democratic government. Even though the right has been a true and tested option in Venezuelan politics, there is little sympathy from these lower strata for rightist parties; this preference is in many cases a reaction against leftist authoritarianism.

Neither do we find Venezuelan workers very susceptible to rightist authoritarianism. More importantly, it cannot be said that the workers are the most authoritarian group. To be sure, a plurality of workers prefer the right, but only by a margin of four percentage points over the left. In addition, the group that seems to be consistently rightist is the group of low status agricultural workers. Whether one examines their preferences as a stratum (agricultural poor) or as a reference group (peasants), they always turn out to be predominantly rightist. In terms of the literature of Latin American politics, the authoritarian threat is perceived from the right as a response to liberal or populist inability to cope with a host of problems that have advanced the popularity of the left. Thus, if a rightist orientation is predicated on preference for more authoritarian forms of government, this is to be found among the poor and among women, not among workers or middle-class identifiers.

We fail to detect strong middle-class support for the right. The preferences of the middle class are not that markedly rightist, for although the value of the index of rightist dominance is $+9$, the difference between rightist and centrist preferences within the class is a mere two percentage points. Furthermore, the middle-class strata cannot really be labeled rightist, except perhaps the lower white-collar strata, the most heterogeneous of these. A centrist

Social Context of Political Experience

Table III-2. Ideological Orientation by Major Socioeconomic Cleavages

	Left	Center (percentage points)	Right	(A)[1]	(B)[2]
Classes, eta = .15					
Poor (323)	26	22	52	+26	.13
Middle class (663)	28	35	37	+9	−.06
Strata, eta = .22					
Agricultural poor (143)	25	16	59	+34	.25
Manual poor (197)	29	24	47	+18	.05
Manual middle class (255)	28	25	47	+19	.06
Lower white collar (151)	29	31	40	+11	−.04
Upper white collar (93)	28	40	32	+4	−.12
Professional (157)	31	43	26	−5	−.24
Reference groups, eta = .11					
Peasants (82)	26	23	51	+25	.15
Workers (242)	35	26	39	+4	−.12
Housewives (213)	15	27	59	+44	.37
Common people (194)	31	33	36	+5	−.11
Middle class (171)	23	39	38	+15	.01
Students (132)	42	29	29	−13	−.35

Note: Numerals in parentheses are frequencies.

[1] Index of rightist dominance = (percentage on right − percentage on left).

[2] Deviation from population mean (2.14) in standardized units.

orientation is more frequent here. The preferences of the combined white-collar strata (upper and lower) are right 37 per cent, center 34 per cent, and left 29 per cent, while the preferences of the combined manual strata (poor and middle class) are right 46 per cent, center 25 per cent, and left 29 per cent. Thus, whether in absolute or comparative terms, one cannot treat the ideological preferences of the Venezuelan middle class as rightist.

In short, there are relatively accentuated differences between the ideological preferences of socioeconomic groups in Venezuela. Such differences may be summarized as follows. First, there is an undeniable preference for the right among the lower classes and strata, especially the poor and the peasants. Second, women as a group are very rightist and their distribution throughout the strata contributes to the observed strength of this ideological orientation, regardless of its social context. Third, it cannot be said that workers are more rightist, although the manual strata seem to prefer it. However, the former cannot be perceived as more authoritarian except under the most generous of definitions. Fourth, the middle sectors cannot be suspected of explicit preference for the right; the higher the status, the more frequent the identification with the center. Finally, a relatively strong preference for the left can only be found in terms of group identifications, not class images or social stratification, and it is the students and the workers who turn out to be more leftist.

Social Inequality and Political Participation

Observable differences in evaluations, policy preferences, and ideological orientations of major social groupings in Venezuela can be discussed, with a degree of latitude, within the parameters found in the literature. Classes and strata may or may not, in fact, be associated with particular clusters of attitudes and orientations, but apparent gaps between theory and reality do not require much reevaluation of the premises of contemporary social science. Environmental and contextual differences probably suffice to explain such gaps. At the same time, Latin America's political experience suggests that the paradigm of Western political development, in its liberal and Marxist varieties, falls short of satisfactory theoretical explanation and actual political relevance. When one turns to the area of political participation, defined as "behavior oriented to influence the distribution of public goods,"[40] it becomes necessary to go beyond contextual differences and question some of the premises found in the literature.

We believe that the Venezuelan political system provides a valid context for the study of participation; one finds a type of political behavior there which justifies usage of the definition of participation: elections can produce turnover of the party in power, political opposition is considered legitimate, and a wide variety of political preferences have the available institutional mechanisms to organize and offer themselves as alternatives. However, two features of that context, a system of compulsory suffrage and the predominant role of parties in the political process, produce a kind of participatory behavior that seems to contradict much of what has been taken for granted in analyses of participation in industrialized societies.

In previous commentary and discussion we have shown that the Venezuelan public has complied with compulsory suffrage, a fairly common feature of Latin American electoral systems, to the extent that *there are no differences in the rate of electoral participation of the classes and strata.*[41] The threat of legal sanction, the ability of the major parties to organize and mobilize the electorate, the perceived efficacy of electoral campaigns, and a high level of support for the institution of elections are the probable reasons behind this uniformity. In addition, we have also shown that in the area of campaign participation, socioeconomic differences are limited to individual exposure to campaign stimuli, while they have very little impact on individual participation and on the perceived efficacy of electoral campaigns.[42] In summary, our evidence suggests that *there is no relationship between social inequality and electoral participation in Venezuela.*

This in itself would not be noteworthy were it not for the fact that until the publication of Verba and Nie's seminal work the literature of political participation had come to assume the universality of the nexus between higher socioeconomic status, a more "civic" orientation to politics, a greater sense of personal political efficacy, and higher rates of participation. Studying the Venezuelan case, we have come to the conclusion that this nexus, described as the "standard socioeconomic model" by Verba and Nie,[43] may be more characteristic of systems with voluntary participation and/or without strongly articulated parties.[44]

In addition, we found that the rates of activity in other participatory modes is higher for individuals of lower socioeconomic status. Partisan participation, the formal membership or militancy in a political party, is more frequent among the lower strata: 43 per cent for the agricultural poor, 42 per cent for the manual poor, 37 per cent for the manual middle class, 31 per cent for the lower white collar, 23 per cent for the upper white collar, and 28 per cent for the professional. In essence, *in Venezuela, the rate of party membership decreases with increasing socioeconomic status*. The significance of this is best understood in terms of Verba and Nie's qualified utilization of the standard socioeconomic model:

> If the socioeconomic model "works" and there are no additional forces that cause deviation from it, the result is that citizens of upper social status participate more than those of lower social status. The consequences of such a situation would, of course, be significant in terms of government response to participation.
> . . . Therefore, the consequences of participation for social and economic equality might differ substantially if what brought individuals to participate were high socioeconomic status rather than some other force. . . .[45]

A host of theoretical questions emerge from this deviation concerning the rest of the components of the model.

We have some reservations about the concept of political efficacy. Ever since Angus Campbell and his associates first formulated this concept in 1954,[46] political efficacy has been measured in the same fashion, asking individuals whether they feel that they can influence the government, whether the government cares about what people like themselves think, and so forth. At issue here is whether there are "correct" responses to these kinds of questions, and whether the absence of the "appropriate" response can be treated as a failure of the respondent to understand the political process. Study after study has shown that in general, the poor and the ill-educated feel less efficacious than their more affluent counterparts.[47] The problem is that, for the most part, these studies attribute this low sense of efficacy to ignorance, inexperience, and lack of empathy with civic norms conducive to participation which are learned through political socialization.[48]

This mode of thinking betrays a profound misunderstanding of the experiences that individuals and groups of different social standing have in dealing with the government, as well as a blind eye for situations in which the nature of the regime prevents a valid application of the definition of participation. In short, the current theoretical standing of the concept limits its applicability to the political experiences that middle-class or higher-status groups have in dealing with government officials. It forgets that the disproportionate participation of the latter is "significant in terms of governmental response." We prefer to speak of personal *political capacity* instead of sense of personal political efficacy. We measure the former with questions on efficacy but do not assume that there must be a "correct" response indicating successful experiences in dealing with government officials. We limit ourselves to recording whether or not this has been the case, defining personal political capacity as "the extent to which individuals believe that they can influence the distribution of public goods."[49]

The Venezuelan case is relevant because, despite a pattern of participation that does not fit the standard socioeconomic model, one finds that *the level of political capacity increases with socio-economic status*. The evidence presented in figures 8 and 9 is conclusive in this regard, showing a trend that fits the postulates of the standard socioeconomic model concerning greater levels of political capacity with increasing socioeconomic status. Differences within the manual strata (II and III) and within the white-collar strata (IV and V) are not statistically significant, but this does not seem to affect the linearity of the relationship between these two variables. The poor feel singularly incapable, although there is a substantial number of incapables among the middle class. The same low level

Figure 8. Levels of Political Capacity of the Classes

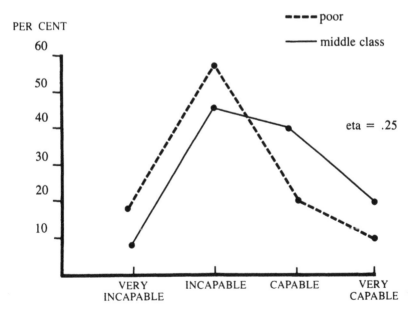

Figure 9. Levels of Political Capacity of the Strata

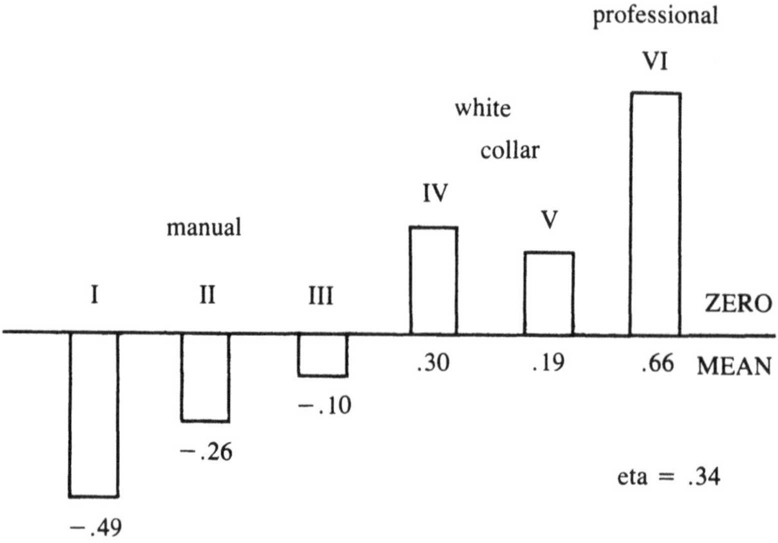

Note: Values in standardized (Z) scores.

of capacity is observable for the agricultural poor. In short, the Venezuelan case presents a situation in which greater levels of political capacity are not accompanied by greater participation in the electoral, campaign, and partisan modes.

If the greater sense of political capacity of the upper strata cannot be explained in terms of higher involvement in the aforementioned participatory activities, what is really the impact of successful experiences? We have shown that even though they participate more on the partisan mode and at levels comparable with the upper strata on the electoral and campaign modes, the lower strata feel less capable. Consequently, if there is a relationship between political capacity and political participation, this does not include voting, campaigning, and membership in a political party. After all, such activities do not have a direct, immediate impact on the distribution of public goods. Therefore, one has to attribute higher levels of capacity to successful experiences in other participatory modes, such as contacting public officials and involvement in community problem solving.

We do not have additional data concerning these modes of participation.[50] Therefore, we cannot really test the relationship for these kinds of activities. However, we have maintained the view that the items utilized to measure "trust in government" measure individual experience in dealing with the government. At the same time, our treatment of political efficacy follows a similar orientation. In essence, we treat trust in government as evaluation of what the government does, while we interpret capacity as evaluation of what the individual can make government do. If we combine the two, we obtain a two-dimensional configuration of what can be treated as *participatory mood*. The work of William A. Gamson,[51] among others, suggests that certain combinations of trust and efficacy, or capacity and evaluation as amended in our usage, are conducive to different varieties and rates of participation. Dichotomizing the categories of these two measures into high and low capacity and negative or positive evaluation of government action, we constructed a fourfold typology of participatory moods, as follows: (1) *supportive*, characterized by high capacity and a positive evaluation of regime policies, (2) *deferent*, predicated on positive evaluation and low capacity, (3) *discontent*, combining negative evaluation and low capacity, and (4) *critical*, a combination of negative evaluation and high capacity believed optimal by Gamson.[52] To be sure, participatory mood is not actual participation but is a relevant measure of actual experiences involving the ultimate target of participation—that is, what the government does.

Figure 10. Participatory Moods of the Classes

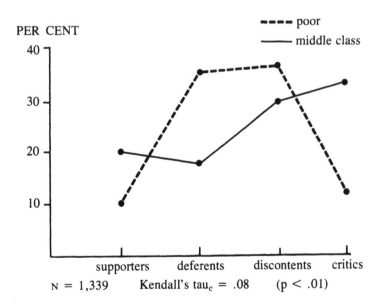

PER CENT

- - - - poor
——— middle class

N = 1,339   Kendall's tau$_c$ = .08   (p < .01)

Social Context of Political Experience

The distribution of the four types of participatory moods among the classes and strata are presented in figure 10 and table III-3. The former shows the predominance of deferents and discontents among the poor, while discontents and critics prevail within the middle class; supporters appear in relatively short supply. Table III-3 shows that the professional stratum contains the greatest proportions of critics and supporters, which implies a high potential for conflict and cleavage. Critics are a plurality of the lower white collar stratum, while discontents constitute the plurality of the agricultural poor, the manual poor, and the upper white collar. These distributions seem to contradict Gamson's hypothesis to the extent that participation rates seem to be greater for the strata with the higher proportions of discontents, not critics. In other words, critics do not seem to play the role of complete activists in Venezuela.

One obvious inference is that the relationship between participation and participatory mood may be the reverse of what one would imagine. The literature suggests that, in general, persons of lower socioeconomic status participate less since they feel less efficacious. However, Cornelius, and others, have asked whether the feeling of political efficacy is a result of a participatory act, and not a precondition for the act.[53] Our data suggest that the lower strata, even though they do not have the participatory moods more conducive to participation, participate more. In short, we find a reversal of the causal sequence postulated by the standard socioeconomic model.

It could be argued that the critics and discontents of the upper strata participate less because they can afford to, since their higher levels of capacity reflect successful experiences in other areas. By

Table III-3. Participatory Moods of the Strata

	I	II	III	IV	V	VI
Supporters	8	14	19	18	19	29
Deferents	38	31	32	20	18	12
Discontents	42	39	32	26	33	19
Critics	12	16	17	36	30	40

Note: All of the figures in row percentages.
Kendall's tau$_c$ = .06 (p < .01).
N = 1,364.

70

contrast, the lower strata, in spite of their less successful experiences, seem to maximize their participatory rates, especially in the partisan mode, as if to create conditions of obligation that may allow them greater access to influencing public policy. That is, their involvement suggests an attempt to create a network of influence, not available otherwise due to their low social condition.

Lacking data on the rest of the modes of participation, we cannot further refine our analysis; that is, we cannot probe the sources of participation input in those modes. However, we can try to detect the sources of withdrawal from participation under hypothetical conditions. This would be possible by comparing rates of electoral participation of the classes and strata if compulsory participation were abolished in Venezuela. In addition, similar comparisons are possible with respect to another form of withdrawal, namely, the likelihood of "null voting" in any given election, a type of behavior often associated with protest and discontent.

One certain way to demobilize the Venezuelan system would be to adopt a system of voluntary suffrage. This could cut the rate of electoral participation in half, reducing electoral turnover to about 48 per cent, with a group of about 4 per cent conditioning their participation to the relevance of the election. It appears that only the upper white collar and the professional strata would continue to participate in elections by a proportion larger than the majority, 52 and 58 per cent, respectively. The manual poor (at 41 per cent), the lower white collar (at 45 per cent), and the agricultural poor and the manual middle class (each at 46 per cent) would be less likely to continue participation. In short, *under voluntary suffrage the standard socioeconomic model would work in the Venezuelan case—that is, electoral demobilization would introduce socioeconomic distinctions in voting turnout.* Whether the model would be applicable in toto is a different proposition, since comparable declines in the rates of other participatory modes would have to be registered as well. For example, this would not be likely in the partisan mode, since even though the lower strata would vote less if not compelled to do so, they have higher rates of partisan participation at the present time. In addition, one would have to examine the relationship between participatory rates, efficacy, and civic attitudes, and there are unresolved theoretical problems concerning the relationship between voluntaristic participation and civic attitudes. By this we mean that it is difficult to treat as civic, which we read as a surrogate of altruistic, the motives behind behavior intended to influence the distribution of public goods.[54]

Consider the problem in relation to the motivation that leads individuals to affiliate with a political party in Venezuela. If we classify the reasons offered by the 547 respondents who are party members in terms of personal and institutional or, better, patronage versus principle, we find that individuals from the lower strata cite personal reasons with greater frequency. There is a drastic decline from the 58 per cent of party members among the agricultural poor who admit to patronage considerations for their affiliation to the 28 per cent of the professional. But *camburismo*, the relentless pursuit of patronage, is a very common phenomenon in Venezuela, and we view these differences with some skepticism, reading the evidence to mean that the upper strata are less dependent on the political parties to satisfy some basic needs such as employment, housing, and adequate health care. We saw that these were dominant policy concerns among the lower strata and believe that their higher rates of party membership reflect the attempt to secure access to these public goods, otherwise unavailable to them through the private sector. This is the basic difference, which needs no hypothetical situation for clarification. Thus, with compulsory suffrage, voting becomes a legal obligation without socioeconomic differences. Under voluntary suffrage, voting would perhaps become more directly related to civic attitudes, but this would not change the present rates of partisan affiliation which favor the lower strata.

Concerning "blank" and "null voting," conventional wisdom has stressed the element of protest, suggesting that ". . . blank voting is indicative because the voter is clearly motivated to vote but frustrated in not finding any alternative appropriate to express his own political identification. By blank voting he withdraws from the decision making process for the purpose of making his dissatisfaction known. . . . Blank voting may represent more than alienation, it may represent an active hostility to the regime. . . ."[55] Although there is considerable truth in this explanation, several problems are associated with it. First, there is the element of voting turnout. We believe that nonvoting in relatively low turnout situations, as in the United States, simply cannot be equated to nonvoting in a high turnout, compulsory voting situation like Venezuela's. The explanation does not take into account the different turnout rates postulated by the standard socioeconomic model. Second, although blank voting and null voting may be instruments of protest, error seems to be a more important component in the variation of the latter.[56] Third, the explanation is too biased in favor of rational theories of voting, which are, of course, but one of the plausible explanations of the voting act.[57] Finally, the fact that a blank ballot and a ballot which becomes nonvalid because of an infringement of electoral rules are not differentiated in the official reporting of the vote does not prove that there is no difference between them.

We probed the reasons why 409 of our respondents would consider voting null in a given election. Those who specifically mentioned protest constitute but 8 per cent of this group, while dislike of the candidates or parties was the more frequent reason adduced by 45 per cent. More importantly, the probability of null voting increases with socioeconomic status, although not in a monotonic fashion: 21 per cent of the agricultural poor, 19 per cent of the manual poor, 27 per cent of the manual middle class, 36 per cent of the lower white collar, 35 per cent of the upper white collar, and 31 per cent of the professional strata would consider the null vote as a viable alternative in an election. Thus, the element of protest is not very prominent even though, during the Venezuelan campaign of 1973, the argument was advanced that the *voto nulo* opened "significant possibilities to the armed revolutionary movement," constituting the ideal avenue of protest against the "militarized" Venezuelan democracy.[58] Our data suggest that this type of withdrawal from electoral participation would be more likely to reflect the momentary dissatisfaction of the strata with the largest proportions of critics, namely, the lower white collar and the professional. These more capable individuals would abstain from electoral participation if unable to support candidates and programs, while their lower-status counterparts would do so on more permanent bases if voting were no longer a civic obligation supported by legal sanction.

What is the applicability of the standard socioeconomic model of political participation to the Venezuelan case? Undoubtedly, the more appropriate strategy to test the model would be to weigh the causal importance of the different factors for several participatory modes. Elsewhere we have shown that, under present conditions of compulsory suffrage, little can be explained in rates of electoral participation, and that socioeconomic factors have very limited impact on electoral withdrawal and null voting.[59] We have discussed the applicability of the model to campaign participation in a separate effort, concluding that while the standard socioeconomic model is not totally inadequate in explaining campaign activism in Venezuela, some of the better-known links predicated by the model cannot be substantiated.[60] Also, we prefer to postpone discussion of the causality of partisan participation until chapter 6.

On the evidence reviewed thus far, we can conclude that, while allowing for the fact that any model of participation should be tested in as many modes as possible, the standard socioeconomic model is found more adequate in explaining differences in participatory rates than in applying subsidiary assumptions emphasizing the importance of efficacy and civic-mindedness. Our data show that, under compulsory suffrage, differences in participatory rates are minimal or in a direction opposite that postulated by the model. Differences would emerge between rates of participation of classes and strata if voluntary suffrage were introduced. In general, our view is that partisanship and not the social circumstances of individuals may provide a more relevant baseline. However, in the light of the Venezuelan example, our most serious criticism of the model involves the supposed linkage between efficacy, trust, and participation. Neither is efficacy as crucial as it is purported to be, nor lack of trust in government such a decisive deflator of participation.

Stratification and Political Party Preference

For many years, the topic of political parties and partisanship was foremost in the minds of political scientists. However, as Martz commented more than a decade ago (and as remains largely true today) Latin Americanists never approached the disciplinary trend in their attention to the topic.[61] Without entering into a full discussion of the central role of parties in Venezuelan politics until later (in chapter 6), we will describe the more obvious overlappings between party sympathies and socioeconomic inequality. The exercise will not exhaust the question of class and party but will at least sketch the more fundamental aspects of the Venezuelan case.

Our first observation is that, as witnessed by the evidence in table III-4, there are no strong linkages between class and party in Venezuela. Second, our data show that party support is less variable than party opposition across the strata. For example, the upper stratum is more unique in its profound dislike of Acción Democrática (AD), than in its support of the Social Christian COPEI. The lower stratum is very hostile to leftist parties, especially the Movimiento al Socialismo (MAS). Third, opposition to leftist parties like MAS and the Communists (PCV) decreases with increasing socioeconomic status, while opposition to the Social Democratic AD and the Social Christian COPEI shows somewhat less fluctuation. At the time of our survey (fall 1973) we found that a plurality of party identifiers, who themselves represented about two-thirds of the electorate, identified with COPEI. The newness of the bonds of party identification in Venezuela, the outcome of the 1973 elections, and the manner in which party identification is measured lead us to doubt the accuracy of this datum, but differences between the strata are of sufficient

Table III-4. Stratification and Party Preferences

				Strata				Popula-
		I	II	III	IV	V	VI	tion
Opposed to . . . [a]	AD	10	17	23	26	34	37	24
(eta = .16)	PCV	46	44	48	33	29	25	38
Hostile toward . . . [b]	AD	44	45	55	55	54	65	53
	COPEI	53	53	43	39	36	33	44
	MAS	81	80	72	62	55	47	67
Identify with . . .	AD	49	42	32	30	43	22	36
(eta = .13)	COPEI	33	36	42	47	46	49	42
	MAS	6	8	11	11	6	19	10
	MEP*	7	6	6	8	2	6	6
	CCN*	5	8	8	4	2	3	6
Polarization . . . [c]	AD	63	62	46	42	45	33	50
(eta = .21)	COPEI	37	38	54	57	55	67	50

		Peasants	Workers	House-wives	
Polarization . . . [c]	AD	54	54	52	
(eta = .12)	COPEI	46	46	48	

		Common people	Middle class	Students	
	AD	52	41	38	50
	COPEI	48	59	62	50

Note: All table values are row percentages. Data on opposition and hostility do not include the complete cross-tabulations with stratification.

[a] As measured by response to the question "Is there any party in Venezuela for which you would *never* vote . . . ?"

[b] Measured by thermometer responses indicating "no sympathy whatsoever. . . . "

[c] Responses to the question "Suppose that there were only two political parties in Venezuela, Acción Democrática and COPEI. Which of these two would you vote for?"

*MEP is Movimiento Electoral del Pueblo; CCN is Cruzada Cívica Nacionalista.

magnitude and are repeated with enough frequency to suggest that, in general, *the distribution of support for and sympathy toward AD and COPEI duplicates*, to a limited degree, *the classical type of overlap between party preference and socioeconomic status.*

This becomes more evident by focusing on the hypothetical situation of a two-party system in which the choices would be limited to AD and COPEI. This kind of two-party polarization, presented at the bottom of table III-4, would divide the poor (I and II) versus the middle-class strata (III through VI), with AD favored by the former and COPEI by the latter. Class and stratification differences would both be relevant in this regard, as suggested by a two-way analysis of variance performed on the data to determine whether class differences would overshadow differences between the strata.[62] This result is particularly relevant since there is a tendency to deemphasize programmatic and socioeconomic differences of the constituencies of the two parties.[63] To be sure, both are centrist and more or less populist, and subject to the catchall tendency suggested by students of Western European party systems[64] and by observers of the North American case.[65] However, in spite of the relative accuracy of the observation that AD and COPEI are very similar in many respects, the strata do not see it that way. That is, given a situation in which opinion was forced to polarize between AD and COPEI, such polarization of party support would considerably overlap class and stratification cleavages.

Additional evidence concerning the reference groups confirms that this would be the case. The cleavages are not that pronounced but do overlap with class and stratification differences. Finally, if the comparisons of polarized support for AD and COPEI are conducted in terms of the manual versus the white-collar strata, the result would be 54 to 46 per cent in favor of the AD within the manual, and 56 to 44 per cent in favor of COPEI within the white collar. Thus, the evidence is consistent in showing a configuration of considerable polarization of party preference along class and stratification lines.

It has been argued, with considerable justification, that the dominance exerted by AD and COPEI in the Venezuelan party system reduces the overlap between social inequality and party preference.[66] We do not wish to exaggerate the degree to which the classes and strata would become polarized if their partisan choices were limited to these two. After all, 24 per cent of the population would abstain from endorsing either if such were the case. On the other hand, we are not certain whether a two-party system would be better for Venezuela than the present multiparty configuration.

Social Context of Political Experience

With only AD and COPEI to choose from, class and stratification differences would become more explicit, but this does not necessarily mean that Venezuelan politics would become radicalized as a result. However, at the present time, the parties of the left have managed to produce comparable cleavages in terms of the opposition, not the support, they generate.

Even though the multiparty nature of the system and the dominance of the populist parties tend to diminish the cleavage potential and extant differences between classes and strata, the linkage between the two would be strengthened by the polarization of support for the two dominant parties. Only the MAS is capable of generating a comparable pattern, as seen at a glance in the evidence presented in table III-5. Thermometer scores[67] measuring the affective distance between the individual and the political parties were standardized to compare differences between the strata. These summarize support, as well as opposition to the parties. We found that they were statistically significant only for AD, COPEI, and MAS. With the exception of the position of the upper white-collar stratum (V) in a hierarchy of increasing level of sympathy for these three parties, sympathy toward them varied with stratification. The relationship is strongest for MAS, suggesting that by itself it is the only party

Table III-5. Stratification and Party Sympathy

AD		COPEI		MAS	
.19	(I)	.21	(VI)	.45	(VI)
.14	(II)	.18	(V)	.16	(V)
.03	(V)	.11	(IV)	.11	(IV)
−.06	(III)	−.01	(III)	−.05	(III)
−.09	(IV)	−.14	(II)	−.24	(II)
−.22	(VI)	−.21	(I)	−.25	(I)
eta = .14		eta = .15		eta = .23	

Note: Values presented in the table are standardized (Z) means computed from those obtained in multiple range (one-way) analyses of variance. Positive values indicate sympathy, while negative ones suggest antipathy. Horizontal bars separate strata (identified with parentheses) that differ in their mean values of sympathy for the parties.

capable of producing relatively strong reaction along class and status lines. AD and COPEI would produce such reaction, as suggested above, but only in opposition to one another, only when they are contrasted to one another.

In conclusion, although our evidence suggests that the relationship between status and party preference is not presently very strong in Venezuela, there are sufficient elements to suggest that the relationship is relevant and that it could become even more so. It is difficult to predict whether this duo-centric dominance of the AD and COPEI will continue, whether one of the two will become dominant, or whether a third party will attain comparable levels of support. As far as the classes and strata are concerned, that third party could count on the support of the upper, not the lower, strata if on the left. It is doubtful whether a rightist party could take advantage of this kind of situation and count on the support of the lower strata. However, it is clear that the policy performance of the regime would play a large role in determining the actual outcome, since this is the filter through which the two dominant parties would have to pass in order to continue with majority support.

4

Cultural Diversity and Political Cleavages, I:
The Community Context

Introduction

For those who might deliberately choose to downplay the importance of class conflict in order to examine other important sources of societal cleavages, the literature of sociocultural sources of political conflict is germane. Robert A. Dahl was so inclined when he complained that

> . . . a preoccupation with class conflict and often an unarticulated assumption even among sophisticated social theorists that classes are somehow the "real" basis of differences in an industrial society, to which all others are "ultimately" reducible, has tended to deflect attention from other sources that give rise to durable subcultures into which individuals are socialized: these are differences in religion, language, race, or ethnic group, and region.[1]

Reviewers of the literature of "cultural segmentation" underline the fact that profound socioeconomic cleavages interact with those based on broad ideological or religious foundations to create the patterns of political conflict that are characteristic of *segmented pluralism*.[2] Our analysis of cultural cleavages is less a symptom of scholarly sophistication than an attempt to examine potential sources of political conflict beyond the socioeconomic. This implies two related tasks—the identification of areas where cultural differences are significant, and of factors which confound or reduce such differences.[3]

Unlike North American pluralism, which rests on horizontal or crosscutting patterns of institutional loyalties, segmented pluralism is conducive to ". . . the organization of social movements, educational and communications systems, voluntary associations, and political parties along the lines of religious and ideological cleavages. . . ."[4] In a subculturally segmented society, institutional solidarities are vertical. Therefore this kind of pluralism poses the problem that these cleavages tend to reinforce one another, creating a network of vertical solidarities that isolates different groups or pillars in the society.[5] Students of this phenomenon have offered the concept of *verzuiling* ("pillarization") to describe the tendency to establish organizational networks based on vertical solidarities.[6] The result is the emergence of clearly distinguishable pillars (*zuilen*) or blocs which come to represent the institutional expression of socially isolated and generally antagonistic subcultural groups.[7]

Although the literature of comparative politics does not offer a lengthy list of possible or actual sources of cultural segmentation, the relationships among these lines of cleavage are rather complex. Religion, language, and regionalism comprise preponderant lines of cleavage in culturally segmented societies. However, these three do not always appear in the same order of importance, nor do they represent a constant factor: in Belgium, linguistic and religious cleavages seem to be more relevant;[8] in Switzerland, linguistic, religious, and class cleavages;[9] in Austria, ideological and religious cleavages;[10] and in the Netherlands, religious and class cleavages.[11] Thus the different *zuilen* (Netherlands), *familles spirituelles* and *Weltanschauungsgruppen* (Belgium), and *Lager* (Austria)—which posed formidable threats to the national integration of these societies—can all be conceptualized as cultural conflict groups, but their internal composition is not always the same, nor have they responded to the same hierarchy of cleavages.[12]

Lipset and Rokkan's attempt to deal with the interaction between economic and cultural sources of societal cleavages and their impact on the politics of national integration in Western Europe departs from the premise that there is ". . . *a hierarchy of cleavage* bases in each system and [that] these orders of political primacy not only vary among polities, but also tend to undergo changes over time. . . . [Moreover] we rarely find one criterion of alignment completely dominant. . . . But we often find differences between regions in the weight of one or the other criterion of alignment. . . ."[13] It should be remembered, moreover, that cultural diversity is not necessarily conducive to fragmentation or segmentation. Obler and Steiner are helpful on this point: "By cultural diversity we mean simply that the members of a political system differ with regard to cultural attributes, such as language and religion. The people sharing the same cultural attribute may or may not form a subculture in the sense of subcultural segmentation. The latter concept should also not be confused with subcultural hostility; the existence of subcultures does not necessarily mean that there is hostility among them. . . ."[14]

There is little in the literature of Latin American politics to suggest that the concepts in these prefatory remarks have much applicability there. Some of the cultural revisionists have alluded to the fragmentation of Latin American societies in order to "show" that this fragmentation differs from North American pluralism.[15] Our caveat is that if the analyses of the theorists of consociationalism show that fragmentation and intricate patterns of cultural solidarities can be overcome, then the case of the cultural revisionists—and their assumptions about the influence of Hispanic culture on Latin American political integration—is much weaker. In addition, we are well aware that Venezuela is not territorially small, speaks but one language, and lacks politically relevant ethnic diversity. Thus we will proceed with caution.

Cultural Diversity in Venezuela

Analysis of the politics of national integration in Latin America has focused on *caudillismo*. After all, the politics of *caudillismo* is perhaps the major difference between the politics of integration in Western European "center" nations and the "peripheral" countries of Latin America. During much of the nineteenth century, regionally based *caudillos* monopolized the key decisional structures of the Venezuelan Republic.[16] Nonetheless, as Frank Safford has suggested recently, "to identify a government with its principal figure is to substitute a metaphor for serious description of a system."[17] *Caudillismo* is simply too important to be left out of the politics of national integration in Venezuela. Still, *caudillismo* was the natural result of the patterns of conflict in the politics of the period, for there were great issues that mobilized people along the major lines of societal cleavage, providing the justification for interest conflict.

During the nineteenth century Venezuela was convulsed by the "classical issues" of the national period of Latin America:[18] separation of church and state and the simmering dispute over *patronato* rights;[19] the agrarian question;[20] protracted controversy which pitted federalist against centralist, ultimately leading to the Federal War and the destruction of the Conservative party and the oligarchy;[21] the issue of slavery, settled in 1854 by abolition but without great social consequences of an immediate nature;[22] and the conflict between planters and *comerciantes*.[23]

These do not offer conclusive proof that Venezuelan society was segmented along regional, religious, or ideological lines. Rather, they attest to the fact that regionalism, ideology, and religion have been historical cleavages in Venezuelan politics and that, at one time or another, society was polarized along these lines. One cannot talk about "denominationalism" in Venezuela because Catholicism is still the religion of the majority of believers; therefore, this "trait cleavage"—to use the language of Rae and Taylor[24]—is not likely to produce "pillarization" in Venezuelan politics. In fact, it could be argued that although the education issue has crystallized this cleavage on two occasions within the last thirty years, partial pillarization of the Catholics and the reduced number of intense secular antagonists on this issue has kept such religious conflict within manageable bounds.[25] On the other hand, although the Catholic Church has been traditionally weak in Venezuela, this has not led to the emergence of a rival denomination.[26]

Regionalism, admittedly less important than it once was, is still a factor.[27] Integration and the emergence of a strong central state dealt a death blow to provincial *caudillos*, but regional factions can still be found within the major political parties and organizations, and the regions have consistently reflected distinct political preferences in national elections. Ideology was sufficiently salient to precipitate the radicalization of the Venezuelan left during the early sixties, while parties and candidates still boast about their commitment to nationalism and social democracy, if not to socialist redistribution. In short, there are indications that, although religion, ideology, and regionalism do not produce the profound divisiveness which is characteristic of segmentation, they are elements of cultural diversity in Venezuela.

More recent analyses of cultural diversity in Venezuela have focused on "cultural dualism," defined in terms of two phenomena: first, the coexistence of two adjacent cultures under the same system of political power, and second, the coexistence "within one social stratum of individuals with attitudes typical of two or more basic patterns of value orientation . . . individuals with modern personalities and others with traditional personalities."[28]

To summarize, the literature suggests three cultural cleavages in Venezuela: regionalism, of notorious historical standing but apparently diminishing in importance; ideology, which is often mentioned but has not been clearly applied to specific areas of opinion or behavior; and religion, which has played an intense but limited and occasional role. In this chapter we attempt to measure the actual importance of regionalism as a source of cleavage in contemporary Venezuelan politics, comparing its impact with that of other cultural cleavages, and testing for possible spuriousness or interactive effects.

Cultural Diversity and Political Cleavages

The study of societal cleavages, cultural or otherwise, cannot proceed cleavage by cleavage but must analyze constellations of conflict lines within each polity. Regionalism has been the most frequently mentioned source of societal cleavage in Venezuela,[29] and thus provides a convenient starting point. Furthermore, regionalism can serve as a baseline or axis along which we may examine other cultural factors related to this territorial dimension.

Two initial problems must be faced. First, there are as many classifications of Venezuelan regions as there are authors who have addressed the topic. Second, purely quantitative methods may not be sufficient. Results of extensive factor analyses showed us that the emerging configuration of regions, based on factor scores, did not fit the more conventional of the extant regional typologies;[30] these have been based primarily on geographic and cultural factors that are both elusive and difficult to quantify. Sharing Simeon and Elkins' conviction that regionalism is not simply the result of an uneven geographical distribution of demographic and socioeconomic characteristics, and that routine attitudinal differences resulting from such a distribution do not constitute the "political culture" of those regions,[31] we were disturbed by these factor-analytic results. In their analysis of the political heterogeneity of Canadian provinces, Simeon and Elkins have argued that regions are essentially containers, and that other factors are necessary to account for variations in their content. In short, if it means anything at all, regionalism represents a conduit for the expression of "the ethos or community norms of an area deriving from particular historical forces and events."[32] We embrace this analytical orientation in our treatment of Venezuelan regionalism.

Most typologies of Venezuelan regionalism emphasize factors related to the terrain and to the relative isolation of the different regions from the center. Few would dispute the salience of at least three distinct major geographical areas: the Andes, the plains, and the coastal regions. On the other hand, not all the outlying regions had the same type of interaction with the capital in terms of center-periphery relations.[33] Furthermore, the overall process of social change has homogenized the different regions and may have re-

Table IV-1. Typologies of Venezuelan Regionalism

Caldera administration (1969)	DATOS, C.A. (1973)	Martz (1966)	Baloyra and Martz
(1) Capital region: Caracas metropolitan area, Federal District, Miranda	(1) Caracas: Federal District, Miranda, Guárico, Apure	(1) Metropolitan Center: Federal Dist., Aragua, Miranda	(1) Center: Aragua, Carabobo, Federal Dist., Miranda
(2) Central region: Aragua, Carabobo, Cojedes, Guárico	(2) La Línea: Aragua, Carabobo, Cojedes, Lara, Portuguesa, Yaracuy	(2) Plains-Guayana: Anzoátegui, Apure, Barinas, Bolívar, Cojedes, Guárico, Monagas, Portuguesa	(2) Plains: Apure, Barinas, Cojedes, Guárico
(3) Center-West: Falcón, Lara, Portuguesa (*except* Sucre district, and *municipio* Guanare, Guanare district)	(3) Oil region: Falcón and Zulia	(3) Coastal: Carabobo, Falcón, Lara, Nueva Esparta, Sucre, Yaracuy	(3) West: Falcón, Lara, Portuguesa, Yaracuy
(4) Zulia	(4) Andes: Barinas, Mérida, Táchira, Trujillo	(4) Maracaibo: Zulia	(4) Zulia
(5) Andes: Barinas, Mérida, Táchira, Trujillo; *plus* Sucre district and *municipio* Guanare of	(5) East: Anzoátegui, Bolívar, Monagas, Nueva Esparta, Sucre	(5) Andes: Mérida, Táchira, Trujillo	(5) Andes: Mérida, Táchira, Trujillo

Table IV-1. Typologies of Venezuelan Regionalism (*Continued*)

Caldera administration (1969)	DATOS, C.A. (1973)	Martz (1966)	Baloyra and Martz
Portuguesa; *plus* Páez district, Apure (6) North-East: Anzoátegui, Monagas, Nueva Esparta, Sucre (7) South: Apure (*minus* Páez district) plus Cedeño district, Bolívar (8) Guayana: Bolívar (minus Cedeño district)			(6) East: Anzoátegui, Bolívar, Monagas, Nueva Esparta, Sucre

Note: We have excluded the federal territories of Amazonas and Delta Amacuro, but they are included in all typologies.

duced some of their more idiosyncratic features. On the bases of these considerations we opted for the typology that appears in table IV-1; for the sake of contrast, we have included others developed by the Caldera administration,[34] DATOS, C.A. of Venezuela,[35] and a previous typology offered by Martz.[36]

It could be that our typology is unrealistic in failing to preserve the "true diversity" found among Venezuelan regions, and that our results will be but an artifact of the aggregate characteristics of the clusters of respondents grouped into our six regions. Given the size of our sample, we could not conduct the analysis by state and thus avoid assumptions about the "true" configuration of the different regions. Following this line of reasoning, states could have been grouped in terms of the patterns of similarities and differences between them.[37] However, this would have led us to identify a set of regions which lacked geographical continuity, thereby rendering impossible any assumptions about the fact that these regions share a common historical or community ethos. Moreover, the fact remains that, at the present time, there is no accepted configuration of the regions. To be sure, all typological exercises introduce an inevitable amount of distortion. However, we felt it was more important to emphasize the status of the regions as communities than to create clusters of regions in terms of similar socioeconomic characteristics. If anything, we have tried to preserve the integrity of the units as identified by social historians and commentators on the politics of nation-building in Venezuela. Thus the factors related to the political role of the different regions during the process of national integration were emphasized,[38] and the identity of the units was preserved. In summary, *our typology aims at emphasizing the status of the regions as communities*.

Linz and de Miguel distinguish between "cutting points," such as the cleavages that we have alluded to, and "actual social units."[39] They qualify this dichotomy and its empirical usefulness with the following contention:

> Ideally, the "operationally" defined units based on systematic indicators should coincide to a certain degree with actual social units perceived as "real" by the participants, with historical, administrative, and political continuity, self-consciousness, and solidarity. . . . The historically, geographically, and socially more "real" units sensitize us to new contextual variables and serve as ad hoc explanations of differences observed when people in identical positions, playing comparable roles, differ greatly in their behavior or attitudes. The implicit assumption is that they

are involved in some form of interaction or communication that would account for a certain climate of opinion, shared even by those we would not expect to be predisposed in such direction.[40]

We not only followed this mode of thinking, but also experimented with an alternative typology that included urbanization as a very prominent factor, lending total credence to the contention that urban-rural differences have overshadowed regional ones in Venezuela. The results derived from this alternate typology were essentially the same,[41] with the aggravating factor that, given the territorial discontinuity of the units of this typology, we could not assume that the regions were communities; little theoretical muscle remained to explain the results. Those results allowed us to bring territorial factors into focus, but still left much to be desired. Thus we decided to stay with our initial typology.

To compare the impact of these sources of cultural cleavages we correlated regionalism, ideological tendency, and religion with regime evaluation, institutional evaluation, political participation, and partisanship. Urbanization was added to reflect another cultural cleavage, albeit of more recent historical standing. It has been argued that, in Venezuela, urbanization rather than industrialization has been the primary axis of the unfolding process of modernization. In other words, urbanization is employed as a surrogate for industrialization in mapping the impact of the major cleavages generated by socioeconomic development. In addition, urbanization has been identified as one of the factors contributing to cultural conflict in Venezuela.[42]

Inspection of the correlation coefficients of the matrix presented in table IV-2 suggests that Venezuelan patterns of cultural sources of political cleavages are both limited and complex. First of all, regionalism seems relatively unimportant. Its impact appears confined to regime evaluation and political participation. Second, *urbanization* exerts a more extensive and marked influence, including evaluation, participation, and partisanship. This is accentuated on actual participatory behavior. Third, *ideology* figures more prominently in connection with partisanship, although its impact is also detectable on evaluation and participation. Finally, *religion* exerts a mild influence that appears the least relevant.

Cultural Cleavages and Community Context

This preliminary evaluation would seem to confirm the widespread impression of the diminishing importance of the influence of region-

Table iv-2. The Impact of Cultural Cleavages

	Regionalism[a]	Urbanization[b]	Ideology[c]	Religion[d]
Regime evaluation and regime norms				
Opinion about one-party system	.02*	.03*	-.13	.02*
Opinion about opposition criticism	-.03*	-.03*	.00*	.03*
Opinion about most powerful group in Venezuelan politics	.16	.16	-.05*	-.02*
Evaluation of regime policies[e]	.00*	-.01*	-.15	-.10
Opinion about role of the military in politics	.09	.04*	.04*	.00*
Opinion about coups d'etat	.02*	.00*	.13	.01*
Evaluation of political institutions				
Opinion about politicians[e]	.06*	.07*	-.08	-.09
Criticism of elections[e]	.13	.17	-.08	-.03*
Evaluation of Caldera's policies[f]	-.01*	-.09	-.17	-.01*
Level of political information[g]	.01*	.07*	.08	.02*
Political participation				
Actual membership in political parties	.20	.22	-.11	-.07
Membership at any time	.18	.24	-.05*	-.09
Voting under voluntary suffrage	.05*	.04*	.00*	.06*
Null voting	.00*	.00*	-.13	-.06*
Participatory mood[g]	.03*	.00*	-.16	-.13
Political capacity[f]	.04*	.07	-.04*	-.02*
Exposure to the 1973 campaign[e]	.01*	.11	-.06*	.10
Involvement in the 1973 campaign[e]	-.11	-.16	.02*	.08
Perceived efficacy of the 1973 campaign[e]	-.13	-.12	.02*	.01*

Table IV-2. The Impact of Cultural Cleavages (*Continued*)

	Regionalism[a]	Urbanization[b]	Ideology[c]	Religion[d]
Partisanship				
Polarization between AD and COPEI	.06*	.09	.16	-.02*
Sympathy toward AD	-.05*	-.08	-.04*	.03*
Sympathy toward COPEI	.03*	.08	.21	.05*
Sympathy toward MAS	.08	.10	-.28	-.15
Sympathy toward MEP	-.01*	.05*	-.18	-.05*
Sympathy toward PCV	.02*	.06*	-.20	-.09
Sympathy toward CCN	-.01*	.04*	.02*	-.02*

Note: All table values are Pearson's product-moment correlation coefficients. Asterisks identify those that are not significant for P = .05. Sample size is 549 for all computations.

[a] Regionalism is measured in terms of the typology presented in table IV-1. Categories have been reordered in terms of center-periphery.

[b] Community size, as follows: (1) rural (smaller than 5,000), (2) intermediate (between 5,000 and 25,000), (3) urban (between 25.000 and 100,000), and (4) metropolitan (larger than 100,000).

[c] Choice of position in terms of left, center or right.

[d] Combines denomination preference and frequency of worship, as follows: (1) atheists and agnostics, (2) Protestant, (3) nominal Catholics, and (4) practicing Catholics.

[e] Guttman scale described in appendix F.

[f] Standardized (Z) scale.

[g] As presented and discussed in chapter 3.

al variation. It seems that as a result of the homogenization brought about by the tremendous onslaught of urbanization, the distinctiveness of the regional outlook has been decisively undermined. In other words, the process that has made the regions more similar in a number of demographic and socioeconomic characteristics seems to have reduced whatever cultural variation remains, as this could be perceived through its impact on political behavior and political opinion. In contrast, the ideological element suggests greater influence of partisanship than previously attributed to it by scholarly opinion.

However, in order to verify the plausible conclusion that the "remnant," which Simeon and Elkins pinpointed in the Canadian case[43] does not play an important role in Venezuela, more rigorous testing is required. This is produced by a partial correlation analysis of the relationships between regionalism and the four aforementioned areas, controlling for the other cultural factors. This would indicate whether (1) apparent differences between the regions disappear with such controls; (2) differences emerge when the similarities between the regions are controlled; or (3) the introduction of such controls does not affect the relationships. We control for the other three cultural factors plus stratification, since the latter may be closely related to the center-periphery criterion utilized to reorder the regions for the correlation analysis.

Following this line of reasoning, we introduced controls for all the relationships presented under the first column of table IV-2, in order to determine their actual nature. Admittedly, the analysis by partials is weaker than the path-analytic method, but given the large number of relationships involved we had to opt for the former.[44] In table IV-3 we present those cases for which we found that: (1) the magnitude of the zero-order correlation coefficient between regionalism and the attitude or behavior in question was unaffected by the introduction of controls, and thus remained statistically significant; (2) a significant relationship disappeared with the introduction of controls; and (3) the introduction of controls made the relationship significant. Reviewing the evidence presented in table IV-3 it is apparent that even though degree of urbanization tends to reduce the impact of regional differences, these do not for the most part disappear nor lose their statistical significance. Regional differences in opinion about the role of the military, support for elections, party membership, involvement in the 1973 campaign, and perceived efficacy of that campaign do not disappear when we control for degree of urbanization. In addition, regional differences emerge in levels of exposure to the 1973 campaign and in sympathy toward

Table IV-3. Cultural Cleavages and Regional Location

Zero-order correlation between regional location and . . .	Zero-order correlation between regional location and . . .	First-order partials controlling for . . .				
		Urbanization	Ideology	Religion	Stratification	All
Opinion about the role of the military	.09	.09	.10	.09	.09	.09
Criticism of elections	.14	.07	.12	.13	.12	.06*
Actual membership	.16	.10	.15	.16	.14	.09
Membership, ever	.16	.08	.15	.15	.13	.07
Exposure to '73 campaign	.01*	−.08	.00*	.01*	−.04*	−.09
Involvement in '73 campaign	−.06	−.05	−.07	−.06	−.09	−.06
Perceived efficacy of '73 campaign	−.12	−.11	−.11	−.12	−.12	−.11
Sympathy toward MAS	.10	.03*	.09	.09	.06	−.01*
Sympathy toward MEP	−.02*	−.05	−.03*	−.03*	−.04*	−.08

Note: All the variables measured as described in table IV-2. Stratification measured as discussed in chapter 2. Asterisks identify coefficients not significant at .05. This table should be read across, comparing the magnitude of the zero-order coefficients with those of the first- and fourth-order partials.

the Movimiento Electoral del Pueblo (MEP) when such controls are introduced. Thus, degree of urbanization may have become a more important aspect of community differences than their regional ethos, but there are areas on which the latter continues to exert influence independent of community size. In short, these differences between the regions suggest the permanence of a "remnant" which expresses a uniqueness of the regional communities, translated into the way they perceived the proper role of the military in the political process, levels of support for the institution of elections, and patterns of party membership and campaign participation.

To be sure, these differences do not indicate a marked impact of the regional factor, although they include highly significant aspects. The fact that urbanization, a variable related to one other aspect of community differences, is the more frequent intervening factor minimizing the impact of regional differences suggests the resilience of cultural variation pertaining to another aspect of community ethos. What may be at work here is a case in which the community size has become more relevant than its regional location. That is, the community context may have come to replace the regional as a relevant frame of reference, creating a uniqueness which is not reducible to its demographic or socioeconomic composition. This would imply a change from relatively broad and continuous geographic areas creating a distinctive configuration in attitudes and behavior to noncontiguous communities of similar size sharing a common outlook which is yet to crystallize and mature. The question thus becomes: "are differences in the size of communities really more important than their regional location?"

In an earlier analysis[45] we have shown that when the influence of community size is subject to the same type of control procedures utilized with regionalism, the latter tends to reduce the impact of the former on a number of relevant aspects, such as opinion about elections and political participation. In addition, some differences attributable to community size are revealed as a mere reflection of the type of social stratification found in such communities, a result which we did not observe when this manipulation was applied to the regional factor (see table IV-3). We summarize the more relevant results of the analysis by partials performed on urbanization in table IV-4.[46]

To begin with, community size appears to correlate with higher levels of criticism of the institution of elections, independently of any other factor. Its impact is more relevant in the area of political participation, where most indicators suggest decreasing levels of participation with larger community size.[47] Apparent differences in

Table IV-4. Cultural Cleavages and Community Size

Zero-order correlation between community size and . . .		First-order partials controlling for . . .				
		Region	Ideology	Religion	Stratification	All
Criticism of politicians	.07*	.04*	.05*	.05*	.10	.07
Criticism of elections	.17	.10	.14	.14	.12	.07
Evaluation of Caldera's policy performance	−.09	−.08	−.10	−.08	.02*	.00*
Actual membership	.22	.10	.15	.16	.13	.06
Membership at any time	.24	.13	.18	.19	.14	.08
Null voting	.00*	−.02*	−.04*	−.04*	−.06	−.07
Political capacity	.07	.07	.08	.08	−.05*	−.05*
Exposure to '73 campaign	.11	.18	.15	.16	.07	.11
Involvement in '73 campaign	−.16	.00*	−.03*	−.03*	−.08	−.04*
Opinion about efficacy of '73 campaign	−.12	.02*	−.04*	−.04*	−.05	.00*
Polarization AD-COPEI	.09	.07	.10	.09	.02*	.02*
Sympathy toward AD	−.08	−.06	−.08	−.08	−.03*	−.02*
Sympathy toward COPEI	.08	−.07	.10	.08	.01*	.02*
Sympathy toward MAS	.10	.12	.12	.14	.08	.05*
Sympathy toward CCN	.04*	.04*	.04*	.05*	.06	.06

Note: All variables coded as in table IV-2. Asterisks identify coefficients not significant at .05 level.

level of political capacity are shown in fact to be the result of differences in the type of social stratification found in communities of different size, while differences in the involvement and efficacy modes of the campaign of 1973 are attributable to the other three cultural factors. Finally, differences in party preferences are traceable to other characteristics of the communities, not to their size.

Thus, if regionalism seemed to diminish in importance when examined in the light of the size of the communities found in the regional "containers," size of community lacks the character of a "remnant" which might be treated as that irreducible element of community ethos which goes beyond the demographic and socioeconomic characteristics of the community. Thus, we have a somewhat perplexing set of results: (1) there is a causal network in which one intervening factor, urbanization, tends to reduce the impact of regionalism; but (2) it seems to lack an independent causal status of its own, its effect being decomposable in terms of the characteristics that are associated with the size of the community; (3) such characteristics, however, are not in themselves capable of producing the same effect on the impact of regionalism when they are controlled for. The most significant differences between regions can be diminished by their degree of urbanization, and not by their cultural or socioeconomic characteristics. Yet differences due to size of community are really a reflection of the impact of one or more of the latter.

In reality, the emerging case suggests that regionalism and urbanization exert a reciprocal influence more symmetrical than could have been anticipated from previous results. Certainly the two factors correlate fairly strongly (their Pearson correlation coefficient is .53), but not enough to justify substitution of one for the other. We should not lose sight of the fact that their separate impact on most areas of opinion and behavior is scarcely robust, and that introduction of controls reduces these to trivial magnitudes. However, it is possible further to clarify the nature of the linkages between these two factors, following the route provided by analysis of variance, a technique which allows circumvention of the problem of order between the regions. Analysis of variance does not require any assumption about the order between different categories of a variable and permits their qualitative treatment.[48] This is particularly welcome in our case since, in order to perform the correlation analysis, we had to order the regions according to their location on the center-periphery continuum. In essence, we are asking if the regional location of the community is as significant as its size, or whether one is more so than the other.

The results of this procedure were presented in considerable detail elsewhere[49] and need not be repeated. However, two important inferences were derived which require some comment. First, interaction between these two factors is limited to opinion about elections and to party membership. Consequently, they do not for the most part have an interactive type of impact on political opinion and political behavior. Second, we found that differences between the regions prove to be as significant as those between communities of different size when their impact is inspected simultaneously through two-way analyses of variance.

A Theoretical Blemish: Community Context and Participation

The nature of the interaction between regionalism and urbanization sounds a very discordant note against the theoretical backdrop of an impressive body of literature concerning the linkage between modernization and participation.[50] The implications of this interaction, however, are easier to reconcile with the literature of Venezuelan politics. At issue here is the principle that, in general, peripheral and less modern communities will participate less in politics and proffer more "parochial" orientations to politics.[51] Interaction between regionalism and urbanization, as well as significant differences between regions and communities in other participatory modes, can be used to challenge the validity of the principle for the Venezuelan case. The fact is that high levels of support for elections and greater frequency of party membership are more characteristic among the residents of the more peripheral and rural regions, no matter how one examines them. In cases where the two factors are significant and independent of one another, or even when only one is significant, the evidence points to higher levels of political participation in the rural and more peripheral communities.

Perhaps the best illustration appears in figure 11, where we have depicted the percentages of party members among residents of communities of different sizes and regional locations. Since this is a case involving interaction between the two factors, we have collapsed their respective categories in order to better illustrate the relationship. Notice how their separate impact measured by the beta coefficients adds up to their combined interaction, as this is measured by the eta coefficient derived from cross-tabulating this combined dimension with the dependent variable, party membership. Furthermore, note that the metropolitan areas of the Center and the two

Figure 11. Community Size, Regional Location, and Party Membership

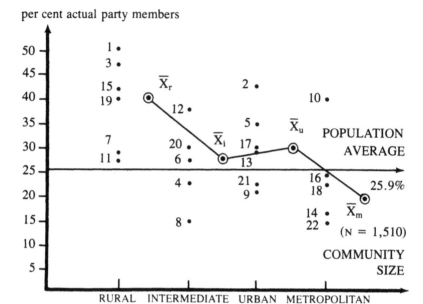

Note: Values of beta as follows: .13 (for regional location), .13 (for community size), and .26 (for combined dimension).

Key to symbols: 1: rural, Plains; 2: urban, Plains; 3: rural, Andes; 4: intermediate, Andes; 5: urban, Andes; 6: metropolitan, Andes; 7: rural, West; 8: intermediate, West; 9: urban, West; 10: metropolitan, West; 11: rural, East; 12: intermediate, East; 13: urban, East; 14: metropolitan, East; 15: rural, Zulia; 16: intermediate, Zulia; 17: urban, Zulia; 18: metropolitan, Zulia; 19: rural, Center; 20: intermediate, Center; 21: urban, Center; 22: metropolitan, Center

peripheral regions with closer ties to the Center due to their impor- tance as producers of petroleum, Zulia and the East, have the lowest percentages of party members. It should be mentioned at this junc- ture that we tested for three-way interaction between region, urbani- zation, and stratification for this dependent variable and found this interaction to be nonsignificant. Therefore, this lower frequency of party members in the more important regions and communities goes well beyond their socioeconomic characteristics.

On the other hand, we find that areas less integrated into the national economy and the type of lifestyle evolving from the com- munities of the Center—that is, the rural communities of the Andes and Plains states—have much larger than average proportions of party members. The intermediate and urban communities offer a more complicated pattern, although the latter seem to harbor somewhat larger proportions of party members, judging from the respective means (which have been extrapolated from their respective arrays to simplify interpretation of the figure).

We have been careful to avoid explicit assumptions about the "modernity" of the different regions or areas. Indeed, there was no attempt to measure modernity with our instrument. Moreover, our use of analysis of variance represents an attempt to avoid making any assumptions about underlying dimensions on which the regions could be ranked and allowed us to treat them in more qualitative fashion. Given this orientation we did not want to place a priori emphasis on such a ranking, although familiarity with Venezuela would lead us to suggest that the more peripheral and rural areas—whether conceived of as local or regional communities—are, after all, less modern.

Why, then, do these somnolent, out-of-the-way communities show higher levels of commitment to the system and of activity in a number of participatory modes? Why are the individuals of the Center metropolitan areas, the more modern individuals, less enthusiastic about the political system? How can this be explained in terms of modernization theory or social mobilization theory? Consider the fact that the lowest level of support for the institution of elections is found among the individuals of the metropolitan Center, who are also the least militant in terms of party membership. Contrast this with the fact that the rural communities of the Plains and the Andes, which by all measures have not achieved the degree of modernity of their more affluent and urban counterparts, produce the highest proportions of party militants and the most intense supporters of elections. Could it be that these differences in degree and type of participation are deeply intertwined with the ethos of these communities? Might they be part and parcel of the political style of these communities which, like Venezuelans of low socioeconomic status, must turn to party militancy to seek a piece of the good life denied them by the private sector? We emphasize that this goes beyond any such difference and is no mere reflection of the higher proportion of lower-status individuals among the residents of these communities—by no means.

If we are to believe that participation and voluntarism are almost universal traits of the political behavior of modern middle classes, as the literature of political participation in industrial societies would have it, then it should not be surprising that in a country where urbanization and not industrialization has been the main agent of social change, with class differences more a result of consumption patterns than the individual's relation to the means of production, the more rural and peripheral regions are actually the more mobilized, participatory, and allegiant. The crux of the matter lies in the fact that if we accept the contention that participation and voluntarism are the epitome of middle-class patterns of political behavior, then there is no way to account for the reality that, in Venezuela, residents of the more marginal communities are more civic than their urban counterparts. On the other hand, if we can conceive of situations in which *modernization is not a critical threshold for participation*, relatively little difficulty is encountered in explaining the Venezuelan case. It may well be that participation through political parties and political machines represents a clientelistic style of participation that tends to alienate the more modern individuals, who prefer to participate, if at all, in a less organized fashion. Certain styles of participation may be more characteristic of the peripheral and rural regions while becoming obsolete or unpopular in the metropolitan and Center regions.

The literature of Venezuelan politics offers some responses to these theoretical dilemmas, although by implication a careless utilization of mobilization theory could lead to erroneous conclusions. For instance, consider the well-documented and much-studied "Caracas syndrome." Blank maintains that the

> . . . cleavages most visible in electoral returns are those between urban and rural communities and between the different regions [and that] continued alienation of Metropolitan Caracas from the pre-1958 populist parties, AD, COPEI, URD, remains the most significant sustained electoral cleavage. In the three presidential elections of 1958, 1963, and 1968, these parties did noticeably less well in Metropolitan Caracas than they did in the provincial cities, towns, and countryside. . . . [52]

He contends that the Venezuelan democratic regime is to a large extent a creation of those parties, especially the AD and COPEI, and sentiment for and against these parties is reflected in the evaluation of the *adeco* and *copeyano* administrations of the last fifteen years which, for better or worse, cannot be separated from the evaluation of the democratic regime itself. Our questions on regime evaluation and our Guttman scale of overall attitude with respect to the regime suffer from this difficulty, for some segments of the public may be unable to distinguish between the two.

At the same time, the electoral preferences of the metropolitan core have been very unstable during all this time, especially the preference of the lower sectors. Martz and Harkins concluded that the Caracas syndrome could be characterized by: (1) a lower level of electoral turnout; (2) a greater tendency to protest vote; and (3) considerable variation in the preferences of the class strata.[53] Bonomo found in his survey of 300 *caraqueños* that they lean toward a one-party system (44 per cent), and are relatively neutral with respect to the government (41 gave it a "so-so" evaluation), and that social mobility and support for democratic parties are closely related.[54] Thus it appears that some of the differences in the electoral preferences of residents of metropolitan Caracas reflect a class bias.

Following his careful analysis of the impact of structural cleavages (modern versus traditional, center versus periphery, urban versus rural, and poor versus nonpoor) on partisan loyalties and electoral preferences in Venezuela, Myers concluded that support for the "prosystem" AD and COPEI parties was negatively related to his indicator of modernity (literacy), that support for the "recently attractive" or "antisystem" parties—URD (Unión Republicana Democrática), PCV, FND (Frente Nacional Democrático), FDP (Fuerza Democrática Popular), and CCN—was positively related to modernity, and that urbanization tended to increase support for these parties.[55] Myers' interpretation is congruent with Blank's argument that urbanization ". . . especially the growth of large cities, appears to be providing fertile soil for continual challenges to the party system. As the urban mode of life increasingly penetrates national society, so the rural sanctuary of the established parties is diminishing. . . ."[56] So it seems that the Venezuelan system is predicated on the dominance by two parties which have their stronger historical roots in the rural periphery, and although this cannot be shown directly (since we have no statistically significant differences to report between the regions in party identification) this dominance has tended to alienate more individuals in urban and metropolitan sectors of the Center and of more modern regions. In short, "the civic participants" of the Venezuelan system are in the rural and peripheral communities, areas that have been suspected of producing premodern "parochials" in other countries.

Community Context and Political Cleavages

Despite the fact that our analysis ultimately corroborates the resilience of real regional differences, we should not overlook the fact that the impact of these two cleavages on the attitudes, evaluations, orientations, and behavior of the mass public is very limited. It is one thing to show that a factor—in this case regionalism or urbanization—has significant variation within its categories in terms of a particular attitude, and quite another to utilize that factor to "explain" the total variation of that attitude. The continued salience of regional differences and the increasing importance of urban-rural differences has assuredly been verified, and this is a finding in itself. However, it does not follow that they have a decisive impact on the formation of opinion and on attitudinal and behavioral cleavages among the mass public. Judging from the magnitude of measures of association discussed thus far, the relevance of these two factors seems slight. Our results are particularly dramatic because we refused to consider regionalism as a mere aggregate of individuals in some kind of territorial configuration. On the contrary, we had conceived of regionalism in terms of community heritage, ethos, and geographical continuity. Therefore, careful conceptualization and typology construction, plus a rigorous analysis of its independent impact, lead us to contend that regionalism is no longer a highly significant factor in Venezuelan politics.

A summary of the overall significance of these two territorial factors and their possible interaction suggests that urbanization and regionalism have a rather modest impact on the formation of political attitudes, although it is undeniable that there are significant differences between the regions and areas in terms of a fairly extensive set of opinions, evaluations, orientations, and behavior patterns. The fact that urbanization and regionalism tend to reduce their separate impact on Venezuelan political opinion—but that social stratification only affects the former and not the latter—suggests that these two factors cannot be obviated in analysis without risking oversimplification.

A further implication is that although most differences found between the areas and regions (through ecological analyses based on aggregate data) are not that relevant at the individual level of analysis, most of the differences due to cultural cleavages of a territorial nature are not the result of the socioeconomic characteristics of the individuals who live in those areas and regions. In other words, (major) *political differences between residents of different Venezuelan regions* (notably including the most important) *cannot be reduced to socioeconomic differences nor to differences in their degree of modernity*. Therefore, we have reason to conclude that the residual element relating to the ethos or normative idiosyncrasies of the regions is still a factor in Venezuelan politics.

Finally, it does not escape us that some of the differences expected between the regions in their reaction to the democratic regime and their political preferences either failed to materialize or proved very modest. We will return to the partisan aspect at a later point and prefer to consider, albeit briefly, the salience of another source of cultural cleavage.

Religion: A Change of Skin

The church, the military, and the landed oligarchy were long considered the "three little pigs" of Latin American politics, a sinister trilogy dedicated to unqualified defense of the status quo and adamantly opposed to liberalism and the development of democratic institutions. To a previous generation of scholars, these institutions represented the most formidable obstacles to democratic change and development in Latin America. Several well-documented studies described the problems created by the slowness of the church in adapting to change, its unwillingness to accept the legitimacy of popular rule, and its inability to understand the scope and nature of the secular forces of reform.[57]

Today landed oligarchies are no longer omnipotent contenders in most Latin American countries, while both the church and the military have been undergoing a process of institutional change, thereby forcing scholarly reappraisal of their diverging political roles.[58] The institutional transformation of the church is much too complex to discuss here, but it ". . . has ceased to sacralize the status quo and its official position can no longer be used to rationalize support for established interests. But the ambiguities and tensions operating within and across normative, structural, and behavioral levels in the Church prevent the emergence of a clear line of direction for its future role in society. . . ."[59]

The institutional weakness and dependent character of the Catholic Church during the politics of national integration in Venezuela are a matter of record and require little elaboration.[60] Whatever influence remains is diminished by a trait generally attributed to Latin American Catholicism—a basic shallowness at the mass level. Thus there might seem to be little need to probe for the impact of Catholicism as a potential source of cleavage in Venezuelan politics. However, the presence of a Christian Democratic party, which cannot fail to polarize some segments of the public by mobilizing anticlerical or antireligious biases, and the demonstrated conflict potential of church-state relations concerning educational policy[61] suggest that there may be more than meets the eye. Finally, it is transparent that study of the political idiosyncrasies of Venezuelan Catholics, whatever these may be, would help us better appraise the arguments of the cultural revisionists concerning the relationship between Catholicity and authoritarianism in Latin America.

Our task is simplified by the absence of any other major denominational or confessional group outside the Catholic Church; non-Catholics are not present in sufficient numbers to allow for extensive comparisons. A fairly direct and reliable measure of Catholic religiosity can be constructed from our instrument, enabling us to differentiate *devout Catholics* (1.5 per cent of the population), *participating Catholics* (33.9 per cent), *nominal Catholics* (58 per cent), *Protestants* (2 per cent), and *indifferents* (4 per cent). We collapsed the devout and the participating categories, and refer to the combined category as *practicing Catholics*. Finally, it should be pointed out that *indifferents* include atheists, agnostics, and people who are simply "not interested in religious matters," all lumped together because of their small frequency and the fact that they are not religious.

Because we are not dealing here with Catholic elites and gathered only limited data on content of opinion, we can neither explore the specific nature of the political beliefs of Venezuelan Catholics nor portray the diversity of opinion within the more Catholic group concerning such issues as liberation theology, abortion, and the like. These are not, after all, issues entertained by the "Catholic majority" as such. After considerable manipulation our data could produce some basic differentiation and, following Catholic folklore, we might be able to identify the *vieja beata* (who has never missed a rosary in thirty-five years), the *espiritista* (who has a ritualistic devotion to the *Virgen de Coromoto* for "personal protection" and must obtain a *ramito* on Palm Sunday at any cost), the militant youth (who is annoyed by the whole *ramito* business and is genuinely concerned with finding a political praxis for the Declaration of Medellín),[62] the *cursillista* (who cannot solve the riddle of *Humane Vitae* and "Responsible Parenthood"), and the *caballero de Colón* (who is by no means certain that he is still going to the same church). Following the images that popular folklore offers us of the sociological characteristics of these different types of Catholics, we could find them in our sample but will not try to do so.

That exercise would hold great intrinsic interest but, lacking data on the individual affiliation with different organizations of the church, would be at best an incomplete undertaking. Moreover, we recognize that the Catholic laity has always been an elusive entity, difficult to define on institutional[63] or theological grounds.[64] Efforts to present a clear picture of the normative, behavioral, and attitudinal propensities of the Catholic laity of Latin America have always met with limited success. To date, no one knows what the typical (as distinct from the ideal) Latin American Catholics think about a broad range of issues, primarily because they have seldom been asked to give an opinion. Thus we will be cautious in our treatment.

Demographic Characteristics of Venezuelan Catholics

Our data allow for the elaboration of a somewhat crude sociodemographic profile of respondents identified as "practicing Catholics," who for all practical purposes will be treated strictu sensu as the more Catholic group. Scrutiny of the measure suggests that women comprise some 63 per cent of all the respondents included in the category. Also, women as a group seem to be more devout than men, 27 per cent of whom are practicing Catholics versus 45 per cent of the women, a fact congruent with the conventional wisdom concerning religion in Latin America. In addition, the generational composition of practicing Catholics is consistent with that wisdom, although the relationship between age and religiosity does not follow a smooth monotonic trend. They are more numerous in the 45 to 54 years of age group at 49 per cent; older age cohorts show somewhat lower values (45 per cent and 42 per cent for the 55 to 64 and the over 65 groups, respectively), which might indicate changing levels of church influence over the patterns of socialization of different generations. At the least it suggests greater influence over the middle-aged than the very old. For the three younger cohorts (18 to 24, 25 to 34, and 35 to 44) the percentage of practicing Catholics is in the low thirties, a sign of declining church influence among younger generations of Venezuelans.

The territorial distribution of Venezuelan Catholics confirms previous impressions about greater church influence over the laity of the Andean region. Practicing Catholics were 53 per cent of all those interviewed in the Andes by our field teams; the Plains was a distant second at 41 per cent, closely followed by the West at 39 per cent. The least Catholic area measured in these terms was the East at 29 per cent. If we look at place of residence, it is evident that Catholic religiosity declines in the most urbanized communities while remaining relatively stable in all others. In sum, it seems that *women, the middle-aged, and those who live in nonmetropolitan communities are the most intense Catholics in Venezuela; the Andean group appears the most Catholic of all.*

In table IV-2 we saw that our measure of Catholic religiosity yields but a limited series of statistically significant relationships. These included evaluation of regime policies, evaluation of the role of politicians, partisan participation, participatory mood, exposure to and involvement in the 1973 campaign, and feelings about the Movimiento al Socialismo (MAS). Utilizing larger sample sizes we have observed significant relationships between Catholic religiosity and criticism of elections (Pearson's r = −.13), evaluation of the policy performance of the Caldera administration (r = .12), and feelings toward the Social Christian party (r = .13).[65] Regardless of sample size, these relationships are of similar magnitude and have the same sign as those involving ideology. In other words, even though the relationship between the two is not that strong (r = .15), ideology and religiosity seem to relate to the same kind of political phenomena.

Analysis of the more relevant evidence presented in table IV-5 should depart from the fact that the impact of religiosity is really slight and that this impact is more significant on evaluation than on participation or partisanship. Catholic religiosity correlates negatively with criticism of regime policies, of elections, and of politicians, and this is apparently independent of other cultural cleavages. However, given the magnitude of the coefficients, this seems more relevant in casting doubt on the arguments of the cultural revisionists than as an expression of the uniqueness of the reactions of the more intense Catholics to the Venezuelan regime. On the other hand, since nominal and practicing Catholics account for about 92 per cent of the population, differences between Catholics and non-Catholics would have to be enormous in order for us to observe coefficients of greater magnitude. Even if this were the case, the minuscule non-Catholic minority would have to feel seriously threatened to antagonize the majority.

The fact that regime support seems to increase with religiosity is by no means conclusive proof of the fallacy of the revisionist argument about the incompatibility of Hispanic Catholicism and democratic institutions. We sampled opinion when a Christian Democratic administration was in power, and more conclusive proof would have to be based on similar percentages obtained with a different party in power. Nevertheless, it is important to emphasize that, regardless of region of residence, sex, or ideological orientation, practicing Catholics evaluate the Venezuelan regime more favorably. In other words, if one finds a fairly distinct outlook which

Table IV-5. Cultural Cleavages and Religiosity

Zero-order correlation between religiosity and . . .	Zero-order correlation	First-order partials controlling for . . .				
		Ideology	Region	Comm. size	Sex	Age
Evaluation of regime policies	−.16	−.14	−.16	−.16	−.16	−.16
Criticism of elections	−.11	−.09	−.10	−.10	−.11	−.10
Criticism of politicians	−.09	−.07	−.08	−.08	−.10	−.09
Evaluation of Caldera's policy performance	−.06	−.03*	−.06	−.07	−.07	−.06*
Actual party membership	−.05*	−.04*	−.03*	−.03*	−.06*	−.05*
Membership, ever	−.07	−.06	−.05*	−.05*	−.08	−.06
Participatory mood	−.16	−.13	−.15	−.15	−.15	−.15
Exposure to '73 campaign	.05*	.07	.06*	.07	.08	.05*
Involvement in '73 campaign	.05*	.05*	.03*	.04*	.07	.05*
Sympathy toward COPEI	.12	.09	.12	.13	.12	.12
Sympathy toward MAS	−.17	−.13	−.16	−.16	−.14	−.15

Note: We acknowledge the discrepancy between the magnitude of some of the coefficients included in the two sets of zero-order correlations for religiosity presented in tables IV-2 and IV-5. This is due to different sample sizes resulting from utilization of different sets of dependent variables.

*Not significant.

n = 809 for all computations.

may be traced to religiosity, this concerns greater identification with, not alienation from, the democratic regime. This represents a turnaround from the events of 1948, when some Venezuelan Catholics felt threatened by the policies of the Social Democratic administration.[66]

Equally noteworthy is the fact that religiosity and evaluation of the policy performance of the Caldera administration and feelings about COPEI do not correlate strongly. Moreover, the evidence of table IV-5 shows the relationships weakened when controls for ideology are introduced. Even though the link between religiosity and feelings toward COPEI does not disappear with controls for ideology, the fact that it is weakened is sufficient to cast some doubt on the religious predilections of the rank-and-file sympathizers of the party. Indeed, one finds more devout Catholics within COPEI's leadership than among other parties. However, we must talk in very different terms about the Catholic militancy of COPEI's supporters, for the party's success in widening its base of popular support has meant that this transcends the more Catholic sector of the society. In short, we find that the bond between Catholic religiosity and sympathy toward the Social Christian party, and other political objects or actors related to it, has weakened considerably in contemporary Venezuela.

Given the evidence presented in tables IV-2 and IV-5 concerning the relevance of the religious cleavage, we are forced to conclude that its more distinguished feature is its lack of profound impact among the mass public. In other words, we do not find Venezuelan Catholics to be very different from other Venezuelans in terms of their political opinions and types of involvement in the political process. Thus the overall appraisal would be that greater commitment to Catholicism does not seem to introduce in Venezuela the type of phenomena associated with cultural segmentation resulting from religious "pillars."

A partial explanation may be found by examining similarities between the impacts of religiosity and ideology. This is a particularly relevant facet of the cultural revisionist's hypotheses concerning the connection between preconciliar (pre–Vatican II council) Catholicism and authoritarianism in Latin America. Even though it is difficult to identify an adequate summary of the argument establishing the causal links between Thomistic Catholicism, the organic state, scholastic philosophy, and authoritarianism, a simplistic summary of the connection would have it that, in Latin America, Catholic is conservative and non-Catholic is liberal.[67] This is reminiscent of a previous tendency, denounced by Charles Gibson some time ago, to argue that Latin America's cultural heritage has been perpetuated through conservatism—that is, that anything that has to do with Latin America's heritage *is* conservative—and through "colonial institutions." [68] On a different note, Schmitter has pleaded for confining the usage of the concept of corporatism to a concrete set of institutional practices or structures involving the process of interest representation of observable groups. [69] Finally, one can also challenge the relevance of liberal-conservative distinctions in contemporary Venezuela, arguing instead for other dichotomies such as capitalist versus socialist, leftist versus rightist and so forth. Our own usage excludes reference to liberal and conservative in our treatment of the ideological aspect.

But it is the connection between ideology and religion which may help to explain the limited impact of the latter in Venezuela and put the cultural revisionist argument in sharper perspective, at least for Venezuela. We want to determine whether: (1) ideology and religion have a similar impact but independent of one another; (2) one of the two really has a greater impact than the other; or (3) the interaction between ideology and religiosity is such that their effects cannot be separated. Numerous cases on interaction would fall within the purview of the cultural revisionist argument, while unequal impact, or greater impact on the part of ideology, would to some degree qualify it.

We found two instances of interaction, one involving political capacity, and the other feelings about the MAS. [70] Consequently, an intimate covariation with causal effects is limited to what is probably one of the more ideologically specific actors in Venezuelan politics. Inspection of the magnitudes of the multiple correlation coefficients suggests that this effect is very minor on political capacity (multiple R = .09), while it is more relevant with respect to feelings about MAS (multiple R = .36). Thus, a relevant impact is really confined to the latter, suggesting that the strongest connection between ideological stance and Catholic religiosity is produced by an actor occupying an extreme leftist position on the ideological spectrum, and not by actors, issues, or orientations with less explicit ideological content.

In other cases we found that for the most part ideology was a more relevant causal factor than religiosity. These involved evaluation of regime policies, level of support for the institution of elections, participatory mood, and feelings about the Social Christian party. The results are summarized in figure 12, depicting the standardized causal paths (betas) between the two factors and these four orientations. The explanatory power of the four models is not im-

Figure 12. Causal Effects of Religiosity and Ideology

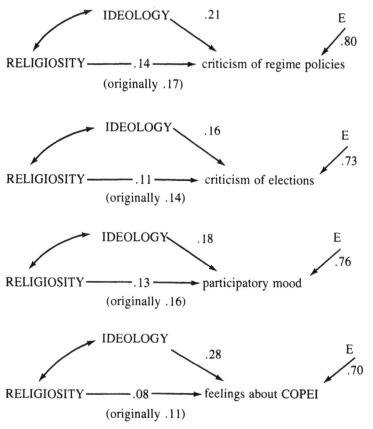

Note: All betas are significant at .01. The simple correlation between ideology and religiosity is about .15 for all models.

pressive, and we have opted to treat the relationship between ideology and religiosity, given by a direct zero-order correlation of about .15 for all four cases, as unanalyzed correlation. The direction of causality between the two is, in itself, a major analytical question which we cannot undertake here. Nevertheless, ideology is clearly the more relevant of the two even for feelings about the Social Christian party, indicating that reaction to the latter is an ideological, not a religious matter.

Not having examined the content of religious beliefs, we cannot advance more definitive conclusions about the connection between Catholicism and political cleavages at the level of the mass public. But it can be noted that the connection between religious observance and political behavior is relatively weak, and that religiosity is not important as a source of political cleavages. This does not deny that for Catholic elites the connection is much stronger (as the historical record would suggest), and that they may hold a set of beliefs standing in stark contrast with those of other elites and/or those of the mass public. However, searching for a response to "what are you in Venezuelan politics," our analysis of three different sources of cultural cleavage suggests that these characteristics, including region of residence, size of community of residence, and religious preference, provide only a modest and incomplete response. By contrast, a factor which has been relegated to a minor role by the scholarly literature seems more relevant. Consequently, we must now consider the impact of ideology.

5

Cultural Diversity and
Political Cleavages, II:
The Ideological Connection

Introduction

In contrast with our discussion on the rather limited impact of
cultural cleavages, presentation of the impact of ideology on the
attitudes of the Venezuelan public is complicated by two types of
considerations. One has to do with theoretical controversies surrounding the contemporary importance, overt manifestations, and
adequate conceptualization of "ideology."[1] The other stems from
methodological debates pertaining to the more appropriate way to
"find" ideology. The nature of our data and our own theoretical
orientation will, to a certain extent, facilitate our task by limiting
its scope. We do believe that ideology can be found in contemporary
Venezuelan politics, and that the Venezuelan public has some ideological characteristics. However, there is uncertainty as to whether,
in the Venezuelan context, ideology should be conceptualized as a
"cultural system,"[2] a set of loosely structured attitudes,[3] or a
belief system.[4] Our evidence is insufficient to allow us such a deter-
mination. We know intuitively that the more rigorous kinds of definitions of ideology ("an explanation of man in the universe, a critique of existing society from the standpoint thus established, and a
description and justification of the good or legitimate political and
social order")[5] are largely inapplicable to the Venezuelan public
but, on the other hand, do not share extant reservations concerning
the apparent ideological incoherence and issue disorientation of
mass publics.[6]

Our presentation departs from a crude measure of individual
ideology based on individual *self-placements* on the left-right continuum, moving through verification and validation of twelve *ideological positions* on the continuum, to their reduction to six *ideological tendencies*. Our basic purpose is to show the salience of
ideological thinking among the Venezuelan mass public, and the
degree to which ideological preferences influence other attitudes
and orientations.

A First Approximation: Self-Placements

Although much existing evidence is based on surveys of student beliefs, research has shown that ideology can be operationalized in terms of the left-right continuum. Finlay and his associates report that the stability and meaningfulness of individual self-placements on the left-right continuum are to a large extent related to the level of development of a political system.[7] Laponce's discussion and treatment of the left-right continuum was predicated on the valida- tion of a scale, measuring individual location on the continuum, with partisan preferences and other data about the individual's ideo- logical predispositions.[8]

Our initial measure of ideology was derived from individual self- placements on the left-right continuum. A majority of our respon- dents were able to respond to our question about individual position on the continuum. Sixteen per cent had no apparent ideological in- clination—those who said that they did not stand anywhere on the continuum. Those genuinely confused about the issue (the "don't knows") constituted 11 per cent of the sample. Only three respon- dents refused to answer the question. In all, 73 per cent were able to place themselves on the continuum: 20 per cent on the *left*, 22 per cent in the *center*, and 31 per cent on the *right*. If these percentages are adjusted to exclude refusals and "don't knows," the proportions are 28, 30, and 42 per cent, respectively. Thus the right seems the modal position of our respondents, with the center and left trailing behind but not too distant from each other. How reliable is this finding?

As mentioned in chapter 3, a study of Caracas *barrio* residents suggested that between 1963 and 1967, modal opinion shifted from the left to the right.[9] By contrast, the CENDES-MIT study of pre- dominantly urban and elite groups put the proportion of rightists at 37 per cent, with other groups as follows: leftists 28 per cent, un- stable centrists (antileft, antiright) 7 per cent, centrists 21 per cent, and permeables (proleft, proright) 6 per cent.[10] The authors of that study were careful to point out that given their sampling methods and the nature of the populations sampled, one should not try to generalize from their data. Moreover, their operational definitions of left, center, and right were not based on self-placement questions but on the patterns of individuals' responses to two different sets of questions.[11] In summary, the distribution of our respondents on the continuum is congruent with the limited evidence with which it can be compared.

How valid is this continuum? Concerning the actual meaning attributed by the mass public to the terms right and left in Venezuela, we can recall evidence presented in a previous report: there are considerable differences in the kinds of surrogate terms utilized, rich versus poor, government versus opposition, democracy versus revolution, and several others.[12] Evidence of the salience of the continuum and of the public's ability to perceive political stimuli in terms of the continuum is provided by public reaction to two leftist presidential candidates during the campaign of 1973. José Vicente Rangel and Jesús Angel Paz Galarraga presented themselves as socialist candidates, basing their campaign communications and messages on avowedly leftist and socialist symbols. Our data show that they were perceived as such by the majority of the public, Rangel by 82 per cent and Paz by 83 per cent. Furthermore, we determined that individual location on the left-right continuum did not distort the perception of these two candidates as leftist. The two were seen as being on the left by similar percentages of individual respondents whether these were located on the left, the center, or the right.

More problematic is the evidence obtained from cross-tabulating individual self-placement by choice of economic system. Even though the *marais*, as Converse calls those without apparent ideological inclination (in our case those responding that they did not stand anywhere on the continuum), were excluded from this cross-tabulation, a significant proportion of our respondents seem to have made incongruent selections (or "inadmissible choices," as Butler and Stokes would call them). Any pair of choices was possible, although some are obviously more congruent or appropriate than others.[13] It is difficult to conceive how one would define the politics of *socialist rightists* (who represent a solid 20 per cent of all the individuals capable of making the two choices) or that of *capitalist leftists* (who account for 5 per cent). One could perhaps search for functional equivalents in other countries, but it seems more appropriate to make their profile more explicit in terms of their role in Venezuelan politics. Yet one should not yield to the temptation of treating these "confused" choices as a symptom of Venezuela's underdevelopment, or of the lack of political sophistication of the Venezuelan public. The literature suggests that such confusion is a relatively widespread phenomenon.[14]

On the other hand, incongruent choices and the inability or at least unwillingness of a large number of our respondents to make two choices suggested that an individual's ability to do so did not necessarily render him or her more congruent ideologically. Many individuals may find one label sufficient and the other redundant. Moreover, considerable information is lost if only those who can make two congruent choices are treated as ideological, while excluding all others. Self-placement correlated more strongly than economic system preference with the rest of the items in our instrument, but this does not necessarily mean that the former is a more reliable measure of ideology, nor that it cannot be improved by further manipulation. Following this reasoning, we folded the two dimensions into one, adding all the single choices to the new dimension and treating the categories as indicators of *ideological position*.[15]

There is additional evidence of the relevance of the continuum in Venezuelan politics. First of all, we should not lose sight of the fact that there seems to be scholarly agreement on the relevance of the continuum. To cite an extreme example, there are even cases in which

> . . . the left-right axis is the enduring yardstick against which the passing parade of parties is measured in most political discourse, and it is natural to wonder if this axis is not also the *commonplace source of enduring orientation to politics* at the mass level. . . . It follows that any party-based classification of voters would be very incomplete, but also is more difficult to track over periods of time than would seem desirable for any close assessment of durable lines of political cleavage. . . .[16]

The Venezuelan case may not be as extreme, but certainly the newness of whatever partisan loyalties exist at the level of the mass public, combined with the changing fortunes of numerous parties, suggests that ideological tendency may be an important source of attitude constraint in Venezuela.[17]

Second, most operationalizations of the left-right continuum have not incorporated individual self-placements on the continuum as a direct categorical measure. Indeed, they have done very little to challenge the notion that, if ideology is conceptualized as a "belief system that is internally consistent [constrained] *and* consciously held,"[18] then the mass public is not ideologically oriented. Butler and Stokes claim that only 2 in 5 voters have any real recognition of the terms left and right in England.[19] Even lower percentages have been found for the United States, France, and Italy.[20] We believe that it is insufficient to present left-right distinctions and that something should be said about the *content* of the continuum.

Third, the relationship between ideological tendency and political party identification has not been satisfactorily clarified for the Venezuelan case. There is some consensus that the AD and COPEI are the two pillars of the post-1958 populist establishment,[21] that there has been a decrease of ideological tensions and stabilization of the system in a conservative direction,[22] that the parties—at least the major ones—have to make pragmatic decisions in adapting to changing conditions,[23] and that the out-groups, electoral protest parties and antisystem parties, really make the party system more kaleidoscopic, with little chance of individual success.[24] But little has been done to try to determine the positions of the parties on the continuum, as well as the makeup of the party clienteles in terms of their ideological tendencies. Since we intend to validate our construct in terms of party preferences and ideological attitudes, we must show that the parties themselves are on the continuum.

There is little question that the parties can indeed be placed on the continuum. Indeed, the mass public sees the parties as being on the continuum. Utilizing thermometer scores of party sympathy and applying techniques of ordinal multidimensional scaling,[25] we can recover the position of the parties on the continuum. This is shown in figure 13, where the three principal dimensions of Venezuelan political space are depicted.[26] Inclusion of the three-dimensional configuration in this discussion is intended to emphasize that we do not believe that the left-right continuum is the only relevant dimension of that space. However, when the thermometer scores obtained for the national political parties, candidates in the 1973 presidential election, and former presidents are subject to multidimensional scaling techniques, the left-right dimension never fails to materialize, regardless of the number of dimensions recovered and type of configuration selected for a particular dimensionality.

There are several ways to approach the configuration presented in figure 13. First of all, notice the centrality of the position of then incumbent President Rafael Caldera. Notice how COPEI and its (1973) presidential candidate, Lorenzo Fernández, are very close to Caldera's position near the intersection of the two hyperplanes (XY-XZ). Notice the extremity of Rómulo Betancourt's position on the Y axis, the nonpartisan-partisan continuum. His position on the Z axis is also fairly extreme, being surpassed only by that of José Vicente Rangel; this is the elitist-populist dimension. By contrast, the extreme locations of Unión Republicana Democrática (URD), Fuerza Democrática Popular (FDP), and URD's Jóvito Villalba add some validity to the nature of the second and third dimensions. Notice that URD and Villalba are on relatively modal range on the Y

Figure 13. Three-dimensional Configuration of Venezuelan Political Space

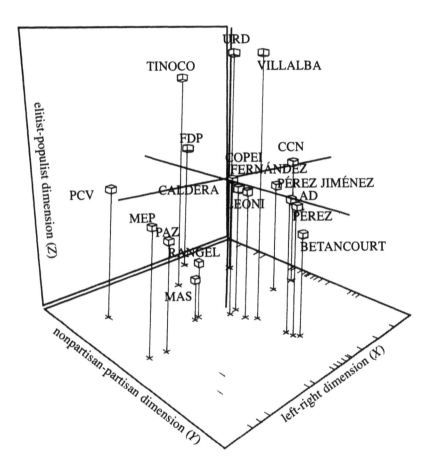

axis. However, having gained very little from party competition, they have moved into a nonleftist, antipopulist type of opposition to the system. Both the URD and the FDP have tried to combine the advantages of party machines with "antiparty," "antipolitician," and "antisystem" slogans designed to appeal to the "independent majority." By organizing heterogeneous electoral coalitions and placing notable independents on their presidential tickets, Villalba and FDP leader Jorge Dáger have tried, sometimes together, to reap the benefits of public discontent without renouncing their tight control of what is left of their parties' machines. In recent years the strategy has backfired, driving both parties to the verge of extinction.

Probably, if URD, FDP, and Villalba had been deleted from the analysis, our results would have been more robust. However, we wanted to include them since their electoral *componendas* (patronage-oriented attempts to build winning electoral coalitions) represent a source of confusion for the electorate. In addition, they, as well as other minuscule nonparty groups who follow similar strategies, occupy a portion of Venezuelan political space. However, there are other, ideologically oriented or at least more ideologically consistent actors, like MEP, MAS, and PCV, which are relatively central on the partisan position, but very extreme on the ideological. The fact that they are on the extreme opposite Cruzada Cívica Nacionalista and Marcos Pérez Jiménez lends considerable validity to our treatment of the X axis as the left-right continuum. Not only that, but the position of the 18 different actors on the X axis is very congruent with other results obtained in our analysis, as well as with intuitive interpretations of left and right in Venezuela. *Adecos* and *copeyanos* are more or less in the center, flanked on the left and the right by those actors whom one would suspect of being where they are on this dimension. Thus, considerations of left and right do not monopolize Venezuelan political space but lend a certain coherence and serve as a basic frame of reference for the orientations of the public with respect to relevant political actors.

After all, the parameters of figure 13 were derived from individual feelings about the parties and their leaders, as measured by the thermometer items, and they obviously include an implicit reference to left-right distinctions among them. We have obtained more direct indication of the public's perception of the position of the leaders by asking where these stand in Venezuelan politics—that is, posing the self-placement question applied to others. Ranking the responses from left (score of 1) to right (score of 3) we recovered the following pattern of leaders' positions on the continuum (in means): José Vicente Rangel (1.26), Jesús Paz Galarraga (1.25), Carlos Andrés Pérez (2.31), and Lorenzo Fernández (2.54). We counted at least 72 per cent of our respondents (and as high as 80 per cent) among those willing to identify these leaders' positions. We obtained less convincing results and higher proportions of "don't know" responses for less visible figures. Thus, we feel justified in treating the parties as being located on the left-right continuum, and in utilizing these locations for validating our measure of individual ideology.

Ideological Position

The configuration presented in figure 13 offers a relevant frame of reference for further exploration of the contextual meaning of different ideological positions in Venezuelan politics. Our first step consists of measuring the consistency of these positions in terms of their partisan preferences. The positions themselves are the unordered (nominal) categories resulting from individual self-placements on the left-right continuum and choice of economic system in all their possible combinations, including single choices. Given their refusal to place themselves on the continuum, the *marais* are of special interest to us, for this may respond to ideological motivation such as a shared value stressing the rejection of political labels. We will show that the *marais'* refusal to use ideological labels also extends to party labels; 75 per cent of the persons in the category classified themselves as "independent" or "apolitical" when asked to select one of three labels which would define their overall attitude toward politics in general (the third possible choice being "partisan"). Consequently, the *marais* can be utilized as a control group in the analysis. Their location relative to others' may be indicative of the true configuration of the continuum, which may or may not include them. Finally, we want to determine through these comparisons if the *marais* are ideological in spite of their resistance to being classified as such in operational terms.

Concerning partisan preferences which may characterize the different ideological positions, we should observe those identified by leftist and/or socialist labels to be more antagonistic toward status quo or "prosystem" parties such as the AD and COPEI, while demonstrating sympathy toward leftist and "antisystem" MAS, PCV, and MEP. One could also expect CCN to be more popular among individuals in rightist positions and, to a lesser extent, the *marais*.

Figure 14 delineates the patterns of sentiment toward the more important parties that seem to predominate within the different ideological positions. The horizontal axis represents the left-right dimension recovered in the solution presented in figure 13. The locations of MEP, PCV, MAS, AD, COPEI, and CCN are those identified in that figure; other actors have been omitted to simplify the discussion. Perpendicular to these six party locations we have plotted standardized (Z) mean sympathy scores of the twelve positions. The locations of the ideological positions of these perpendicular plots confirm our first assumption: socialists and leftists are more antagonistic toward prosystem parties. Positions most hostile to AD and COPEI include communists and leftist socialists in both cases, with the *marais* conspicuously close. All of the socialist positions are below average in their sympathy toward the AD; however, loosely defined leftists (those making this choice without any commitment to type of economic system) are shown to be the most *adeco* of all. Sympathy for COPEI is also low among these positions, although rightist socialists are the most enthusiastic *copeyanos*, this being the first datum about the character of this "incongruent" position.

Furthermore, feelings toward AD and COPEI are highly consistent and stable: leftist socialists, communists, *marais*, centrists, and socialists are below average in their sympathy toward these two parties. On the other hand, rightists and capitalists tend to be above average in their sympathy toward the AD and COPEI, with rightists especially warm toward the latter. Much has been made of the ideological trajectory of the leaders of the Social Christian party away from the right since its creation; however, the party continues to attract the support of conservative elements of the Venezuelan public. Ironically, it seems that support for the AD reveals quite the opposite trend: even though the AD has drifted to the right in the recent past, the party continues to attract the favor of the left. With a touch of audacity we could contend that, defined in ideological terms, the more intense *adecos* are leftists who can reconcile themselves to varying degrees of state intervention in the economy, while their *copeyano* counterparts accept an active participation provided this is not legitimized with leftist slogans. In short, feelings toward establishment parties are as anticipated, with only minor variation. Leftists and socialists tend to favor neither, while higher levels of support for both tend to come from rightist and capitalist elements, especially in the case of COPEI.

Figure 14. Partisan Preferences of the Ideological Positions and the Left-Right Continuum

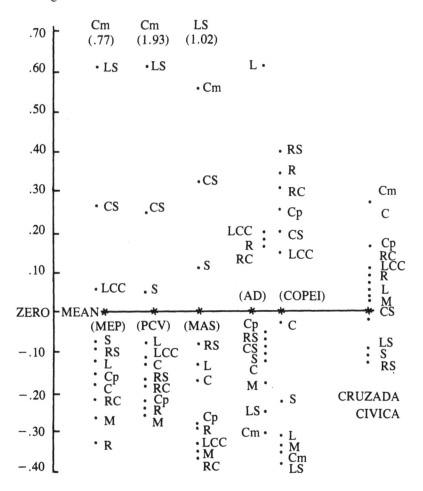

Key to symbols in figure 14:
M *Marais*, L *Leftists*, C *Centrists*, R *Rightists*, S *Socialists*, Cm *Communists*, Cp *Capitalists*, LCC *Leftist and centrist capitalists*, RC *Rightist capitalists*, LS *Leftist socialists*, CS *Centrist socialists*, RS *Rightist socialists*

Note: Standardized (Z) scores greater than .70 are not on scale, all other plots represent a scale of .10 z units for .75 inches. Asterisks (*) depict the position of the parties on the continuum, as this was recovered in the three-dimensional plot presented in figure 13. The parties are identified at the bottom of each array of perpendicular plots.

Eta values between ideological position and sympathy for these parties are: .29 (for MEP), .35 (for PCV), .46 (for MAS), .19 (for AD), .30 (for COPEI), and .06 (for CCN). With the exception of the latter, all are significant at the .01 level.

Sample size for these different computations varied as follows: 1,370 (for MEP), 1,364 (for PCV), 1,367 (for MAS), 1,377 (for AD), 1,379 (for COPEI), and 1,372 (for CCN).

The scores were computed from means obtained in multiple-range (one-way analysis of variance) comparisons. Thus, the location of the parties may be interpreted as the solution sets to each of the values of the plots.

Turning to sentiment about the antiestablishment parties, our findings seem congruent; that is, support for these parties from the different ideological positions tends to be consistent with the location of the parties on the left-right continuum. Furthermore, there appears to be a better fit between feelings about leftist parties and their location on the continuum; this is scarcely surprising, given the fact that MEP, PCV, and MAS provide more explicit ideological stimuli than AD and COPEI, which in contrast seek to attract much broader and therefore more ideologically heterogeneous segments of the public.

The data presented in figure 14 leave little room for doubt; there is a virtual reversal in the partisan preferences of the ideological positions when one moves from prosystem to antisystem parties. Three positions are consistently above average in their sympathies for parties of the left: the centrist socialists, the leftist socialists, and the communists. Their locations vary somewhat due to factional rivalries within the Venezuelan left but are nonetheless consistent. The socialists drop in and out of the above-average range of sympathy depending on whether we are discussing the MAS or the PCV; they are above average in their sympathy toward these two parties but below it with the MEP, yielding their location to leftists and centrist capitalists, who seem less threatened by MEP than by other parties of the left. Of the three leftist parties, MAS receives the warmest endorsement (the mean [raw] sympathy scores are slightly higher with respect to MAS).

Only the *marais* and the centrists seem to maintain their locations at the lower levels of sympathy, suggesting a more or less generalized antiparty stance that embraces both the pro- and antisystem parties. The leftists are also relatively stable: anti-MEP, anti-MAS, and anti-PCV, a fact explainable in terms of their *adeco* proclivities. Capitalists and rightists are consistently below average in their sympathy scores; they are grouped into rather tight clusters of positions antagonistic to the parties of the left, especially the MEP and the PCV. The pattern of feelings toward the MAS produces a similar clustering but allows easier discriminations between ideological positions. Capitalists in all of their combinations are particularly antagonistic toward MAS. However, the general pattern is very systematic: capitalists and rightists are antileft, socialists and leftist socialists proleft.

In summary, the partisan preferences of the ideological positions, as measured by their sympathies toward the political parties, are consistent with the location of the latter on the left-right continuum.

In addition, the intensity and direction of feelings toward the parties correlate significantly with the location of each ideological position on this dimension and, by implication, with the position of the parties on the continuum; the CCN provides the only case to the contrary.

The status and significance of the Cruzada Cívica Nacionalista (CCN) requires additional comment. The Cruzada is decidedly anti-system and its association with exiled dictator Marcos Pérez Jiménez explicit. Cruzada represents, if anything, the type of authoritarian option now in power in the major South American countries. It claims continuity with the *nuevo ideal nacional* of Pérez Jiménez which dominated Venezuelan politics in the 1950s. However, feelings toward CCN do not correlate with ideological position. In fact, the range of sympathy scores for the CCN is the narrowest, going from a low of 1.45 to a high of 1.75. This is reflected on the pattern of perpendicular plots obtained for the CCN and depicted in figure 14. Contrary to every reasonable expectation, it is the communists who are warmest toward the Cruzada. On the other hand, it is the rightist socialists who show the lowest level of sympathy toward that party.

On the other hand Cruzada bases its appeal, to a greater extent than URD and FDP, on being a movement against party politicking; thus it should attract greater than average support from those ideological positions more adverse to parties in general. Yet the *marais* cannot be construed as sympathizing with the Cruzada; although slightly above average, individuals in this group are within the cluster of positions antagonistic to it. Only the centrists seem to be enthusiastic about this option, and not very much at that.

In summary, our findings show that *the partisan preferences of our respondents are congruent with their ideological position and with the position of the parties on the continuum*. In addition, the findings validate our measure of ideological position, for if our respondents had expressed their ideological preferences without regard for politically relevant criteria, the labels chosen to characterize ideological position would not have been so consistent with partisan preferences. That is, *the congruence between ideological position and party preference cannot be adequately explained without the assumption that the former constitutes a valid measure of individual ideology*. This means that no matter how awkward or incongruent the combinations of labels utilized to describe ideological position, these are clearly related to such an important attitudinal area as party preference.

Ideological Attitudes and Ideological Position

There are some difficulties embedded in further validation of our measure of individual ideology. These include not only problems of validity and reliability, but also theoretical issues concerning the extent to which elements of an ideology or belief system tend to "hang together," and their constraining influence on political behavior. Prothro and Chaparro showed that shifts in the preferences of the Chilean electorate toward leftist parties were not accompanied by increases in the ideological content or left orientation of Chilean public opinion.[27] Sartori warns that "per se the ideological mentality is not necessarily conducive to an active involvement and thereby to 'ideological activism.' . . ."[28] Be that as it may, where ideological linkages between constrained attitudes are concerned, one of the two elements—either the behavioral or the attitudinal—may be missing.

There is also the problem of the relationship between individual ideology and party preference. First, there are instances in which the former is a better predictor of opinion than party affiliation. Note the remarks of Converse and Pierce concerning the French case:

> In most modern democracies with any history of mass voting, the tracing of political cleavages in the population is entirely straightforward. At least three-quarters, and often 90–95 per cent of the electorate can be shown to have adopted a more or less abiding sense of allegiance to one of the nation's political parties. . . . Where France is concerned, this is much less clearly the case . . . while every French party enjoys the support of firmly engaged partisans and activists, the proportion of French voters who keep themselves adrift from such anchors or points of orientation in evaluating the political scene is noteworthy. . . .[29]

This typifies a situation in which the relationship between party preference and individual ideology is predicated on the dominance of the former over the latter. In Venezuela, where parties enjoy the support of firmly engaged partisan activists, there is a fairly robust link between party identification and ideological position (eta = .47 for 892 party identifiers, considering ideology the dependent variable). However, this tells us nothing about people who do not militate in the parties.

One does not find much guidance in the literature. Most of the discussion centers on the elite's ability to manipulate the poorly articulated beliefs of the public. Sartori views ideology as a crucial lever at the disposal of elites for obtaining political mobilization and for maximizing the possibilities of mass manipulation.[30] This view is in accord with that of Converse and represents one side of the ongoing controversy on the degree to which mass publics are ideological. However, its inability to account for instances where ideology exists outside such a frame of reference diminishes its usefulness. For example, Converse does not utilize the French case, where a considerable proportion of voters maintain themselves "adrift from partisan anchors" to try to reformulate the paradigm. In addition, another advocate of this interpretation, Herbert McClosky, utilized his findings on divergence of opinions between party leaders and followers to stress the looseness and incoherence of the latter's opinions.[31]

Granted, people are not equally ideological, and there is a plethora of definitions of ideology. However, a more basic problem is the apparent unwillingness to perceive some attitudes and actual behavior of ordinary citizens as ideological, even though these may fall considerably short of (1) a dogmatic and closed cognitive structure (ideology as psychological phenomenon), (2) a rationalistic, doctrinaire, and nonpragmatic orientation (ideology as cultural phenomenon), or (3) emotional responses resulting in political mobilization (ideology as normative phenomenon), to invoke only the more notorious elements associated with ideology.[32] To be sure, the mass public lacks a weltanschauung and, as Putnam has shown, even among elite ideologues one may no longer find the dogmatism, unwillingness to compromise, hostility to pluralist norms, and total antagonism to political opponents associated with ideological thinking.[33] If these are the standards of proof we would then have to concur with the "end of ideology" thesis. But is this really ideology?

Mullins argues that the starting point of any empirical investigation of ideology

> . . . is to distinguish between those people who hold ideologies and those who do not; or between those people who have the capacity for thinking ideologically, and those who lack it. . . . In my conception . . . there are four elements that are fundamental . . . *logical coherence* (or, in Converse's terms, "constraint"), *historical consciousness and action orientation* (ability to conceive of fundamentally different arrangements of the social structure), *cognitive competence* (ability to conceptualize how things get done in politics), and *evaluative competence* (applicable to present and imagined social arrangements). . . .[34]

This would not deny, of course, that

> . . . there is a difference between the articulated, differentiated, well-developed political arguments put forward by informed and conscious Marxists or Fascists or liberal democrats on the one hand, and the loosely structured, unreflective statements of the common men. . . .[35]

However, it runs contrary to the view that ideology belongs only in the realm of the former.

In addition, one must determine the substantive nature of the symbol or label capable of influencing a person's attitudes, evaluations, and political behavior and making it more similar to that of others who identify or could be identified with the same symbol or label. Obviously, these will vary with the extant pattern of cleavages which predominate in the society. In Northern Ireland, religious affiliation provides sufficient information about the political preferences of individuals. Venezuelan Catholics would need additional qualifiers to convey more specific meaning in their political context. The point is not that religion is ideological in Northern Ireland; instead, religion is *the* primary basis for the formation of political cleavages. Once individuals are identified in this manner, we start to observe differences between Catholics and Protestants which seem ideological in nature. Thus, what is important is not the symbol or label but its ultimate relevance, and the extent to which it can produce an ideological cleavage.

It is extremely difficult to find ideology with a sample survey. One of the more marked differences between the two schools of thought concerning mass ideologies refers to the use of the survey[36] versus in-depth interviews.[37] The latter is a more adequate tool for the analysis of ideology at the level of ordinary citizens, but a very expensive one if utilized with large samples. Working within the limitations of a survey instrument, it is possible to tap some aspects of ideology, especially ideological tendency or any other such summary measure of ideological preferences, and then to explore its cleavage potential and operational validity in terms of other attitudes believed related to ideology. We have shown that, in Venezuela, 73 per cent of the public can relate to the left-right continuum, while 37 per cent could not be characterized at all in terms of their choice of one type of economic system. On the other hand, our foregoing analysis suggests that combinations of the two are analytically useful and congruent with partisan preferences. This procedure allows us to examine the ideological tendencies of some 92 per cent of the

Venezuelan electorate. What else can we say which is firmly grounded on theoretical reasoning or historical evidence to show that the left-right continuum is relevant, and that the position of the individual on the continuum provides a fairly reliable index of that individual's ideological preferences?

We showed that parties and candidates, along with other political figures, are perceived on the continuum. If we could show that reaction to events and institutions varied with position on the continuum, a more impressive case could be made. We have additional evidence which may permit us to do so. This includes opinion about the Chilean military coup of 1973, military coups in general, evaluation of the institution of elections, and participatory mood.

The Chilean military coup of September 11, 1973, which resulted in the death of President Salvador Allende, destruction of his regime, and inauguration of a fascist military dictatorship, bears all the characteristics of an event capable of producing a profound cleavage of opinion along ideological lines. Whether examined in terms of its domestic genesis[38] or international implications,[39] reaction has taken on predominantly ideological themes.

The impact of this event on Venezuelan politics can hardly be exaggerated. The candidacy of Dr. Jesús Angel Paz Galarraga, of MEP, was being supported by a Popular Front—the Nueva Fuerza —whose basic strategy was an attempt to repeat in Venezuela the formula which gave Allende and his Unidad Popular coalition their 1970 electoral victory. Not only was the Paz candidacy seriously undermined by the Chilean coup, but the reaction affected Rangel's candidacy as well, even though the reaction of the parties supporting the latter was to disclaim concern and deny any strategic similarity with the "Chilean way." The Social Christians were presented with an insoluble dilemma in the middle of a hard-fought campaign. Given the suspicion of Christian Democratic involvement or tacit approval of the coup, the Caldera administration had to move very cautiously in order to minimize criticism of its Chilean coreligionaries while condemning the coup.[40] It is no exaggeration to say that, with the possible exception of France and Italy,[41] in no other country did the Chilean military coup of 1973 have an impact comparable to that in Venezuela.

Unquestionably the coup polarized Venezuelan opinion along ideological lines, and reaction to the Chilean event was congruent with the ideological positions of individuals. The evidence is presented in figure 15, where we display the standardized means obtained for each position's orientation toward the coup. Clearly, support for the coup came from all capitalist as well as rightist posi-

Figure 15. Ideological Position and Opinion about the Chilean Military Coup of 1973

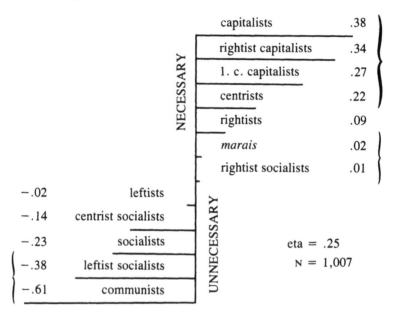

capitalists	.38
rightist capitalists	.34
1. c. capitalists	.27
centrists	.22
rightists	.09
marais	.02
rightist socialists	.01

NECESSARY

UNNECESSARY

−.02	leftists
−.14	centrist socialists
−.23	socialists
−.38	leftist socialists
−.61	communists

eta = .25
N = 1,007

Note: Brackets identify groups of standardized scores that are not statistically different from one another (p < .01).

QUESTION: "Recently, the president of the Republic of Chile, Dr. Salvador Allende, was overthrown by a military coup. Are you aware of this event? [No = 14 per cent.] How would you evaluate this coup? Do you believe that this was necessary [22 per cent] or unnecessary [42 per cent]?" Other responses: "depends" (5 per cent), "do not know" (17 per cent).

tions. It should be stressed that the predominant view was condemnation of the coup; however, rightists tended to perceive the coup as "necessary." On the other hand, leftists and socialists were for the most part strongly opposed to the coup. Communists and leftist socialists shared a level of greatest opposition, which put them in a stance clearly antagonistic to that taken by all capitalists and the centrists, the ideological positions relatively most supportive of the coup.

In one of his most celebrated essays, Marx analyzed the causes and consequences of the coup de main of Louis Napoleon, hoping to eliminate the concept of *caesarism*. His discussion of the consequences of the coup d'etat of December 2, 1851 help illustrate the reasons why the left cannot rely on this type of strategy in its struggle for power.

In parliament the nation made its general will the law, that is, it made the law of the ruling class its general will. Before the executive power it renounces to an alien force. . . . The executive power, in contrast to the legislative power, expresses the heteronomy of a nation, in contrast to its autonomy. France, therefore, seems to have escaped the despotism of a class only to fall back beneath the despotism of an individual. . . . The struggle seems to be settled in such a way that all classes, equally impotent and equally mute, fall on their knees before the rifle butt. . . . Only under the second Bonaparte does the state seem to have made itself completely independent. . . . But let there be no misunderstanding. The Bonaparte dynasty represents not only the revolutionary, but the conservative peasant. . . .[42]

Contexts and times may change, but history shows that, in general, the left has little to gain from coups. In Venezuela, the coup of October 1945 meant the end of a successful collaboration between the communists and the Medina administration.[43] The coup of January 23, 1958, which put an end to the Pérez Jiménez regime and ushered in the democratic era, restored the predominance of the Social Democrats and is regarded by the Venezuelan left as a missed opportunity.[44] Thus, while one may find variation in levels of support for these coups among different sectors of Venezuelan opinion, the left tends to be more consistently opposed to coups.

Confirmation comes from the data presented in figure 16, based on standardization of the scores of a scale measuring overall individual attitude about coups. The scale includes opinion about the coups of 1945 and 1958 as well as responses to two general questions concerning coups d'etat and the role of the military in politics. Location of the different ideological positions on the continuum presented in figure 16 suggests the presence of the "historical consciousness" discussed by Mullins,[45] for these data not only reflect "institutionalized beliefs that someone may pick up," but reactions congruent with the historical impact of coups on the different ideological positions. We do not wish to stretch the evidence beyond its analytical possibilities, but these include an ordering which puts the left against coups and the right in a more supportive attitude. Whether one looks at reaction to the Chilean coup or at opinion about coups in general, the more leftist—communists, leftist socialists, and socialists—oppose coups while the more rightist—capitalists in general—tend to be more supportive. Whether one views ideology as inflexible dogma or as loosely constrained beliefs, it is clear that the more extreme positions are the more consistent. On the other

Figure 16. Ideological Position and Overall Attitude toward Military Coups

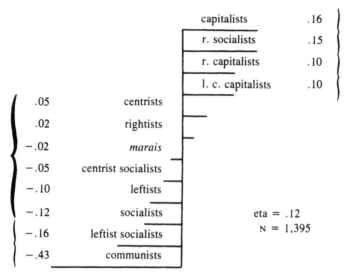

capitalists	.16
r. socialists	.15
r. capitalists	.10
l. c. capitalists	.10

.05	centrists
.02	rightists
−.02	*marais*
−.05	centrist socialists
−.10	leftists
−.12	socialists
−.16	leftist socialists
−.43	communists

eta = .12
N = 1,395

Note: Brackets identify groups of standardized scores that are not statistically different from one another (p < .01). The ordinal scale on which these scores are based included items 97, 99, 100, and 101 presented in appendix B. The scale itself appears in appendix F.

hand, if the magnitudes of the scores reflect "intensity," the left is more adamant in its opposition to coups in general than the right in favoring them, although both ends of the left-right continuum seem equally intense in their reaction to the Chilean coup. This suggests two possible inferences. First, individuals in rightist ideological positions seem more capable of accommodating to situations created by coups than leftists. Second, unless one treats a preference for capitalism as a symptom of traditional Catholic values, the putschist impulse against the pluralist Venezuelan regime is more likely to come from capitalists, not unreconstructed "traditionalists."

The position of the *marais* on the continuum of opinion concerning coups is noteworthy. One could anticipate that this staunchly antiparty group would be relatively receptive to military coups. However, its location with respect to coups falls within modal range, .02 for the Chilean coup and −.02 for coups in general. Although they seem to loathe political parties, this does not translate into a greater receptivity toward military coups. On the other hand, it should not pass without comment that those ideological positions feeling "warmer" toward prosystem parties seem somewhat more inclined to support coups. Thus, if intense sympathy toward these parties does not inculcate unqualified opposition to coups, since those parties have benefited from coups in Venezuela, a total lack of support for parties is not conducive to a conspiratorial stance supportive of military regimes. Finally, judging from their reaction to coups—which seems grounded in doctrinaire reasons as well as in actual historical experience—the more "subversive" positions of the left cannot be construed as the more "conspiratorial." This is true whether one looks at opinion about a reactionary-fascist coup which *had* to arouse leftist condemnation, or at opinion about coups in general.

The fact that some ordinary Venezuelans understand the problem of right versus left as a problem of government versus opposition reflects recent historical events. Undoubtedly the most consistent, concerted, and visible source of opposition and criticism of the Venezuelan regime has been the left. This has gone beyond condemnation of the reformist character of a regime unable to cope with the problems of dependency and underdevelopment[46] that functions as a "neocolonial" appendage of international capitalism.[47] Leftist criticism of the regime, especially during the 1960s, focused on repeated violations of Article 58 of the 1961 Constitution[48] as a symptom of government's unwillingness to apply such provisions to Venezuelan communists and radicals suspected of guerrilla or any similar form of subversive activities.[49] The policy of pacification pursued by COPEI following its electoral triumph in 1968 diminished the salience of the human rights issue but obviously did not change the overall perspective of the left on the regime.[50] Finally, leftists' participation in recent elections[51] has done little to change a consistently critical interpretation of this route,[52] of the difficulties that it creates for leftist unity,[53] and of the realization of their own very limited opportunities for success.[54] Thus, leftist criticism has been sustained concerning the nature and possible outcomes of the regime, as well as the manner in which the electoral process has been conducted. How have these views "filtered down" to the rank-and-file, and what do they say about an inflexible attitude of the left with respect to its basic orientation toward the regime?

In figure 17 we present evidence which addresses these questions. We include standardized scores for opinion about regime policies as well as policies of the Caldera administration, along with opinion about elections. Locations of the different ideological positions on these continua are plotted perpendicular to the line represented by a common zero mean for the three standardized distributions. First of all, ideological position is related to the three areas of opinion which deal with the relevance of ideological preferences at the level of the public. That is, ideological reaction to the regime is not confined to the elite. Second, insofar as the left is concerned, ordinary citizens in leftist positions—especially communists, leftist socialists, and socialists—have patterns of evaluation which suggest awareness of the appropriate response, or at least a certain inflexibility in their negativism about the regime, the administration in power, and elections. Third, one tends to find a similar consistency among rightist positions, and in general among those that seem closer to the pro-system parties. A common configuration seems to hold for the three aspects of regime evaluation: socialists and leftists critical, rightists and capitalists more supportive.

Shifts in location are experienced by the (pro-*adeco*) leftists whose criticism of regime policies $(Z = .19)$ is less intense than their very critical evaluation of Caldera's $(Z = -.44)$. The *marais* shift from a relatively modal location concerning the regime $(Z = .07)$ to a moderate level of criticism of Caldera $(Z = -.24)$, and a high level of criticism of elections $(Z = -.42)$. The capitalists also experience a shift when it comes to their evaluation of the institution of elections, dropping out of a relatively well knit cluster of rightist positions. In short, the capitalists are more critical of elections than could be anticipated from their party preferences.

The locations of the positions on the continuum of opinion concerning the Caldera administration parallels their location concerning feelings about COPEI: the left in general is very negative, the rightists and the capitalists more favorable. Thus we gain relatively little information from inspection of the reaction of the ideological positions in this sense, except to confirm the rigidity and extremity of the location of the communists and the leftist socialists. Even though the Caldera administration legalized and, to a certain extent, reincorporated these positions in the political process, their evaluation of COPEI's policies is about as negative as their evaluation of the regime.

Discussing the roots of political alienation, a concept of long standing in the Western intellectual tradition, Robert Lane has suggested that this is best understood as

> . . . the tendency to think of the government and politics of the nation as run *by* others *for* others according to an unfair set of rules. It is more than a traditionalist's sense that these things are part of the natural order over which he has no control, for the traditionalist has no belief that it could or should be otherwise. He does not feel alienated from his government because he never felt allegiant or integrated. . . . The politically alienated man is aware of the alternatives and grieves over his losses. . . .[55]

Figure 17. Ideological Position and Political Evaluation

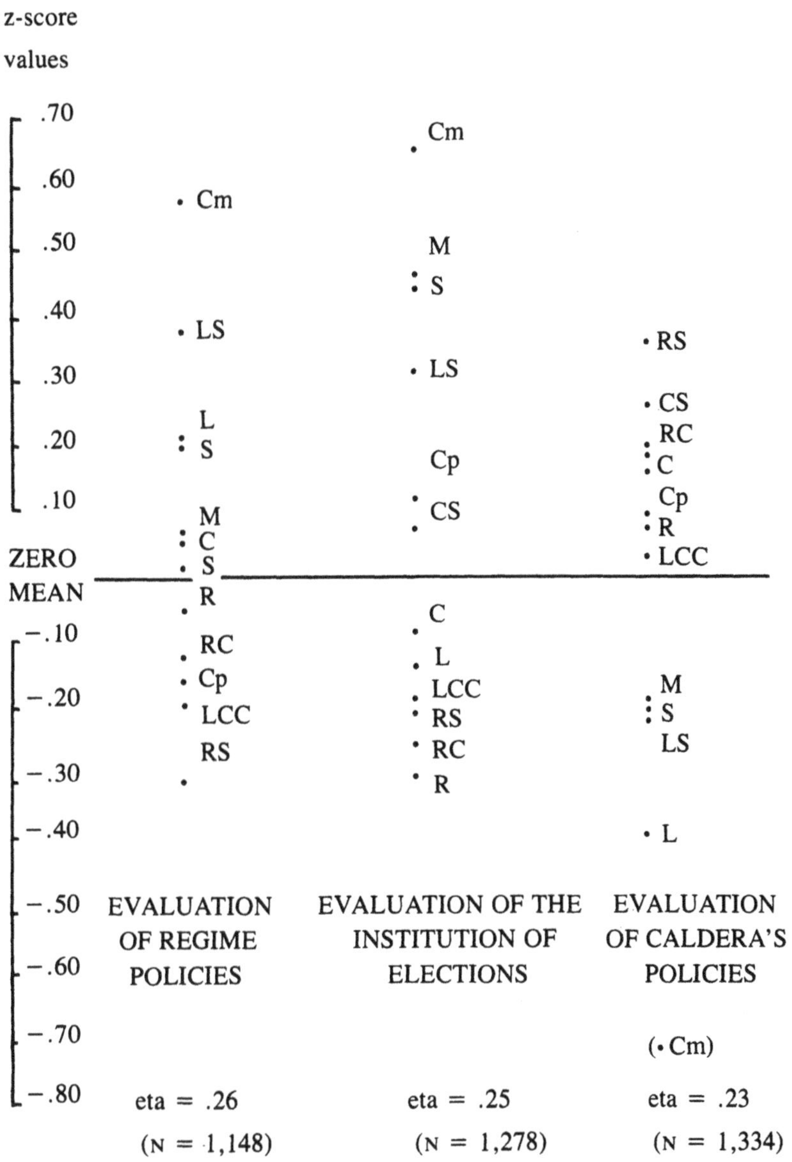

z-score
values

```
 .70                        Cm
                             •
 .60      • Cm

 .50                         M
                           • S
 .40      • LS
                                              • RS
 .30                 • LS
                                              • CS
          L                                   . RC
 .20     : S                                  : C
                           Cp
 .10                       • CS               Cp
          M                                  • R
         : C
ZERO     . S                                  • LCC
MEAN     ─────────────────────────────────────────────
         . R
−.10                        C
         . RC              •
       • Cp                . L
−.20     • LCC             . LCC              M
                          • RS               : S
         RS               • RC               LS
−.30     •                • R

−.40                                         • L

−.50   EVALUATION      EVALUATION OF THE    EVALUATION
       OF REGIME       INSTITUTION OF       OF CALDERA'S
−.60   POLICIES        ELECTIONS            POLICIES

−.70                                        (• Cm)

−.80   eta = .26       eta = .25            eta = .23

       (N = 1,148)     (N = 1,278)          (N = 1,334)
```

Note: Scores for the regime and for elections reflect increasing levels of criticism; those for Caldera reflect increasing approval. Ideological positions identified as in figure 14. All eta values are significant at the .01 level.

Allegiance to the political regime, treated as "diffuse support" by David Easton[56] and operationalized as "trust in government" by Almond and Verba,[57] has been related to a high sense of political efficacy or "subjective competence." However, in their five-nation study Almond and Verba found that Mexico deviated from the general pattern in that competent Mexicans were not more likely to evaluate actual government performance positively.[58] William Gamson pioneered the effort to combine trust and efficacy in order to explain rates of political involvement.[59] Seligson's review of efforts to test the trust-efficacy hypothesis suggests that this has not been sustained by existing data, although the main difficulty seems to reside in Gamson's failure to specify the modes of participation to which the hypothesis was applicable.[60]

One additional explanation could depart from the relationship between efficacy and participation, as well as from ideological differences between participants. Ideology may sustain a relatively high level of personal capacity despite the lack of immediate success stemming from participation. In Venezuela as in other countries where the short-term electoral prospects of the left do not include victory, leftist activists may interpret the outcome of their efforts on a different timetable than partisans of AD or COPEI, who can develop more immediate expectations and have the memory of successful experiences in dealing with government officials. Thus electoral participation through compulsory voting need not diminish the political capacity of leftist activists, since they may not consider this their more fundamental mode of participation. In short, ideology may sustain political capacity despite unsuccessful participation. On the other hand, the operational types evolved from Gamson's hypothesis have been examined along more or less dichotomous conceptions of participation—normal versus protest, conventional versus unconventional, and so on. It would be interesting to consider ideology an intervening variable in these relationships.

We do not intend to test the hypothesis except to underscore the fact that, to our knowledge, no one has tried to probe the relationship between what we call participatory mood, that is, the combination of high and low levels of efficacy (capacity), with high and low levels of trust (evaluation) and ideology. Our own fourfold scheme is most similar to that proposed by Simeon and Elkins,[61] although most typologies evolved to test the trust-efficacy hypothesis are much alike.[62] Given their consistently negative evaluation of the policy outcomes of the regime, their criticism of elections, their affective distance from the establishment parties, and their highly negative orientation to political objects related to the regime, we expect the ideological positions of the Venezuelan left to be dominated by *critics* and *discontents*.

In chapter 3 we saw that although there are differences between classes and strata in terms of their prevalent participatory moods, the strength of the measures of association between social inequality and the former did not suggest that the social circumstances of individuals play a large role in determining this important attitudinal orientation. What is the situation with respect to ideological position? First of all, the relationship is significant and much more robust than that just mentioned.[63] Second, following Gamson and assuming that leftist ideology fosters discontent in Venezuela, we standardized the values of the variable for the different categories of ideological position. On the right side of figure 18 we present the standardized score of each ideological position, and these tend to increase with rising leftist orientation.[64] Third, looking at the relative strength of each mood within each position, it becomes apparent that among the rightist positions in general, dissatisfaction with the regime leads to discontent, not criticism. Similarly, the deferents appear more numerous than the supports among these positions, which suggests that a more favorable orientation to the regime (greater trust) is not necessarily conducive to greater capacity (greater efficacy or subjective competence). In other words, a rightist orientation produces more favorable evaluation and reduces dissatisfaction, but does not increase capacity. By contrast, a leftist orientation produces a predominantly critical mood and virtually shuts the door to a combination of allegiance and capacity, as shown by the reduced area of supporters within leftist positions. Thus, within the left, capacity is mostly found in combination with criticism, suggesting that negativism about the regime, the "grief over one's losses," and the realization that immediate improvement is not at hand does not diminish capacity. We feel justified in calling this "ideological thinking" and in arguing that our evidence on some key attitudinal preferences of different ideological positions shows a great deal of congruence, cognitive and evaluative ability, and historical consciousness. In summary, we believe that the ideological positions of individuals make a difference in their attitudes and preferences.

To recapitulate, our findings show that combining individual self-placements on the left-right continuum with preferences about economic system (or in North American terms, degree of state intervention in the economy), twelve ideological positions can be discriminated among the Venezuelan public. *These positions are on*

Figure 18. Ideological Position and Participatory Mood

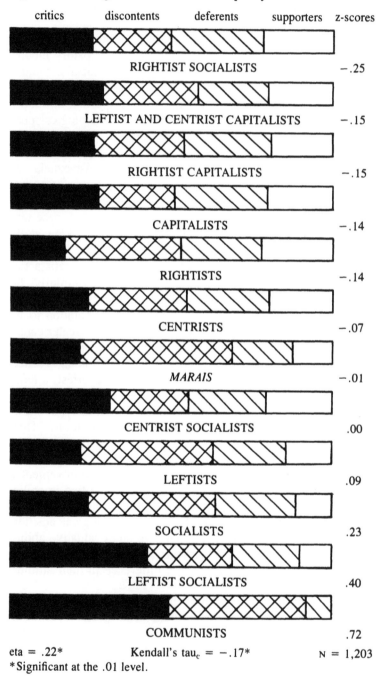

critics	discontents	deferents	supporters	z-scores

RIGHTIST SOCIALISTS — -.25

LEFTIST AND CENTRIST CAPITALISTS — -.15

RIGHTIST CAPITALISTS — -.15

CAPITALISTS — -.14

RIGHTISTS — -.14

CENTRISTS — -.07

MARAIS — -.01

CENTRIST SOCIALISTS — .00

LEFTISTS — .09

SOCIALISTS — .23

LEFTIST SOCIALISTS — .40

COMMUNISTS — .72

eta = .22*   Kendall's tau$_c$ = -.17*   N = 1,203
*Significant at the .01 level.

the left-right continuum, and their partisan preferences and more ideological attitudes are congruent with differences that can be perceived between left and right in the Venezuelan context, as well as in a broader historical perspective.

The analysis allows for qualification of a series of well-known views of the Venezuelan political public. First of all, there are contradictions within the right: greater allegiance to the system and a more supportive attitude toward the Chilean coup suggest selective ideological thinking in applying democratic rules of the game. This raises questions about rightist unwillingness to accept a leftist government. Second, leftist disaffection and criticism of democratic institutions reveals the rigidity and inflexibility associated with ideological thinking on the left and seems linked to a mood of criticism, not discontent. The left, in other words, feels relatively capable in Venezuela. Third, the terms "leftist" and "rightist socialist" can be used as proxies, respectively, for *adeco* and *copeyano*. Given the broad support for a large state role in economic affairs, this is scarcely incongruent. Fourth, conservative preferences appear more attached to capitalist than to rightist positions. In other words, the preference for a "market economy" seems to increase individual conservatism in the Venezuelan context. However, that context lacks the historical and partisan referents that would justify applicability of the terms "liberal" and "conservative" to cover as broad a range of phenomena as that implied by left and right.

Our analysis makes clear the unqualified negativism of the *marais*. They are antiright, antileft, antiparty, and largely antiestablishment as well, which would suggest they are really not on the continuum. However, their orientation seems to have more in common with leftists than with centrists. Thus, it may be useful to include them as the least ideological of the positions. The overlap of partisan and ideological preferences suggests that although the presence of two broad-based, multiclass parties like AD and COPEI tends to lower the salience of their supporters' ideological frame of reference, they have not managed to diminish the salience of the left-right continuum. Left and right are clearly discernible and distinct from one another, but there is considerable variation within their constituent positions.

The Left-Right Continuum in Venezuela

The partisan preferences and dominant ideological orientations of the twelve positions can be utilized to determine their exact location on the left-right continuum. This can be accomplished if all the items presented in figures 14 through 18 are recoded to reflect antigovernment or antiregime bias, standardized, and summed to obtain a measure reflecting the content of the continuum. This content would summarize the location of the ideological positions on the continuum, adjusted for partisan preferences, regime and institutional evaluation, opinion about coups, and participatory mood. Comparison of the standardized mean scores of the positions should give us a clue as to the number of *clusters of positions*, which we will call *ideological tendencies* of the continuum. Applying multiple-range (one-way analysis of variance) comparisons to the standardized added scores we obtain the results presented in table V-1.

The means of the twelve positions cluster into six groups of statistically different tendencies (subsets a, ab, b, bc, cd, and d).[65] The six ideological tendencies are represented in the following proportion: right, 39 per cent, center-right, 10 per cent, center, 10 per cent, center-left, 12 per cent, left, 7 per cent, and radical left, 14 per cent. We are unable to place 8 per cent of the population on the continuum. Utilizing adjusted frequencies, and presenting the results in terms of left, center, and right, their relative strength would stand at 23, 35, and 42 per cent, respectively, which is comparatively close to the 28, 30, and 42 per cent obtained from individual self-placements. The difference comes from adjusting the location of leftists, who are about 4 per cent of the population, to the center-left. Yet this is not the main benefit gained. Not only can we now be more accurate and confident of the meaning of the different labels identifying self-placement, position, and tendency, but in addition can utilize 92 per cent of the population in the analysis. Obviously, utilization of one or another measure would depend on the number of cases and on how accurate the discriminations need be. In short, our measures of individual ideology conform to basic requirements of validity and reliability while allowing us to be assured of accuracy and to confront the problem of disappearing frequencies.[66]

Of the six ideological tendencies the modal tendency is of course the center, but this is quite specific, for it is a tendency that characterizes only the centrist socialists. The left, being monopolized by the socialists, is also a very specific tendency. Thus we have two tendencies that contain only one position. The right, by contrast, is a tendency which includes four different ideological positions, although differences in their z-scores are so small that they clearly belong together (in subset a). Perhaps more surprising is the evidence showing the *marais* sharing the center-left with the leftists. We should not dilute the significance of this similarity with implications about the obvious functional similarity between the two positions. What is more relevant is that, despite the *marais'* refusal to adopt labels, their general negativism, and antiparty biases, they turn out to be within the same tendency as a group of people who use labels and have party preferences but whose views on other matters are very close to theirs. In other words, the *marais* have more in common with leftists than with centrists, and it would probably be erroneous to exclude them from the continuum. It is also noteworthy that capitalists are shown on the center-right, not the right, and that they share this tendency with the centrists. Thus, the latter are more to the right than they care to admit, while the former are less so than it first appeared. Finally, the radical left, which includes the communists and the leftist socialists, is a tendency dominated by the latter, given a numerical strength which far exceeds that of the former, as well as our expectations. The direct implication here is that this tendency is not the domain of the PCV as much as fertile soil for the germination of *masista* and *mirista* loyalties.

Our enterprise has now come full circle. Qualifying individual self-placements on the left-right continuum with economic preferences, we can determine ideological position. Validation of this measure of partisan preferences and attitudinal characteristics seems to meet the requirements suggested by Mullins,[67] which we believe testable at the level of the mass public. Comparisons by multiple-range criteria allow us to establish the order among positions, as well as their clustering into tendencies. Standardization of their cumulative scores allows us to treat the dimension as an interval scale.

In sum, the analysis shows that the left-right continuum in Venezuela presents some of the characteristics suggested by Downs' axioms.[68] The continuum is not unidimensional, but allows for cumulation of ordered partisan preferences and attitudes toward the regime along its axis. There seems to be a common reference between elite and mass concerning the position of the parties on the continuum. However, we cannot say how stable the positions are, except to cite evidence suggesting a shift of modal opinion to the right of the continuum. There are other ways of measuring the position of individuals on the continuum: whether by comparison with their peers,[69] selection of a score from a range of 0 to 100 from left to right,[70] or reference to categories thought to overlap left-right

Table v-1. The Left-Right Continuum in Venezuelan Politics

IDEOLOGICAL POSITION	Absolute frequency	Relative frequency[a]	Adjusted frequency[b]	Mean	Mean set	Z-score	IDEOLOGICAL TENDENCY
Rightist capitalists	133	8.7	9.5	2.33	a	−.30	Right
Leftist and centrist capitalists	130	8.5	9.3	2.34	a	−.28	Right
Rightist socialists	160	10.5	11.5	2.38	a	−.22	Right
Rightists	165	10.8	11.8	2.38	a	−.22	Right
Centrists	94	6.2	6.7	2.45	ab	−.10	Center right
Capitalists	61	4.0	4.4	2.48	ab	−.05	Center right
GRAND MEAN	—	—	—	2.51	—	.00	MODAL
Centrist socialists	151	9.9	10.8	2.52	b	.02	Center
Marais	127	8.4	9.1	2.57	bc	.05	Center left
Leftists	54	3.6	3.9	2.57	bc	.10	Center left
Socialists	105	6.9	7.5	2.69	cd	.30	Left
Leftist socialists	199	13.1	14.3	2.78	d	.45	Radical left
Communists	16	1.1	1.1	2.95	d	.73	Radical left

Table v-i. The Left-Right Continuum in Venezuelan Politics (*Continued*)

IDEOLOGICAL POSITION	Absolute frequency	Relative frequency[a]	Adjusted frequency[b]	Mean	Mean set	Z-score	IDEOLOGICAL TENDENCY
Others[c]	126	8.3	—	—	—	—	—
Standard deviation of the grand mean	(N = 1,395)			.60			

Note: The scores are the weighted sums of the responses to the items presented in figures 14–18. Items pertaining to feelings about prosystem parties and the Caldera administration were recoded to reflect antiestablishment sentiment. The *position* of the groups on the continuum is inferred from the groups' mean scores. The *tendencies* grouping different positions were inferred from the comparisons between the mean scores.

[a] Percentage of total sample.
[b] Percentage of those making at least one choice plus *marais*.
[c] Refusals and "don't know" responses.

distinctions.[71] One might be tempted to compare their explanatory power, as well as that of the three different measures of individual ideology discussed thus far. We are content, however, to observe that a more pressing concern dictates analysis of the overlap between individual ideology and societal cleavages, and of the degree of constraint exerted by ideology on other attitudes.

Sources of Ideological Orientation

Discussion of the genesis of individual ideology is complicated by the rather large number of definitions and approaches to the concept, as well as by the ideological nature of most such discussions. We adopt the position that, as with most other fundamental political attitudes and value structures, ideology is largely determined by the life experiences of individuals, whether directly or through vicarious identification with group experiences. In view of the mammoth task implied by an inventory of extant relevant propositions, we will proceed with some callousness by going directly to results of a path-analysis of ideological tendency based on major social cleavages. These are straightforward and can be summarized as follows. First, party sympathy seems most relevant of the causal factors examined, including class images, social status, and group identification, region and size of community of residence, gender role, and generation. The explanatory power of this model, presented in figure 19(a) is within reason, and we interpret its substantive implication to mean that, in Venezuela, the parties sustain the expression of ideological tendency, with gender role and within-family role serving as secondary influences. The model is predicated on the order of the parties on the continuum and, consequently, the categories of the variable party sympathy have been recoded, placing "no preference" in a mid-point category between leftist and rightist preferences. In other words, this model maximizes the observed relationship between party preference and ideological position.

By contrast, the model presented in figure 19(b) attempts to identify the sources of ideological tendency beyond the constraining effects of party preferences. In order to minimize the latter, we excluded all individuals who declare themselves "militants" or "members" of parties, as well as the variable party sympathy from all computations. The model produced in this fashion would imply the perfect ideal type, with class images, religiosity, and generation the more relevant factors. In short, the classical differences between

Figure 19. Path-analytic Models of Ideological Tendency

(a) With party sympathy as on left-right continuum:[a]

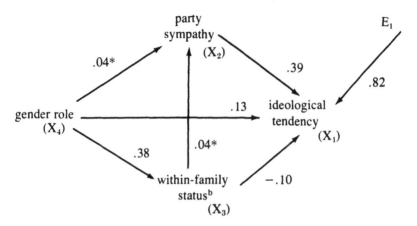

[a] Party preference coded as follows: 1 = MEP, 2 = MAS, 3 = NONE, 4 = AD, 5 = COPEI, 6 = CCN, 7 = other.
[b] Head of household or dependent member.

N = 665
Multiple R = .42
*Not significant at .01 level.

$\rho_{12} = \beta_{12}$
$\rho_{13} = \beta_{13.24}$
$\rho_{14} = \beta_{14.2}$

(b) Excluding party sympathy:[c]

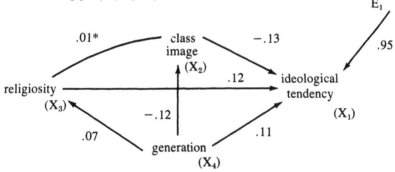

[c] Results based on cases of "independent" and "apolitical" individuals; party sympathy excluded from all computations.

$\rho_{12} - \beta_{12}$
$\rho_{13} = \beta_{13.2}$
$\rho_{14} = \beta_{14.23}$
*Not significant at .01 level.

N = 326
Multiple R = .22

up and *down*, *sacred* and *profane*, and *young* and *old* are most significant. But how much variance do these factors explain? All they can account for is 5 per cent.

We do not interpret these results as proof that ideology does not exist beyond the manipulation of party elites in Venezuela. Looking at the parameters of the first model, it is obvious that the most important factor—party sympathy—is far from being a necessary and sufficient source of ideological tendency. To be sure, it far outweighs all other factors, but does not preempt the possibilities. The low proportion of variance accounted for by the exogenous variables of figure 19(b) is not so much an indication that these are relatively trivial, as it is a reflection of a highly capricious pattern of cleavages. Converse and Dupeux's comments on the French case are germane to ours: "It seems that French political differences are *homogeneously spread* through the social structure in a degree that is both notable and can be suspected to have important implications. . . ."[72] Thus, it is a matter of people with very similar characteristics showing great diversity in their ideological positions, as seemed to be the case with people of similar social status holding diametrically opposed views.[73] However, there are a series of additional considerations to be borne in mind.

First, Venezuela's population is predominantly young, urban, and concentrated in the metropolitan Center. This means that, other things being equal, young persons of the metropolitan Center may come to represent at least a plurality of any imaginable category of respondents. For example, the metropolitan Center has some 38 per cent of the population. It is hardly startling, therefore, that this region contributes a plurality of the respondents included in each ideological tendency. A similar observation could be made with respect to residents of metropolitan communities, which account for about 46 per cent of the population. However, our cross-tabulations suggest that there are no major differences in the distribution of the tendencies across communities of different size. Finally, we have no doubt that *the right is the dominant tendency in Venezuela at this point*. It represents at least a plurality of any conceivable group into which one can subdivide our sample. One implication is that we may say that the radical left is predominantly male and young, but in this, as in other cases, the plurality of males and young people are on the right. In short, attempts to characterize the overlap between ideological tendency and societal cleavages are complicated by the configuration of the latter as well as by the demographics involved. However, we can attempt to sketch a profile of the more notable

Cultural Diversity and Political Cleavages, II

Table v-2. Ideological Orientation and Major Cleavages

	Radical left	Left	Center left	Center	Center right	Right	eta
GENDER ROLE							.09
Male (50)	+15	−5	−7	+8	−1	−3	
GENERATION							.14
18–24 (29)	+13	+10	−8	−1	+2	−5	
REGION							.12
Andes (12)	−1	−4	−8	−3	0	+4	
East (16)	+5	+2	−1	+1	−5	0	
Zulia (12)	+2	+7	−3	+7	−2	−1	
Center (39)	0	−6	+14	−5	+5	−3	
COMMUNITY SIZE							.08
Metropolitan (47)	0	+10	+8	+1	+3	−6	
CLASS IMAGE							.06
Middle class (67)	+4	+5	−1	+10	−6	−2	
STRATIFICATION							.10
Manual poor (20)	−3	−4	+4	−6	+8	0	
Professional (15)	+7	+4	−6	+8	+3	−3	
GROUP IDENTIFICATION							.21
Housewives (22)	−15	+2	0	−5	+4	+4	
Students (13)	+12	+15	−6	−1	−3	−4	
RELIGION							.14
Practicing Catholic (35)	−9	−5	−3	−5	+5	+5	

Note: All table figures are percentages, except the eta coefficients; all these are significant at the .01 level. Figures in parentheses identify the percentage of the category in the population. The rest of the figures indicate how much above (+) or below (−) their population averages are, in terms of their proportion within the specific tendency.

features of the tendencies by looking at the degree to which the characteristics represented in them differ from their true proportion in the population.

The evidence in table V-2 attempts to etch this profile. Categories were selected for which we found deviances of at least 5 percentage points from their true proportion in the population; omitted categories came very close to the latter. Looking at the larger deviations, we can attempt to characterize the individuals grouped under the six ideological tendencies as follows.

The Radical Left
Population groups overrepresented are men, young people, residents of the East, persons in the professional stratum, and students. Housewives and practicing Catholics are underrepresented.

The Left
This tendency is predominantly female and young, with residents of Zulia and metropolitan communities and students also overrepresented. Residents of the Center and practicing Catholics are underrepresented.

The Center Left
Males, young people, residents of the Andes, persons of professional standing, and students are found in less than average proportions here. Residents of the Center and of metropolitan communities are overrepresented.

The Center
This tendency does very well among men, Zulia residents, middle-class identifiers, and professionals. Residents of the Center region, the manual poor, housewives, and practicing Catholics are underrepresented.

The Center Right
Easterners and middle-class identifiers are underrepresented, while residents of the Center, the manual poor, and practicing Catholics are overrepresented.

The Right
Perhaps the least unique of the tendencies in that it is most difficult to characterize for under- or overrepresentation, the right has more practicing Catholics than its due share, while it seems less attractive to the young and residents of metropolitan communities.

Looking at the data of table V-2 and trying to relate the deviations found therein to the path diagrams of figure 19, it becomes evident that the distribution of population groups among the different ideological tendencies is relatively close to their proportion. In cases in

which the magnitude of the eta coefficients suggest greater deviations, these affect categories which do not add up to a majority. This
is the case for group identifiers and generational groups, which
deviate considerably in terms of their support of leftist tendencies.
However, young people, on the one hand, and housewives and students, on the other, are not numerous enough for their reaction to
the left to make a more robust impact on the overall pattern. In
short, we cannot conclude that there is a substantial overlap between
ideological preferences and societal cleavages; this may explain
why partisan preferences constitute the only factor capable of reducing the constraining effect of ideology on other political attitudes
and orientations.[74]

The Scope of Ideological Constraint

Discussion and consideration of the adequacy of Downs' axiomatic
propositions on the left-right continuum leads invariably to a focus
on the content of the continuum. Like Barnes, one can adopt a
perspective that views the continuum as an "open space," its
meaning determined by the respondent's contextual interpretation.[75] Alternatively, like Stokes, one can try to distinguish between
"valence" and "position" issues in order to limit that content to the
latter, since the former involves a state of affairs (good government,
integrity in office, and the like) or condition (abatement of inflation,
full employment) desired by consensual opinion.[76] In addition,
inquiry into the issue content of the continuum involves an operational test of the degree to which opinions and attitudes reflect a left-
to-right order, that is, the degree to which they are constrained by
ideology.

Given the close connection between ideological disposition and
party sympathy, and aware that the major societal cleavages do not
seem to diminish the scope and intensity of ideological constraints
in Venezuela,[77] we will concentrate on the former, in determining
the extent to which party preferences, coded in terms of the parties'
location on the continuum, preempt any additional effect attributable to ideology. Thus, we will engage in a simultaneous analysis of
ideological constraint, substantive content of the continuum, and
the autonomy of ideological posturing beyond the partisan realm.

Table V-3 contains a detailed and extensive set of data which
should throw light on these questions. First of all, we present unadjusted (eta) and adjusted (beta, for party preference) scores for the

link between ideological tendency and a host of evaluations, orientations, and participatory patterns of the Venezuelan public. The third column of the table presents the multiple correlation coefficients obtained with tendency and party preference. Comparison of these three sets of figures should give us some idea about how robust the constraining effect of tendency really is, and how much it is deflated (or inflated) by its overlap with partisanship. This portion of the table is extremely important, since we maintain that parties provide "containers" for ideological dispositions, whether "cooled" or "warmed up" therein. In addition, although we established and validated the locations of the parties on the continuum separately, these were included in the aggregate indices utilized to test differences in location of the *tendencies* and the *positions*. Thus, we could not evolve a test utilizing empirically valid criteria which made the two coincide to such an extent. In other words, these data provide an acid test for the independent effect of ideology. Approached in this manner, the relationship between ideological tendency and party preference is gauged at .45 for eta (treating both as nominal measurement), and at .48 for Pearson's r (assuming interval measurement).

A cursory inspection of the first three columns of table V-3 suggests that, for the most part, party preferences tend to deflate the constraining effect of ideological tendency but do not make it disappear altogether, even in blatantly partisan areas of opinion. Interaction between the two factors is relatively limited, but the areas in which it occurs are significant. These include primarily participatory aspects, but also partisan and policy concerns. The former involve the suffrage, how it is viewed, whether it would be worth it if voluntary, and whether to utilize null voting; two of the campaign modes, exposure and involvement, are also affected by this interaction, which is also detectable in the actors identified as having the responsibility and ability to solve national and individual problems, polarization between AD and COPEI, and sympathy toward the two most leftist parties, MEP and the PCV.

The attitudes concerning policy matters appear relatively free from both partisan and ideological concerns. This indicates the degree to which the problems perceived and the goals proposed have come to be regarded as valence issues. For after all who in Venezuela favors (or could afford to favor) unemployment, inflation, and delinquency? On the other hand, most people agree that it is the government, not the private sector, which can and should solve these problems. It is amazing to find that there are indeed some differences in this respect, at least of degree, although we cannot elucidate whether these are partisan or ideological, due to interaction.

Much less surprising is the fact that people of the most extreme tendencies (radical left and the right) would be more likely to continue to vote than those of more moderate persuasion, other than those who endorse the prosystem parties. Interaction involving evaluation of the suffrage is congruent with our findings on left-right differences in this respect.

Ultimately, partisanship tends to reduce the impact of ideological constraints, but not in a manner suggesting that Venezuelan parties are the only guides and repositories of ideological concerns.

The last three columns of table V-3 are the product of somewhat heterodox treatment. In most discussions of left-right the center is largely overlooked. Frequently it is difficult to determine what the center really stands for, how much "intensity" is to be found, and whether it is in fact ideological. Consider the comments of Converse and Dupeux: "While it is probably true that some of these people are convinced 'centrists' in a thoughtful and genuine sense, it seems that the vast majority of voters who choose this way of indicating that they either know little about or at least are not particularly engaged by the preeminent cluster of issues that the axis reflects. . . ."[78] To be sure, the center includes the *marais* but, in our case, the three centrist tendencies embrace five of the twelve ideological positions. Lack of significant relationships could not be attributed here to a lack of variation of the independent variable. Instead, this could stem only from a great homogeneity of opinion reflected on a small range of variation in the dependent variables. Thus, if a case is to be made for the center being less ideological, we could provide an ideal scenario.

That this seems to be true is confirmed by an overwhelming number of nonsignificant (Pearson's) correlation coefficients. In other words, the center in Venezuela does not seem engaged by the issues. Yet we detect a certain tug-of-war effect in a number of areas in which the "pull from the left" seems to predominate over the "pull from the right" and vice versa. These show the center taking sides on matters involving evaluation of regime and Caldera's policies, one-party rule, and the Chilean coup; overall policy preferences and political capacity; and, very important, opinions about which party governs best, AD-COPEI polarization, and sympathy toward AD and toward COPEI. Thus, the center is not a cumulation of indifference although it can only be aroused, appar-

Table v-3. The Scope and Nature of Ideological Constraint

	Across tendencies			Within tendencies		
	(eta)[a]	(beta)[b]	(multiple R)[c]	Left[d]	Center[e]	Right[f]
Evaluation						
Of regime policies (S)	.24	.12	.39	−.20	−.12	(.01)
Of elections (S)	.23	.14	.32*	(−.05)	(−.05)	(.03)
Of politicians (S)	.23	.16	.34	(.02)	(−.07)	(−.04)
Of Caldera's policies (S)	.21	.12	.59	(−.09)	−.18	(.00)
Of one-party rule	.13	.06	.37	(−.04)	−.10	(.03)
Of opposition criticism	.10	.08	.17	.15	(−.02)	(−.02)
Of Chilean coup	.29	.26	.31	.11	.10	.11
Of coups in general (S)	.19	.20	.24	(.05)	(.06)	(.02)
Policy orientation						
Overall policy preference	(.08)	(.07)	(.12)	.12	.09	(−.02)
National problem	(.13)	(.14)	(.23)	(−.02)	(.06)	(.05)
Agent for resolution	(.06)	(.06)	.12*	(−.05)	(.01)	(−.04)
Personal problem	.15	.13	(.20)	.25	(.02)	(−.02)
Agent for resolution	(.09)	(.08)	.11*	(.02)	(−.05)	(−.05)
Other political orientations						
Political capacity (S)	.14	.13	.25	−.16	.09	(.02)
Political agility (I)	(.08)	(.08)	(.17)	.18	(.02)	(−.12)
Participation						
Voluntary suffrage	.16	.11	.31*	(.05)	(−.02)	(.02)
Null voting	.21	.13	.31*	(.06)	(−.06)	(.05)
Actual party member	.20	.09	.46	.13	(.01)	(−.02)
Ever a party member	.20	.12	.38	.15	(.02)	(.04)
Reason for membership	(.19)	(.20)	(.27)	(−.09)	(−.01)	(.02)

Participatory mood (S)	.18	.13	.26	−.14	(−.06)	(.00)
Exposure to '73 campaign (S)	(.09)	(.09)	.19*	−.11	(−.04)	(.07)
Involvement in '73 campaign (S)	.24	.14	.46*	−.27	(−.04)	(.02)
Perceived efficacy of '73 campaign (S)	.29	.16	.56	−.29	(.03)	.09
Partisanship						
Party that governs best	.24	.08	.81	−.26	.10	(.02)
Polarization AD-COPEI	.15	.05	.82*	(.01)	.19	(−.04)
Party for which they would never vote	.20	.16	.31	.19	(.02)	.16
Voting intention in '73	.29	.11	.73	−.24	(.04)	(.05)
Sympathy toward AD (T)	.12	.04	.76	.11	−.10	(.01)
Sympathy toward COPEI (T)	.30	.12	.76	(.09)	.17	(−.05)
Sympathy toward MAS (T)	.45	.22	.68	−.25	(.02)	(−.05)
Sympathy toward MEP (T)	.27	.15	.62*	−.22	(.01)	.09
Sympathy toward PCV (T)	.31	.20	.40*	−.29	(.01)	(.02)
Sympathy toward CCN (T)	(.05)	(.06)	.42	(−.04)	(.04)	(.03)

[a] With ideological tendency, unadjusted.
[b] With ideological tendency, adjusted for party sympathy.
[c] For tendency and party sympathy.
[d] Zero-order correlations for positions included in the radical left and the left.
[e] Zero-order correlations for positions included in the center left, center, and left.
[f] Zero-order correlations for positions included in the right.
* Interaction detected between tendency and party sympathy.
( ) Not significant at .01 level.
(S) Scale measurement.
(I) Index.
(T) Thermometer measurement.

ently, by the most salient and the most ideological objects and issues; it seems relatively uninterested in the rest.

By contrast, the right contains four ideological positions, implying considerable variation on our independent source of constraint, yet lack of significant relationships cannot be interpreted as with the center. The issue extremity and preference patterns of the right suggest anything but disinterest or inability to make choices. Thus, lack of significant covariation can only mean a high degree of consensus here—minimal variation in attitudes and orientations across ideological positions of the right. We interpret this as evidence of active constraint, of the emergence of a configuration of opinion based on consensus. The data of the last column of table V-3 suggest a consensus that only breaks with respect to opinion about the Chilean coup, the perceived efficacy of the 1973 campaign, and the party for which one would never vote.

Finally, the often-heard complaints about lack of leftist unity in Venezuela seem well grounded as viewed through the magnitudes of the array of Pearson's correlation coefficients presented in the fourth column of the table. The left seems as disunited as the right is united. Even though the two tendencies of the left include only three ideological positions, the diversity of views is such that we can observe the largest number of significant relationships found in any tendency. These are as numerous as one could expect to find within a center which was under severe pull from both left and right. The differences are very extensive and include all areas, while somewhat less pronounced where relating to evaluation and electoral participation. These seem the aspects more constrained by leftist orientation. In others we find substantial differences between left and radical left.

It would be possible to illustrate more pointedly certain of the relationships presented in table V-3 in graphic or cross-tabular form, but this would be largely repetitious. Thus we must await another opportunity to deal with some specific aspects in greater detail. However, in closing, certain conclusions bear restatement. There is evidence of patterns of ideological thinking among a substantial number of Venezuelans, as suggested by their ability to place themselves and other actors on the left-right continuum. Their locations seem congruent with the manner in which parties are ordered on the continuum. There are a number of issues which fit this configuration of ordered left-right positions and tendencies. Admittedly, we have not demonstrated that the Venezuelan public is deeply influenced by the most rigorous and well-integrated "ideology" in its strictest definition. Yet we have been able to put substantial theoretical and empirical validity behind what appeared on first impression to be an uninformed, unsophisticated, and simplistic fashion in which some Venezuelans summarize left-right differences: "It's all a matter between the government and the opposition." As Lane suggests, this only makes sense if we know what it really means.

6

Partisanship
in Venezuelan Politics

Some Assumptions

Partisanship and party politics have attracted a great deal of attention in the literature of Venezuelan politics. The genesis of the present party system,[1] its contemporary configuration,[2] and the more salient features of its principal members[3] are topics studied with care and discussed with passion. The centrality of parties in Venezuelan politics is undeniable. We agree with Levine that ". . . Venezuelan politics can be described as a party system. The basic vehicles for political action are parties, the fundamental legitimate power resource is mass consult and votes, and power is transferred through elections. A crucial norm in Venezuela is organizational concentration: *the parties are monopolists of political action. . . .*"[4] Thus it is difficult to discuss Venezuelan politics without mentioning the political parties, for party opposition and competition constitute the central axis of the political process, and the presence of parties is felt in all areas of national and local political life.

Organizational concentration was possible because parties came to fill a severe institutional vacuum in Venezuela, preceding most associational groups and in many cases creating those groups on their own initiative and impulse.[5] Such penetration of partisanship into associational life is reinforced by the parties' structural characteristics, which follow the blueprint of the European socialist parties. Through their ancillary organizations and specialized functional branches or *fracciones*, the parties have come to control associational life, especially the trade unions, the professional associations, and the secondary and university student associations.[6]

From the standpoint of internal organization, the largest Venezuelan parties follow what Duverger once called the "strongly articulated model," which relies on internal discipline enforced by specialized organs and on strict functional adherence to the structural blueprint. To the individual party member, ". . . adhesion to the party is relatively formalized, although in practice the boundary between *militants* and *sympathizers* withers away sometimes; the rights and duties of the members are stipulated clearly in the [party] statutes and, albeit with little success, there is the attempt to maintain a permanent register of party members. . . ."[7] Thus *Venezuelan parties conform to the European model in organizational style, and members experience a more intimate relationship with their party than their counterparts in the United States.* However, from the very beginning the parties tried to attract a wide base of support, so that they would not "represent a restricted or particularized clientele"[8] and instead "depend on an electorate much larger than their militancy."[9]

Finally, on purely impressionistic grounds, it appears that partisanship and party militancy are not matters reserved for the better-educated and more affluent segments of the mass public. Among the marginals, party politics are

> . . . a constant ingredient in *barrio* affairs. They play a strong role in determining the way the neighbors relate with one another. Close acquaintanceships among men are as likely to be based on common party affiliations as on the fact that they live on the same street, hail from the same region of the country, or work for the same company. Party affiliations determine not only with whom one should associate, but also with whom one should not associate. . . . Concern with party politics is found in many, seemingly irrelevant, phases of daily life. . . .[10]

Even peasant activities are penetrated by party loyalties: "Leaders of the Peasant Federation at all levels manifest a considerable history of affiliation with the political parties of their choice. . . . They are party leaders, holding party offices at local, state, and national levels. . . ."[11] In short, there is considerable evidence that parties are extraordinarily conspicuous in the Venezuelan political arena. But our task is not to dwell on these familiar and relatively well researched themes. Instead, we want to concentrate on the phenomenon of partisanship at the level of the individual member of the mass public, and to offer evidence concerning the more relevant parameters of this phenomenon.

Our first assumption holds that, in Venezuela, it is more appropriate to utilize the concept of partisanship than the related notions of affiliation and identification. Venezuelans do not declare a partisan preference at the time of registration, thereby weakening the relevance of the former. Furthermore, the concept of party identification, firmly entrenched in North American analytical practice, offers problems of its own.[12] First of all, the concept is usually defined in such loose terms as "a psychological identification which can persist *without legal recognition or evidence of formal member-ship and even without a consistent record of party support.*"[13] This definition, although perhaps well suited to United States conditions, is of limited value for cases in which partisanship is influenced by organizational discipline, adherence to a formal party line, and the functioning of permanent party structures.

Furthermore, the definition becomes too inclusive for cases in which party loyalties imply little beyond what is considered partisan under the terms of the definition. Some argue that for Venezuela, individual concern with patronage leads people to join a party as a matter of convenience.[14] Although we find this view somewhat exaggerated, it is undeniable that such considerations figure promi-nently in the calculus of an individual's party loyalties.[15] Moreover, the constant proliferation of parties suggests that party loyalties may be somewhat unstable and superficial. Given this possibility, it would be ill-advised to examine partisanship in Venezuela with as lax an operational definition as that suggested by the concept of party identification.

Our second assumption is consonant with the historical record and aims to improve the kind of inferences that may be drawn from our data. This holds that the political socialization of the generations of 1928, 1948, and 1958 have been quite different as a result of the breakdowns suffered by the democratic regime; the unique experi-ence of the generation of 1928 created the conditions that permitted the first democratic experiment. Given these discontinuities in the political process, it seems appropriate to assume not only that gener-ational experiences were diverse, but also that the factors which may have influenced party loyalties changed from one generation to the next.

In an operational sense, the assumption allows us to deal with our inability to meet one basic assumption of causal analysis. As Heise states, ". . . all analyses in cross-sectional statics are based on the premise that the causal systems operating in different cases are equivalent; they have the same organizational and structural param-eters and the causal operators are in working order for each . . . [in short] a single basic causal structure is operative for numerous separate cases. . . ."[16] In view of such considerations, this premise must become one item of our research agenda for the study of par-tisanship rather than an a priori assumption. Therefore, a corollary of our second assumption is that in Venezuela there may not be one single basic causal structure for partisanship and that it becomes necessary to determine this empirically. We will replicate the anal-yses conducted with all the respondents in our sample, with retests designed to verify these general conclusions with the cases of each different generation; this will permit inferences about trends.

Unlike a stable political system in which changes in party loyalty are detectable only through critical or realigning elections, we have a case in which three major discontinuities are posited as having had a lasting influence on political opinion: the military coups of October 18, 1945; November 24, 1948; and January 23, 1958. On each of these occasions, the party or faction deposed by the coup never became reconciled to it, and was subsequently critical of the behavior and attitude displayed during the coup by allies and adversaries who in one way or another benefited from the coup.[17] Partisans of each deposed administration found it difficult to express their political preferences overtly, with a display of such loyalties leading to incarceration and exile. In some instances, two rival parties reached critical thresholds of antagonism, as with Acción Democrática and the Social Christian COPEI following the coup of 1948.[18] Thus a third assumption holds that party loyalties and opinion about military coups d'etat are deeply intertwined. A fourth, which will also require empirical verification, contends that given the multiclass and mass-based nature of the two largest parties, AD and COPEI, cleavage factors of a societal nature are unlikely to figure very prominently in observable partisan cleavages. They may, however, be more prominent for some of the smaller parties such as the Movimiento al Socialismo (MAS) or the Movimiento Electoral del Pueblo (MEP).

Fifth, we have assumed that in analysis of a multiparty situation, it is best to distinguish between general and specific areas of partisanship. The former would include basic differences of a general nature, such as whether a person sympathizes with/is a member of a political party or not. Three aspects of this general area are *party sympathy* (measured as a dichotomous variable indicating whether or not the individual sympathizes with a political party), *membership propensity* (whether the individual has been a formal-legal member of a party at any time), and *actual membership* (whether the individual is a member at the present time or not).

Moreover, we believe that in a multiparty situation, one of the most relevant and precise ways to approach the measurement of party preference and party loyalties is to ask people about their overall political role. We called this role *political self-image* and did not attach a priori characteristics to it. We conceived of this construct in the sense of a filter of preference; before a person is a partisan of a political party he or she must be political, play at least a small political role, and become partisan in a general sense. We hypothesized that people could be classified in this overall sense, and that they would be able so to classify themselves. Given the importance of parties in Venezuelan politics, our respondents' self-perception relative to the parties would say much about their location in the political arena.

The assumption of a single basic causal structure is all the more difficult in a multiparty context. The larger the number of parties, the greater the number of distributions of opinion about them, and the greater the need to treat these separately; thus we must go beyond the discrimination of "hard" or "soft" identification with a particular party.[19] Measurement of *specific partisanship* required the discrimination of different intensities of behavioral commitment (membership), feelings about the preferred party and its principal opponents (sympathy and thermometer feelings), and enduring loyalty (through electoral support). Following standard practice we did not include voting behavior into any of our indices of partisanship. However, it is our firm belief that if partisanship or any measure thereof is to have meaning, it has to be related to voting behavior. We specifically queried our respondents concerning their party preferences, as well as their self-perceptions in relation to parties and politics in Venezuela.

General Partisanship

The Venezuelan case, as suggested by the distribution of political self-images, seems to follow the usual pattern of a small minority of intense partisans among the members of the given mass public. These number 4 per cent, followed at the next level of partisan intensity by 45 per cent sympathizers; roughly one-third, depending on whether one looks at party sympathy or self-image, are nonpartisan. Comparing the two distributions, one could estimate the proportion of partisans at about 5 per cent, sympathizers at 65 per cent, and nonpartisans at 30 per cent.[20] If one examines *actual membership* to evaluate these different estimates of partisanship, we find that 26 per cent of all respondents are or consider themselves members of a political party (scarcely a trivial percentage, considering the significance of party membership in Venezuela). On the other hand, if one combines *membership propensity* with *party sympathy*, the shades of partisan intensity become more precise: 31 per cent have been members, 34 per cent are sympathizer nonmembers, 3 per cent do not sympathize at present but have been members, and 30 per cent are neither.

One aspect that merits some discussion is the extent to which individual self-image provides an accurate and relevant summary of partisan orientations.[21] In other words, are these respondents what they pretend to be when identifying themselves as members or militants of a party, as sympathizers, or as independent or unconcerned? For instance, 37 per cent of those who perceive themselves as unconcerned profess partisan sympathies; this proportion goes up to 42 per cent among the independents. These two groups constitute one-fifth of the electorate, and it would be erroneous to treat them as nonpartisan. They are partisan, since they do express party preferences, but are not firmly engaged party activists. By contrast partisans who *do* sympathize, plus independents and unconcerned who *do not*, constitute the majority of the electorate, a solid 76 per cent. Thus, their party sympathies are congruent with their political self-image. More importantly, sympathy and self-image appear as two closely related but different political orientations. In summary, three-fourths of the Venezuelan electorate adopt political self-images that are congruent with their general partisan orientations. Where do these self-images originate?

An inventory of the causes or determinants of self-image should distinguish attitudinal and trait cleavages of the individual. Our attempt to identify and measure these causal determinants will emphasize the latter for two reasons. First, in a previous effort, the attitudinal factors were included in the explanation, and the models evolved were very similar in their explanatory power to those presented here.[22] In addition, inclusion of the attitudinal component presented us with a tautology of sorts in that adoption of depoliticized images goes together with more critical attitudes. Moods and attitudes are, after all, transient, and less useful in a theoretical sense than more permanent characteristics of the individual which may better inform us about the partisan predispositions of clearly recognizable groups.

Our causal, path-analytic models of political self-image are presented in figure 20. Mindful of the need to verify the assumption of a single causal structure, we evolved four models, one for the electorate and one for each of the three generational cohorts. First, it is evident that the explanatory power of the models is not satisfactory, although comparable to previous ones which included the attitudinal component; the magnitudes of the disturbance or error terms (E_1) are large in each case. Secondly, the actual causal factors identified are what could be expected from a working knowledge of the literature of (early) political socialization, as well as from differences in levels of political activism of Venezuelan men and women. How-

Partisanship in Venezuelan Politics

Figure 20. Path-analytic Models of Political Self-Image

A. *Electorate* (N = 749)

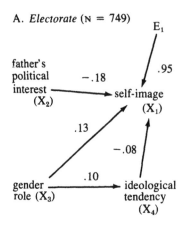

$P_{12} = B_{12} = r_{12}$
$P_{13} = B_{13.2}$
$P_{14} = B_{14.23}$
$P_{23} = r_{23} = .03*$
$P_{24} = r_{24} = .02*$
$P_{34} = r_{34}$

B. *Under 30* (N = 387)

$P_{12} = B_{12} = r_{12}$
$P_{13} = B_{13.2}$
$P_{14} = B_{14.23}$
$P_{34} = r_{34}$
$P_{23} = r_{23} = -.03*$
$P_{24} = r_{24} = .07*$

C. *30–49* (N = 264)

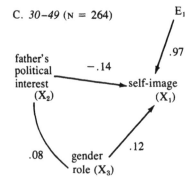

$P_{12} = B_{12} = r_{12}$
$P_{13} = B_{13.2}$

D. *Over 50* (N = 99)

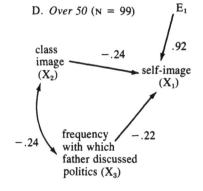

$r_{12} = -.19$
$P_{12} = B_{12.3}$
$P_{13} = B_{13.2}$

*Not represented to simplify the figure.

ever, it is obvious that these explain relatively little. They represent a baseline of sorts and an initial benchmark in need of a more complete set of questions concerning individual political experiences. These may be unique and relatively inaccessible through survey techniques, but we prefer to stress the fact that, perhaps with the exception of the over-50 cohort, *in Venezuela the political self-images of the electorate do not overlap with the more relevant societal cleavages.* In other words, only the male-female distinction seems to have any causal effect, while the *up* versus *down* distinction (middle class versus poor) seems to affect only the older citizens. Ideological tendency appears as a marginal causal factor.

Discontinuities between the political experiences of the oldest and youngest generations are evident and represent a direct challenge to the assumption of a single causal structure. It seems that for older Venezuelans, who you are in a social sense and the influence of the father matters the most at the present time. Discontinuities are also apparent between the under-30 and the *trienio* (30 to 49) generations, with the lack of the ideological connection among the latter representing the most basic observable difference.

Our models of *party sympathy* are somewhat stronger in explanatory power. Given the connection between ideology and partisanship, we recoded the variable measuring party sympathy to reflect the position of the parties on the left-right continuum.[23] It could be argued that this exaggerates the importance of ideology, but our previous analysis in chapter 5 indicates that it does not. Furthermore, the models themselves suggest that ideological tendency is a necessary but not sufficient part of the determinants of party sympathy. The models are presented in figure 21. Ideological tendency appears as the most relevant causal factor for the electorate and for the under-30 and the 30-to-49 cohorts; the model for those over 50, which differs for self-image, shows the only significant influence associated with party sympathy among them.

The model of the youngest cohort deviates somewhat in that religiosity rather than self-image appears as the second-order causal factor required to account for the party sympathies of those under 30. Its explanatory power is the most robust of the four. This contrasts with what is found for the electorate and for the 30-to-49 cohort, which have party sympathies based on ideological tendency and self-image. In all, it appears that nominal identification with right-of-center parties goes together with rightist tendencies and with depoliticized self-images. Thus we find that, for the most part, the factors more closely related to party sympathy are predominantly political; once these factors are accounted for, socialization

Partisanship in Venezuelan Politics

Figure 21. Path-analytic Models of Party Sympathy

A. *Electorate* (N = 749)   B. *Under 30* (N = 387)

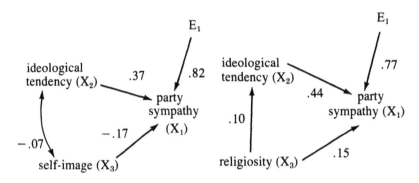

$P_{12} = B_{12} = r_{12}$ $P_{12} = B_{12} = r_{12}$
$P_{13} = B_{13.2}$ $P_{13} = B_{13.2}$
                                              $P_{23} = r_{23}$

C. *30–49* (N = 264)   D. *Over 50* (N = 99)

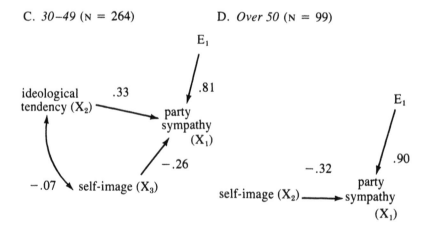

$P_{12} = B_{12}$
$P_{13} = B_{13.2}$

experiences and individual traits do not appear to have a significant (direct or indirect) causal effect.

It does not escape us that we utilized party sympathy to explain ideological tendency at a previous stage of our analysis.[24] The direction of causality between the two is not a matter to be treated lightly, yet their covariation cannot be denied. When trying to determine which other factors accounted for ideological tendency beyond the causal effect of party sympathy, we identified certain individual traits, such as gender role and within-family status.[25] We also found that by excluding party sympathy from the explanation, class images, religiosity, and generation become more relevant, but that the explanatory power of this alternative model was weak.[26] Now in trying to determine what other factors besides ideological tendency have a causal effect on party sympathy, we do not find any traits related to major societal cleavages except the religious. Obviously, we would have required additional questions to determine for each individual respondent which of the two orientations, the ideological or the partisan, weighs most heavily. Lacking this information, we describe the causal factors exogenous to the covariation by looking at it from both ends.

Turning to *actual party membership*, which is an aspect of political participation, one finds the causal effect of self-image to be more sustained and relevant; however, a host of additional factors are required to complete the explanation. These tend to vary with the cohort, more so than those associated with self-image and party sympathy. These intergenerational variations allow us greater analytical latitude in dealing with time-related changes. The models are presented in figure 22 (in order to simplify presentation and discussion, we have omitted all paths and covariations smaller than .10).

In general, one finds that once the causal effect of self-image is accounted for, there is substantial similarity in the impact of other exogenous factors. However, most of that impact is attributable to direct causal effect, in that there is not a great deal of difference between the magnitude of the correlations and the paths. For example, the electorate seems to follow patterns of membership influenced by region of residence, stratification, and ideological tendency to about the same extent. Residents of Center regions, upper-status individuals, and followers of leftist tendencies are generally less partisan in this sense, and report not being members of political parties with greater frequency. This holds true regardless of their political self-images. Whether their fathers were affiliated or not also seems to matter, but not greatly. There is considerable similarity between this model and the one describing the member-

Partisanship in Venezuelan Politics

Figure 22. Path-analytic Models of Actual Party Membership

A. *Electorate* (N = 749)

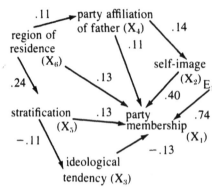

B. *Under 30* (N = 387)

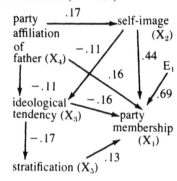

$P_{12} = B_{12}$
$P_{13} = B_{13.26}$
$P_{14} = B_{14.2356}$
$P_{15} = B_{15.236}$
$P_{16} = B_{16.2}$
$P_{24} = r_{24}$
$P_{35} = r_{35}$

$P_{46} = r_{46}$
$P_{56} = r_{56}$
$P_{23} = r_{23} = -.07*$
$P_{25} = r_{25} = -.04*$
$P_{26} = r_{26} = .04*$
$P_{34} = r_{34} = -.03*$
$P_{36} = r_{36} = -.07*$

$P_{12} = B_{12}$
$P_{13} = B_{13.2}$
$P_{14} = B_{14.23}$
$P_{15} = B_{15.234}$
$P_{24} = r_{24}$
$P_{32} = r_{23}$
$P_{34} = r_{34}$
$P_{25} = r_{25} = -.05*$
$P_{45} = r_{45} = .01*$
$P_{35} = r_{35}$

C. *30–49* (N = 264)

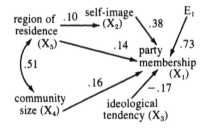

D. *Over 50* (N = 99)

$P_{12} = B_{12}$
$P_{13} = B_{13.24}$
$P_{14} = B_{14.235}$
$P_{15} = B_{15.234}$
$P_{25} = r_{25}$

$P_{34} = r_{34} = -.04*$
$P_{35} = r_{35} = .00*$
$P_{23} = r_{23} = -.07*$
$P_{24} = r_{24} = .08*$

$P_{12} = B_{12.4}$
$P_{13} = B_{13.24}$
$P_{14} = B_{14}$
$P_{23} = r_{23} = -.08*$
$P_{24} = r_{24} = .05*$

*Not represented to simplify the figure.

ship patterns of the youngest cohort. The most outstanding difference comes from the absence of any community-related factor in the latter.

By contrast, the community factor is very conspicuous among those over 30; both the *trienio* and the oldest generations evidence patterns of party membership closely related to the community context. Among those over 50, region of residence becomes more germane than self-image in explaining party membership. In addition, the ideological factor is not a relevant influence among them. Educational level is the only other factor that can be included in this model. The impact of size and of region of residence seems to attest to the enduring relevance of the community dimension, although this seems confined to older generations. Those who came into the electorate after 1958 seem more influenced by socioeconomic distinctions than by the context of their communities. Finally, it is worth repeating that, among the electorate, region and stratification have identical causal effects. Ten years hence the latter may have become more relevant. Our presentation suggests that one must be cautious in applying the assumption of a single causal structure to the analysis of the more general and superficial aspects of the partisan phenomenon in Venezuela. Some relevant differences are found between generations in the manner in which individuals orient themselves to parties (political self-image), their nominal identification with them (party sympathy), and their actual militancy or membership. Clearly, *older Venezuelans have a general orientation to parties which sets them apart from the rest of the electorate*. In dealing with these political orientations in Venezuela, one should treat this cohort separately and make the adjustments necessary to fit them into the general pattern. For self-image and party membership, factors related to socioeconomic inequality become more salient. In other words, differences between political and apolitical, and between party members and nonmembers, are more directly related to social inequality among the old than among their younger counterparts.

A second aspect worthy of greater elaboration concerns the relationship between ideology and party sympathy. Although difficult to determine, the direction of causality between the two probably depends on their relative salience to the individual. Unengaged persons with explicit ideological preferences may choose among the parties as a matter of necessity, especially for voting purposes. Firmly engaged activists may never see discrepancies between party and ideology, although it can probably be assumed that the former is a more basic orientation. Finally, there may be those, like the members of the older generation, who fall predominantly within one ideological tendency (namely the right) and for whom political self-image becomes the only relevant causal factor. The problem of which comes first is thus a matter of breaking into components what seems to be a situation of recursive causation. Obviously, the weak causal link is between ideological tendency and self-image, the strongest between the former and party sympathy, although self-image is also required to account for the latter.

Figure 23 is a path model of the different aspects of general partisanship which we have been discussing, aiming at bringing them together into a common causal structure in order better to understand some of their endogenous relationships (as before, we have omitted paths smaller than .10 in order to simplify the picture). We have not decomposed the causal effects into direct and indirect, but those interested in this aspect may find inclusion of the original correlations helpful.

Clearly, membership, sympathy, and self-image are not strongly related but constitute the endogenous sector of the causal structure. The role of ideology can now be assessed more conveniently. First, it is clear that ideological tendency does not have any substantial *direct* causal effect on the participatory aspects of general partisanship. Such a direct relationship, measured by the zero-order correlation coefficient (at $-.19$) is, for the most part, noncausal. Second, neither does ideology seem to have much impact on self-image; this impact, which is independent of other causal effects, does not vary greatly when the latter are accounted for. Thus, *ideology does not appear to be an important cause of partisan politicization in Venezuela*. Ideology covaries very closely with nominal party preferences (sympathy) but we cannot find any further effects associated with it.

Societal cleavages do overlap with these aspects of partisanship, at least to some degree. Paternal influences can be measured as causal effects on self-image and membership. Women seem to incline to political self-images suggestive of more passive patterns of participation. Upper-status individuals and residents of urban and metropolitan communities militate in the parties less frequently. Yet, with the exception of their impact on self-images, these are relatively secondary influences. Party membership is largely a result of self-image and somewhat less so of party sympathy. Thus, with whom one sympathizes is less important than one's overall attitude toward parties. Finally, a logical sequence seems to underline the model presented in figure 23. The community (size) and societal (stratification) factors appear most remote, with traits (gender role)

Partisanship in Venezuelan Politics

Figure 23. A Model of General Aspects of Partisanship in Venezuela

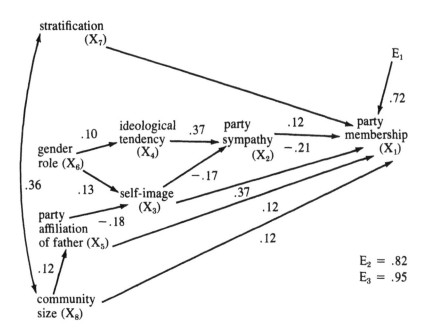

Paths:

$P_{12} = B_{12.3}, (r_{12} = -.30)$

$P_{13} = B_{13.2}, (r_{13} = .42)$

$P_{14} = B_{14.23} = -.08* (r_{14} = -.19)$

$P_{15} = B_{15.23}, (r_{15} = .18)$

$P_{16} = B_{16.23} = .06* (r_{16} = .09)$

$P_{17} = B_{17.238}, (r_{17} = .16)$

$P_{18} = B_{18.237}, (r_{18} = .19)$

$P_{23} = B_{23.4}, (r_{23} = -.20)$

$P_{24} = B_{24}$

$P_{25} = B_{25.34} = .00*$

$P_{26} = B_{26.34} = .02*$

$P_{27} = B_{27.34} = -.01*$

$P_{28} = B_{28.34} = .01*$

$P_{34} = B_{34.56} = -.08* (r_{34} = -.07)$

$P_{35} = B_{35} = r_{35}$

$P_{36} = B_{36.5}, (r_{36} = .11)$

$P_{37} = B_{37.456} = -.04*$

$P_{38} = B_{38.456} = .01*$

$P_{45} = r_{45} = -.03*$

$P_{46} = r_{46}$

$P_{47} = r_{47}$

$P_{48} = r_{48} = -.08*$

$P_{56} = r_{56} = -.04*$

$P_{57} = r_{57} = .01*$

$P_{58} = r_{58} = .12$

$P_{67} = r_{67} = .03*$

$P_{68} = r_{68} = .03*$

$P_{78} = r_{78}$

(*Not represented to simplify the picture.)

and socialization factors representing more direct influences. This makes good theoretical sense, but one must move to more specific aspects of the partisan phenomenon to refine this initial impression.

Specific Partisanship

One of the more appropriate questions for any analysis of partisanship concerns the possibility of elaborating unobtrusive and reliable measures which will unequivocally link partisans with the parties that are the object of their preference. This obviously assumes that there are members of a political public who are partisan. The corollary would refer to partisanship as a phenomenon with distinct attitudinal, normative, and behavioral consequences affecting, at its highest intensity levels, only a minority of the public. By partisans we mean *persons who sympathize nominally or verbally with specific political parties, who proffer high levels of sympathy toward these parties, and who evidence intense behavioral commitments to the parties if not outright militancy, accompanied by a set of electoral preferences congruent with these.*

Suppose that sympathy and membership are combined to approach the identification of the partisans. Looking at the pattern of sympathies and membership for the five largest Venezuelan parties, one confirms from cross-tabulations of the two variables the intuitive impression that they go together. However, sympathy alone does not explain membership, because people with identical levels of sympathy toward a party may not have the same propensity to become members of that party. For AD and COPEI, which have a sufficiently high number of members to make these comparisons meaningful, the split between members and nonmembers is, among those located within the highest categories of sympathy toward these parties, relatively even.

It is clear that the proportion of members declines as the intensity of sympathy diminishes so it seems that membership only appears to be connected to high levels of sympathy. Yet, considering the contrast between members and nonmembers who share identical levels of sympathy, which of the two should be considered more partisan? To determine this, it is apparent that additional characteristics related to the partisan phenomenon are needed. These appear in figure 24, where we have introduced *nominal sympathy, membership in other parties*, and *electoral veto* to provide further discriminations. Three specific types of partisans have been produced by combining the categories of the five dimensions depicted in the

Figure 24. Dimensions Influencing Specific Partisanship

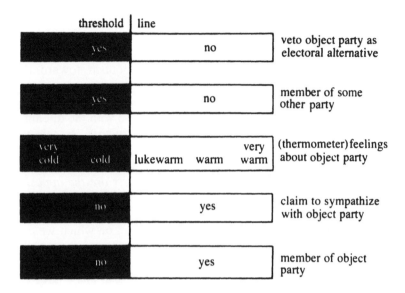

threshold | line

veto object party as electoral alternative

member of some other party

(thermometer) feelings about object party

claim to sympathize with object party

member of object party

Note: The threshold line provides the basic cleavage between those that cannot be included in any of the possible partisan positions toward the object party. Individuals to the left of the line have an antagonistic or at least a nonsympathetic position toward the object party and cannot be included among the varieties of partisans of the party. Taking the combinatory possibilities to the right of the threshold line and reducing these to three intensities of partisanship, we classified individuals as follows:
  (a) militants: members of the party, warm or very warm about it, who identify with it specifically;
  (b) sympathizers: nonmembers who declare specific sympathy and are at least lukewarm about the party;
  (c) potential supporters: nonidentifiers who are at least lukewarm about the party and are not members of any other party.
  None of these categories of partisans contains individuals who veto the party electorally.

figure: *militants, sympathizers,* and *potential supporters.* These were recovered by applying the operational definitions described at the bottom of the figure.

Although not notably rigorous from the standpoint of scaling techniques, and unable to produce mutually exclusive and jointly exhaustive categories in all cases, the typology comes closest to meeting a third criterion concerning empirical validity. The five dimensions are divided into two polar regions by a common perpendicular threshold line. Theoretically, this line divides the dimensions into poles of attraction to and repulsion from different parties. We assume that individuals located to the left of the line on at least three of the dimensions are antagonistic toward the object party, while those situated to the right on a similar number of dimensions are supportive of the party. Clearly, some categories are more significant than others; the dimension pertaining to electoral veto offers a relatively crude and unambiguous check on the others, while membership in some party other than the object party should indicate militancy although not necessarily antagonism toward the object party.

Additional reasons further justify our utilization of the typology presented in figure 24. One is our attempt to cope with the dilemma of the assumptions of a single basic causal structure. In this instance, *we cannot assume that the reasons leading individuals to become partisans of the same party are the same, or that the causes leading others to be antagonistic toward the party are the opposite of the former.* If a party is very salient—and not all parties can claim that they are—large sectors of the public will have an opinion about the party. However, is there one continuum on which we can place all these individuals? Application of the thermometer technique in the United States has shown that there is a continuum of feelings about parties and public figures.[27] Still, can one characterize this continuum as partisan?

Another reason is the need to solve the voting behavior–party identification riddle produced by the frequently well-justified refusal to include voting behavior in the operational definition of partisanship. The import lies in the apparent incongruence between a partisan preference obtained in a nominal and superficial fashion and a voting record which indicates otherwise.[28] Having already criticized the notion of party identification, we seek to untangle the puzzle by use of the electoral veto. The assumption here is that the hardest instance of incongruence would be given by someone who identified nominally with or proffered high levels of sympathy toward a party for which he or she would never vote. Using this restriction, one can have reasonable confidence in the levels of partisanship operationalized following it. In other words, we rule out the possibility of this greatest inconsistency while, as already indicated, treating party preference in more strict fashion than party identification.

A practical test of the validity of the assumption of a single causal structure to specific partisanship is provided by a comparison of societal cleavage correlates of the former as applied to Acción Democrática and COPEI. Both are highly salient political objects and elicit a very wide response from a majority of the mass public. Scrutiny of the coefficients presented in table VI-1 suggests that for the AD there is considerable overlapping between the distribution of specific partisanship, feelings, and opinion toward AD. In other words, the similar magnitudes of the coefficients suggest that *the response to AD follows basically the same lines of cleavage, wheth-*

er we look at partisanship, feelings, or opinion. Moreover, the response to AD cuts across the same population parameters, whether examining *adeco* partisans in their varying intensities or the general public. A more positive reaction to AD, regardless of its qualitative nature, always goes hand in hand with lower socioeconomic status, residence in more rural and peripheral areas, and an ideological tendency within the right.

The distribution of *copeyano* partisanship, and feelings and opinion about COPEI, do not overlap greatly. In fact, a decidedly rightist ideological tendency is the sole common feature of the three. *Copeyano* partisanship appears related to ideological tendency, community size, and region of residence. Feelings about COPEI are intertwined with class images, socioeconomic stratum, group identification, religiosity, and ideological tendency. Finally, opinion about COPEI appears related to the latter and little else.

A possible explanation for the differences between AD and COPEI concerning the applicability of the single causal structure assumption may be found in the status of each party at the time of our survey; AD, as the major opposition party, provoked a fairly homogeneous response from different population groups, regardless of the particular nature of that response. Thus the assumption can be utilized to measure *adeco* partisanship as following the same lines of cleavage of more generalized responses to the party, such as feelings and opinion. COPEI, in contrast, was the government party and perhaps even more salient than AD in eliciting positive and negative responses, both for partisan reasons and in reaction to its governmental role. This may be interpreted that members of the public who liked COPEI or felt "warm" about it did not have the same individual background characteristics as *copeyano* partisans. In other words, general sentiment about COPEI ran along different lines of societal cleavages than specific partisanship toward it. In summary, *adeco* partisanship and reaction to AD run along virtually the same lines of cleavages, while the same cannot be said of COPEI.

Adeco and *copeyano* partisanship can now be explained by regressing the correlates presented in table VI-1, as well as others utilized in the foregoing analysis, on both of these measures of specific partisanship. The contrast between the two sets of results allows us to understand the sources of support for the two dominant parties. A path-analytic model for *adeco* partisanship is presented in figure 25. We find this to be related to political self-image, educational achievement and community size, ideological position, and political party affiliation of the respondent's father. Partisan com-

Partisanship in Venezuelan Politics

Table VI-1. Correlates of Partisanship, Feelings, and Opinion
Concerning AD and COPEI

	Adeco partisanship[a]	Feelings about AD[b]	Opinion about AD[c]
Sex	(−.02)	(.02)	(.03)
Generational group	(.04)	.07	.08
Region of residence	−.12	−.04	−.07
Community size	−.14	−.06	−.10
Class image	(−.06)	−.14	−.14
Socioeconomic stratum	−.10	−.12	−.13
Group identification	−.08	−.06	−.07
Religiosity	(.01)	.04	(.02)
Ideological tendency	.22	.11	.13

	Copeyano partisanship[a]	Feelings about COPEI[b]	Opinion about COPEI[c]
Sex	(.01)	(−.00)	(−.00)
Generational group	(−.01)	(−.01)	.08
Region of residence	−.15	(−.00)	−.07
Community size	−.14	.05	(−.01)
Class image	(.03)	.14	.08
Socioeconomic stratum	(−.04)	.15	.06
Group identification	(.01)	.11	.05
Religiosity	.08	.13	.09
Ideological tendency	.26	.28	.26

Note: All coefficients presented in the table are Pearson's product-moment correlation coefficients. Those in parentheses are not significant for at least $P = .05$.
[a] Includes only the partisans of the party: (a) potential supporters, (b) sympathizers, and (c) militants, as defined in figure 24.
[b] Thermometer scores.
[c] Includes: (a) very negative, (b) negative, (c) positive, and (d) very positive.

Figure 25. Patterns of *Adeco* Partisanship

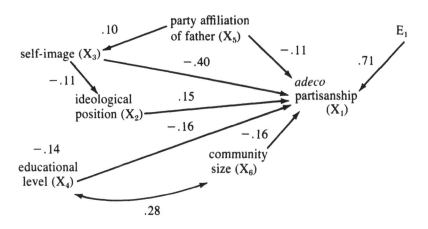

Paths:

$P_{12} = B_{12.346}, (r_{12} = .23)$ $P_{34} = r_{34} = -.01*$

$P_{13} = B_{13.5}, (r_{13} = -.42)$ $P_{35} = r_{35}$

$P_{14} = B_{14.36}, (r_{14} = -.21)$ $P_{36} = r_{36} = .00*$

$P_{15} = B_{15.2346}, (r_{15} = -.13)$ $P_{45} = r_{45} = -.09*$

$P_{16} = B_{16.34}, (r_{16} = -.22)$ $P_{46} = P_{64} = r_{46}$

$P_{56} = r_{56} = .04*$

$P_{23} = r_{23}$

$P_{24} = r_{24}$

$P_{25} = r_{25} = .08*$

$P_{26} = r_{26} = -.08*$

*Not represented.

mitment to AD decreases with community size and educational achievement, while it is more frequent among children of fathers who militated in AD, ORVE (Organización Venezolana), and the PDN (Partido Democrático Nacional). Self-image and ideological position exert the type of causal effect that can be anticipated, increasing *adeco* partisanship with more politicized self-images and right-of-center ideological positions.

By contrast, *copeyano* partisanship is more closely related to religiosity and stratification, once self-image and ideological tendency are accounted for. Community size is the other factor included in the model (presented in figure 26). However, even though we saw that sympathy toward COPEI tended to increase with social status (see tables III-5 and VI-1), *copeyano* partisanship *decreases* with socioeconomic status. Thus, even though the more firmly

Partisanship in Venezuelan Politics

Figure 26. Patterns of *Copeyano* Partisanship

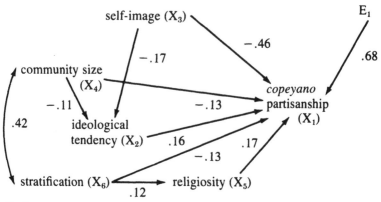

Paths:

$P_{12} = B_{12.34}$, $(r_{12} = .27)$
$P_{13} = B_{13.2}$, $(r_{13} = -.50)$
$P_{14} = B_{14.36}$, $(r_{14} = -.22)$
$P_{15} = B_{15.234}$, $(r_{15} = .16)$
$P_{16} = B_{16.2345}$, $(r_{16} = -.18)$

$P_{23} = r_{23}$	$P_{34} = .05*$	$P_{45} = .04*$
$P_{24} = r_{24}$	$P_{35} = -.01*$	$P_{46} = r_{46}$
$P_{25} = r_{25} = .03*$	$P_{36} = -.01*$	$P_{56} = r_{56}$
$P_{26} = r_{26} = -.09*$		

*Not represented.

engaged activists of the AD can be best characterized by an incomplete education, their *copeyano* counterparts are less affluent than it appeared at first. It is important to stress that we are dealing with rank-and-file citizens, not party elites, and that there is no conflict between this finding and the generalized impression of an edge in the social standing of *copeyano* over *adeco* elites. Our previous commentary on higher levels of system and partisan support for these establishment parties among residents of smaller communities is verified by both models. On the other hand, the religious factor still makes a difference in terms of intensity among *copeyanos*, even though one could anticipate a similar level of religiosity among them. Instead, the more committed *copeyanos* seem to be more religious. This contrasts with the absence of the religious factor among *adecos*, suggesting a gradual decline in the anticlericalism which characterized them in the early days.[29]

Some discussion is necessary concerning specific partisanship as it relates to the cases of three other parties: the Movimiento Electoral del Pueblo (MEP), Movimiento al Socialismo (MAS), and Cruzada Cívica Nacionalista (CCN). We did not recover a sufficiently large number of identifiers for any of these to treat the characteristics of their partisans in the same manner as those of AD and COPEI. What we did was explore the correlates of the different *intensities of feelings* toward the three. These must be treated with some reservation, because we do not know if this distribution is similar to those of partisanship toward each of these three. Following this procedure we developed a profile of the sympathizers of MEP, MAS, and CCN (which we could call *mepistas*, *masistas*, and *nacionalistas* but will not in order to underline the fact that they cannot be treated as partisans of these parties).

Foremost in these profiles were characteristics of a very marked ideological nature; ideological tendency for MEP and MAS, and opinion about the 1958 coup for the Cruzada. Variation of *masista* feelings required a set of four factors to explain about 23 per cent of the variance. Figure 27 presents path-analytic models for MAS, MEP, and CCN.[30] Warm feelings about MAS go together with a leftist ideological preference, high educational achievement, and a negative evaluation of regime policies. Surprisingly, we did not find age and community size associated with *masista* proclivities, although during the 1972 campaign there was the widespread impression, verified through our field observations, that MAS meant urban youth. We found that warm feelings toward MEP were related to ideological position, without any other factor reaching an acceptable level of statistical significance.

The causal effect of ideology on feelings toward MAS and MEP allows us to reconsider the relationship between party and ideology in an entirely different light. These two parties were organized recently, with MEP following the internal squabble within AD at the time of the 1968 campaign, while MAS made its debut in the 1973 race. These parties came into the political arena in an effort to represent the preferences of unengaged leftists. Thus, covariation between party and ideology can be treated with the latter as the antecedent and the former as the consequence in this case. Voters supported MAS because it offered an alternative to the PCV and to the leftist factions of the establishment parties. MEP's support was ample but was reduced, by the time of our survey, to people on the left. Thus, in both cases, the parties sought the favor of leftists without specific militancy. In short, *ideology clearly preceded party preference in this instance*, even though at the time of our survey,

Figure 27. Correlates of Sympathy toward MAS, MEP, and CCN

A. *MAS*

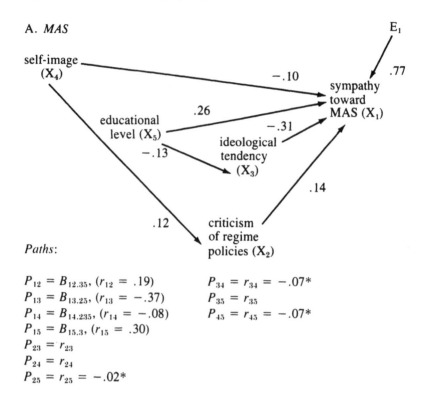

Paths:

$P_{12} = B_{12.35}, (r_{12} = .19)$ $P_{34} = r_{34} = -.07*$

$P_{13} = B_{13.25}, (r_{13} = -.37)$ $P_{35} = r_{35}$

$P_{14} = B_{14.235}, (r_{14} = -.08)$ $P_{45} = r_{45} = -.07*$

$P_{15} = B_{15.3}, (r_{15} = .30)$

$P_{23} = r_{23}$

$P_{24} = r_{24}$

$P_{25} = r_{25} = -.02*$

B. *MEP*   C. *CCN*

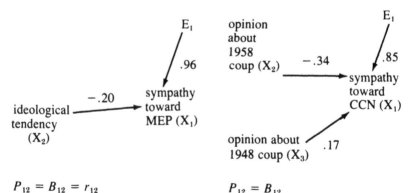

$P_{12} = B_{12} = r_{12}$ $P_{12} = B_{12}$

                                          $P_{13} = B_{13.2}, (r_{13} = .20)$

                                          $P_{23} = r_{23} = -.08*$

N = 430 for all models.
*Not represented.

voters who were more favorable toward them already identified themselves as militants and sympathizers.

Also of notable interest is the fact that none of these profiles unveiled linkages with societal cleavages other than the educational factor, which is obviously related to status. Ideology loomed as the largest and sole societal cleavage connected with the distributions of feelings about these three parties. Finally, we found that among these, feelings about Cruzada were most affected by attitudes molded by past political history—the military coups of 1948 and 1958—which opened and closed the period of the New National Ideal of the dictator Marcos Pérez Jiménez. Perhaps this is a clear indication of the political recidivism of his *nacionalistas*; at least it is the syndrome that best describes them.

In summary, *a close emotional distance between members of the electorate and the more extremist parties is primarily concerned with political ideology, not with sociocultural and economic cleavages.* Unlike the partisanship associated with the parties of the status quo, feelings about these parties produce clusters of ideologically homogeneous sympathizers sharing a common location on the left-right continuum. Having summarized the parameters of those locations, we can now turn to explore the phenomenon of AD-COPEI opposition. In justifying the importance of including this in our agenda to those unfamiliar with Venezuela, we might refer to Colonel Aureliano Buendía's remark that, in Colombia, "the only difference between Liberals and Conservatives is that the Liberals go to mass at five o'clock and the Conservatives at eight. . . ." (Gabriel García Márquez in *Cien Años de Soledad*).

Party Oppositions: Adecos *and* Copeyanos

Contemporary Venezuela cannot match the Colombian experience of civil strife created by party loyalties. There was no colonel to lead 32 unsuccessful insurrections, merely an obscure *bachiller* from Táchira who led the last successful revolt at the turn of the century. Nor was there anything comparable to Colombia's *la violencia*; too few *godos* remained in Venezuela. If anything, part of the problem of party oppositions concerning AD and COPEI stemmed from the latter's *grand peur* that the former might impose a Mexican PRI-type formula in Venezuela. This opposition had something of the clerical versus secular cleavage, and a little of the conservative versus liberal; the times were different and so were the issues. Yet there are more differences between *adecos* and *copeyanos* than the hour they attend mass, and more ideological and socioeconomic distinctions than critics and analysts customarily admit.

To be sure, conventional wisdom points to the *copeyano* Andean stronghold, but that was broken down by the *adeco andino* who became president in 1974. One has the impression that *copeyanos* are a little more affluent, and more oriented to things from the continent. *Adecos* have always presented a *populista* aura, one that smacks of lower socioeconomic status, of *campo* and *ranchería*, and an unabashed admiration for the United States. But 26 years passed since the last time the *adecos* won the city of Caracas in a national election; it was, after all, an *adeco* president who nationalized the oil and iron industries and confronted the wrath of the United States; he had also been considered "safer" by the Venezuelan business community. What, then, *are* the real differences between the two?

The first and more important point to preface these comparisons is that the two sets of people to be identified as partisans of AD and COPEI are not the same. It proved difficult to develop a measure of partisanship that would produce a minimum of overlapping between the two, for the "soft" supporters of both parties overlap to a considerable extent. Having gone through six preliminary versions of the operational definitions of *adeco* and *copeyano*, we settled on a seventh that maintained a similar number of differences found in terms of those which preceded, but also minimized overlapping between the potential supporters and sympathizers of the two parties. This version, utilized in our path analysis of *adeco* and *copeyano* partisanship, is based on the proportions presented in table VI-2.

Our first observation concerning table VI-2 concerns the proportions of firmly engaged partisans of both parties; these militants represent about one-fourth of their partisans and a nontrivial proportion of the electorate (a respectable 21 per cent if both are combined). Second, *copeyano* sympathizers constitute a somewhat larger proportion of total support for COPEI (29 per cent) than their *adeco* counterparts (at 25); the proportions of supporters are identical, at 26 per cent for both. Third, the proportion of potential supporters of both parties is not large but cannot be overlooked if viewed in the context of a closely fought electoral campaign; 6 per cent of the electorate is certainly more than enough to determine the outcome of an election. In addition, these "soft" supporters represent more than twice that amount if calculated as a percentage of the total support for either party, at 17 and 15 per cent, respectively. On the other hand, the wins and losses that each party would

Table VI-2. Levels of Support for AD and COPEI in the Venezuelan
Electorate

	N	Relative frequencies (per cent)		
		Of AD	Of COPEI	Of electorate
Potential supporters of both	96	17	15	6
Adeco supporters[a]	144	26	—	9
Adeco sympathizers, Potential supporters of COPEI	(32)	6	(5)	(2)
Adeco sympathizers[b]	141	25	—	9
Adeco militants	144	26	—	9
Copeyano supporters[a]	170	—	26	11
Copeyano sympathizers, Potential supporters of AD	(34)	(6)	5	(2)
Copeyano sympathizers[b]	190	—	29	13
Copeyano militants	163	—	25	12
Subtotals[c]	1,048	100	100	69
Hostile or indifferent	473	—	—	31

Note: *Potential supporters* do not explicitly identify with the party, but
are at least lukewarm in their feelings about it, and are not members of any
political party; *sympathizers* identify with the party nominally, are not
members, and are at least lukewarm about it; *militants* are party members
who identify with it and are at least lukewarm about it.

[a] Excludes supporters of both.

[b] Excludes sympathizers who can be classified as potential supporters of
the other party.

[c] Excludes those in [a] and [b], and percentages in parentheses.

experience from sympathizers defecting to the other (represented in
parentheses in the table) seem to cancel each other out.

These data suggest that one can place some confidence in the
results of our analysis of the sources of support for these two parties.
We find no overlapping in militants, and only minimal overlapping
in sympathizers. On the other hand, these individuals can be legiti-

Table VI-3. AD-COPEI Opposition among Population Groups

	Electoral polarization[a]	Levels of partisanship[b] Mil.	Symp.	Supp.	All partisans in category[c]
Region of residence					
Plains	−4	−6	0	6	1
Andes	10	3	−10	7	1
West	−10	−4	3	1	−2
East	10	2	−1	−1	7
Zulia	−12	3	−14	11	−2
Center	−8	1	−1	0	−5
Community size					
Rural	8	1	−5	4	3
Intermediate	8	0	7	−7	4
Urban	0	−9	−3	12	1
Metropolitan	−12	2	−4	2	−8
Class images					
Poor	22	5	−2	−3	14
Middle class	−18	−3	−1	4	−14
Stratification					
Agricultural poor	26	10	−3	−7	8
Manual poor	22	−8	6	2	6
Manual middle class	−8	−4	1	3	−2
Lower white collar	−14	2	−11	9	−4
Upper white collar	−10	9	−4	−5	−1
Professional	−34	−5	−4	9	−7

mately included among the supporters of both parties. In short, we believe that the two dimensions are unobtrusive, based on a minimal amount of distortion, and empirically valid. More importantly, whether one utilizes these criteria or follows some other type of measure to differentiate between *adecos* and *copeyanos*,[31] the more basic differences remain. Those which we find using our measures of *adeco* and *copeyano* partisanship are summarized in table VI-3, which presents data on the comparative strength of the two parties among different population groups. The data are based on

Partisanship in Venezuelan Politics

Table VI-3. AD-COPEI Opposition among Population Groups (*Continued*)

	Electoral polari- zation[a]	Levels of partisanship[b] Mil.	Symp.	Supp.	All partisans in category[c]
Group identification					
Peasants	8	16	−11	−5	2
Workers	8	1	−5	4	5
Housewives	4	−6	2	4	1
Common people	4	7	−7	0	2
Middle class	−18	−4	3	1	−5
Students	−36	−6	−8	14	−3
Professionals	−18	0	8	8	−1
Business	−26	−6	−13	19	−1
Ideological tendency					
Radical left	12	0	3	−3	2
Left	12	−4	13	−9	0
Center left	38	14	−2	−12	7
Center	−18	−6	−9	15	−1
Center right	−10	2	−2	0	−2
Right	−12	2	−3	1	−6

Note: All computations are based on differences between percentage AD *minus* percentage COPEI.

[a]Column percentages, % vote for AD *minus* % vote for COPEI.

[b]Column percentages, % of AD partisans of that level *minus* % of COPEI partisans of that level.

[c]Row percentage, % of all AD partisans from the category *minus* % of all COPEI partisans from the category.

percentage differences between the two, controlling for level of partisanship.

Inspection of the levels of party support in the different regions clarifies one aspect of the demographics behind the results of the Venezuelan election of 1973. COPEI lost every state except Zulia, where we see that it enjoyed a solid margin over AD in polarization (−12) and in party sympathizers. COPEI, however, did not draw a much larger proportion of its partisans from the region (only 2 per cent more). COPEI also seemed to enjoy a comparable margin in the Center region, surpassing AD by 8 percentage points in polarization. However, the breakdown by level of party support suggests that such a margin was not very comfortable; both parties were relatively close in militants and sympathizers, separated by a difference of only 1 per cent—this could, of course, be attributable to sampling error. They were dead-even in respective proportions of supporters. In addition, COPEI was more dependent on the Center than AD, as shown by the former drawing 5 per cent more partisans in the region than the latter. Thus, erosion of support for COPEI in the Center damaged the party seriously. A comparable outcome could have obtained for AD in the East, where it enjoyed an advantage of 10 per cent in polarization, while drawing 7 per cent more than COPEI in the region; the two parties were very close in their proportions of militants, sympathizers, and potential supporters in the region. AD's advantage in the Andes seemed unstable, for while the Andes showed a difference of 10 percentage points in polarized votes for AD, this was not based on comparable margins for militants. This was relatively reduced, at 3 per cent, coupled with a margin of 10 per cent in favor of COPEI in terms of sympathizers. Finally, the fact that COPEI lost the Plains states suggests the momentum of AD in the last month of the race, for although the electoral margin favored COPEI by only 4 per cent, the breakdown by levels of partisanship shows COPEI ahead by 6 per cent among militants. In terms of these figures, AD could only overtake COPEI in the Plains by increasing its 6 per cent margin in potential supporters. The *adecos* managed to do that.

Looking at community size, the data of table VI-3 show a substantial margin for COPEI (12 per cent) in metropolitan areas, with COPEI relying more heavily on support from such communities. COPEI's advantage in urban communities can only be observed in terms of militants and sympathizers, given the absence of any electoral margin for either party. AD's support in rural communities and those of intermediate size seemed relatively firm in electoral terms but did not depend on higher levels of militancy. AD was 5 percentage points behind in terms of sympathizers in the rural communities, while it enjoyed a margin of 7 per cent in sympathizers from communities of intermediate size.

In short, viewed in a community context, *differences between AD and COPEI are not as much a matter of militancy as a question of sympathy*. With the exception of the Plains and the urban communities, differences in the proportions of militants are not as large as those between sympathizers. These seemed to favor COPEI, while differences in potential supporters favored the AD. Thus, less than a month away from elections, the parties were evenly matched in the proportions of firmly engaged militants working for them in different communities. However, support for AD seemed to increase with decreasing levels of commitment to either party.

Much has been made of the well-documented support for AD in rural communities, and rightly so. Our data confirm this, at least in part. However, Venezuela is no longer a rural country, and a party which aspires to acquire and maintain majority status cannot rely exclusively on such support. Thus, AD's apparent advantage in those areas by no means makes the party an agrarian movement. Neither could COPEI rely so heavily on its margins in the West and Zulia, as well as in metropolitan communities, for these were not as solid as first appeared.

If the urban-rural and center-periphery contrasts in levels of support for AD and COPEI resist facile characterization, differences of a socioeconomic nature are even more difficult to summarize. To be sure, AD does better among the poor and COPEI among the middle class, but to what extent is this so? The data of table VI-3 depict the *adeco* advantage among the poor in terms of militants. In addition, AD draws 14 per cent more support from the poor. The opposite is true of COPEI, although not among potential supporters. It could be said that the poor are more *adeco* than the middle class is *copeyano*. For example, the breakdowns for level of stratification demonstrate that support for COPEI increases for all partisan categories in combination, but not monotonically. Furthermore, AD has the advantage in potential supporters and also in militants among the white-collar strata. This pattern seems to repeat itself in terms of group identification. The higher the social status of the group, the larger the electoral margin of COPEI, but not among potential supporters.

Our commentary on the data presented in table VI-3 should not pass without noting the extent to which COPEI has successfully established a genuinely *national* base of support. The returns of the 1973 election notwithstanding, COPEI emerged from its traditional Andean bastion to become a party with a very strong presence among all demographic and social groups. This is so pronounced that we are unable to report any differences in sex or age between *adecos* and *copeyanos*. Neither do we find such differences with respect to religiosity. The data seem to sugest that, at the time of the 1973 campaign, COPEI had maximized its support capabilities to their limit. Incumbency and patronage no doubt played a large part. Notice how, for the most part, AD balanced COPEI's advantages in firmly engaged militants with potential supporters. Rómulo Betancourt's favorite expression, "*adeco* is *adeco* until death," should not obscure AD's proven ability to go outside its circle of partisans to attract support, more so than any of its rivals at the present time.

Finally, the data concerning ideological preferences contain few surprises. Basically, AD does better than COPEI among leftists, while the latter does better with rightists. However, if one controls for level of partisanship, the two parties are very close in their respective proportions of militants, sympathizers, and potential supporters from the right and the center right. In addition, AD's advantage among leftists is detectable only among sympathizers from the radical left and the left. However, AD was *behind* COPEI in potential supporters from those ideological tendencies. The true contrast cannot obviate the dependence of each of the parties on support from the different tendencies. For example, COPEI was drawing 6 per cent more than AD, for all partisan categories combined, from the right. AD was relatively more dependent than COPEI in only one ideological tendency, the center left. This should put in doubt the adequacy of COPEI's "shift to the left" during the 1973 campaign.[32] Although this move was not without rational bases, COPEI could not afford to irritate the followers of that ideological tendency on which the party was more dependent. Obviously, COPEI is not a right-wing party, but in 1973 could not realistically hope to gain as much support from potential supporters from the left and the radical left as could be lost from the right, *a tendency in which COPEI did not have that much more support than the AD*. In other words, AD's advantage in the leftist tendencies was not great enough to risk such a bold move. AD only drew 2 per cent more total support from the radical left than COPEI. Both were even in what they received from the left. However, COPEI was more dependent on the right and, as the data of table VI-3 show, did not have guaranteed support of the right.

In summary, we are rather skeptical that COPEI can count on significantly more support from the right than AD. A comparison by levels of partisanship shows the two parties relatively close, much more so than the data on voting intention would predict.

Party Oppositions:
Establishment and Antiestablishment

Students of Venezuelan party politics have consistently alluded to the cleavage between "party and non-party groups,"[33] "recently attractive and historically dominant parties,"[34] or "establishment, electoral protest, and anti-system parties."[35] Even the most partisan analysts admit this basic cleavage of the Venezuelan party system.[36] The cleavage results from the dominance of AD and COPEI, dramatized by the general election of 1973, which gave them a combined total of 85 per cent of the presidential vote. One would naturally wish to explore the differences between partisans and sympathizers of the establishment parties and recently attractive and antisystem parties. To serve that desire we combined nominal sympathizers of AD and COPEI, comparing them with all other members of the mass public. Although this categorization introduces obvious inaccuracies, it fulfills the purpose of contrasting the partisans of these members of the "duo-centric"[37] Venezuelan party system with other individuals.

We identified very few bases on which to distinguish the two groups, much less than those detected between *adecos* and *copeyanos*. Region of residence, educational achievement, father's level of political interest and party affiliation, and individual ideological preferences emerged as the more ostensible and relevant differences. We found partisans of the two establishment parties in greater-than-average proportions among residents of the Plains, Andes, and Zulia regions; among those with relatively little education; among the offspring of parents with high levels of political interest and/or a militancy in AD and COPEI; and among those with a more rightist ideological tendency. We were surprised by the similar socioeconomic characteristics of the two groups, a finding that corroborates our previous inferences concerning the generation of party loyalties and their relative independence from socioeconomic cleavages. Thus it would appear that *reluctance to support the status quo parties and/or the lack of identification with them cannot be explained in terms of the impact of societal cleavages upon these particular attitudes*. Rather, the probability distribution associated with support/nonsupport for these parties seems more a result of individual experiences during the political life cycle than of a set of relatively immutable individual characteristics.

Conclusion

Our analysis shows that the causal structure influencing general partisanship has not changed greatly, although there are notable differences between the generations. In this respect, the 1928 generation seems in every respect more distinct. The assumption of a single causal structure is more difficult to sustain in the case of political self-image, becoming perhaps unrealistic in terms of specific partisanship involving AD and COPEI, and clearly problematic when applied to the more extremist parties. Not only are there intergenerational differences, but also major distinctions in the specific cleavages involved. The assumption is most difficult to sustain as the object of partisan predispositions becomes more specific. In other words, a fairly diverse set of causal factors influences the patterns of general partisan orientations and specific party commitments. Given a multiparty situation, it is evident that the party clienteles are anchored on different attributes of the electorate which cannot be reduced to a common few. Self-image and ideological tendency cannot properly be offered as such since they constitute "thresholds" to partisan orientations and party preferences, respectively. In addition, we were unable to resolve the problem of the direction of causality between ideological tendency and partisanship, except for the parties constituted more recently. As for party oppositions, differences between *adecos* and *copeyanos* are anchored on societal cleavages but resist facile characterization. The two partisan groups are sufficiently distinct, but the two apparently differ more in the potential supporters which they might attract than in terms of the characteristics of their more committed partisans. We would neither rationalize nor justify the limited contrast between *adecos* and *copeyanos* in terms of a shifting or relatively fragile set of partisan loyalties. The important point, however, is that the pattern of support for the two dominant parties in Venezuela has changed considerably in the past twenty years. Old loyalties have eroded, and new bases for loyalty are not yet firmly established. In addition, we can examine only three political generations in the electorate; although we are able to identify certain factors related to patterns of socialization behind the more general aspects of partisanship, these have but a feeble impact. Perhaps one can be born an *adeco* or a *copeyano*, although this does not exhaust the possibilities. However, a very large proportion of the electorate has lacked the opportunity to be one or another (or something else) for many years. Small wonder that their partisan behavior has not yet been cast into a mold of greater demographic and socioeconomic specificity.

7

Summary
and Conclusions

Opinions and Contradictions

Our evidence projects a rather complex and at times contradictory profile of the Venezuelan electorate. There is a solid body of data suggesting that this is a predominantly middle-class electorate (58 per cent), very anticommunist (82 per cent), supportive of *desarrollista* policies (58 per cent), leaning toward rightist ideological tendencies (49 per cent expressed in its simplest form), and fairly critical of its democratic regime (45 per cent). Yet at the same time, the Venezuelan electorate is highly supportive of elections (67 per cent), strongly opposed to military coups (73 per cent) and one-party rule (65 per cent), committed to the need for opposition criticism (75 per cent), and flirting with the idea of socialist economic organization (40 per cent). How can such findings be explained and reconciled? One school of thought would encounter little difficulty. It proffers a view of the mass public as relatively irrational and conditioned by party and class images, possessing attitudes that are contradictory but not very salient in the final analysis, and ultimately held together by the guidance of political elites.

In many important areas of opinion we have found fairly large and consensual majorities, with rather small and intense minorities dissenting from modal views. When they were broken down by the major lines of cleavage, we identified few groups that could be conceptualized as "communities" or even "quasi groups" and that provided an opportunity to locate them at the dissenting end on most areas of opinion. We found such opinion cleavages very similar to those of the electorate at large. For example, there was considerable agreement on the procedural norms necessary for the functioning of the democratic regime, with most relevant cleavages producing relatively little deviance from the general norm. The same was true in those cases wherein a unimodal distribution of opinion did not prevail—as with party identification, individual ideology, policy orientation, and the evaluation of some of the institutions of the democratic regime.

It is clear that one cannot reach beyond these data to confirm or deny the postulates of the cultural revisionists concerning the "monistic tradition" of Latin American political culture. Neither is the evidence sufficiently conclusive to suggest that the Venezuelan public is as disoriented and inchoate as large sectors of the mass publics in the postindustrial democratic regimes. Within the Venezuelan context, many of the seemingly contradictory attitudes have face validity if not political viability. However, determining which of the two types of evidence is more truly characteristic of contemporary Venezuelans is a more arduous task. In short, is this a public ready to support a strong, militantly developmentalist and anticommunist regime, or would its sensibilities concerning democratic requirements prevent it from supporting such a regime? This question is as valid and relevant for Venezuela as for the rest of Latin America, especially in those countries whose authoritarian regimes today claim the consent of the majority of the population. For example, one could argue on purely intuitive terms that these views are very close to those held by the Brazilian public. However, Venezuela has oil and a welfare state, and Brazil presents coffee and the death squad.

Where Venezuela is concerned, both sets of predispositions are instrumental for the solution of the types of problems which most preoccupy Venezuelans: inflation and job security. The electorate by overwhelming majorities wants government to address itself to these, but is dissatisfied with governmental performance to date. In this respect, Venezuela resembles several contemporary regimes of continental Europe, which are as concerned with growth and fiscal viability as Venezuela is with management efficacy and fiscal responsibility. The contradiction stands, and the question devolves upon the point of departure. That is, given the preference for big active government in Venezuela, what type of predisposition is likely to predominate? Given that this is a valence issue, what kinds of societal cleavages could register an impact on this outcome?

In chapter 3 we examined this contradiction in terms of classes and strata. We found the higher strata less critical and cynical, slightly more inclined to support authoritarian solutions, more likely to continue to vote, somewhat more supportive of COPEI, less hostile to the new left, less partisan, and more influential and capable. We interpreted this as a consequence of the close linkages between these strata and the Venezuelan state. By contrast, we depicted the lower strata as more critical and cynical, less likely to continue to vote, less likely to support coups, more anticommunistic, more supportive of AD, more militantly partisan, less supportive of *desarrollismo*, and less efficacious and capable. Thus, *the social aspect of the contradiction is that those who are yet to benefit from*

Summary and Conclusions

the present state of affairs are least likely to support extremist solutions (read coups and communism) outside the framework of the democratic regime. In addition, they seem to participate more as if to compensate for their low level of political capacity. In summary, the standard socioeconomic model affords little insight into political differences between "up" and "down" in Venezuelan politics.

Chapter 4 discussed cultural aspects of the contradiction, focusing on the community dimension and trying to extricate the impacts of regionalism and urbanization. We found these in most cases independent of one another, with their separate impact reduced through simultaneity and their interaction limited to a few instances. We learned that the impact of regional diversity was reduced by the homogenizing effect of urbanization, while the latter represented in some cases but a reflection of differences in stratification. In general, we saw that the more "peripheral" regions and communities yielded higher levels of participation, while this seemed to decline in the more urbanized regions and in the metropolitan Center. We interpreted this as contradicting the standard socioeconomic model. Given the lessened impact of urbanization in the smaller communities, more traditional styles of classical participation have remained viable: militancy in the national political parties, voting in elections, and the like. Since political activation was set in motion before the full impact of urbanization was registered, these communities evolved a political style which fully incorporated classical participation. Thus, *rural Venezuela had participation before modernization*. Ironically, one cannot account for this under the more simplistic formulations of mobilization theory, which posit modernization as a precondition for participation. Such formulations would lead to the conclusion either that Venezuelan political parties are not modern, because they are based on traditional styles of participation, or else that the more affluent sectors of the Center have special reasons for withholding their participation. Granted the less partisan attitude of the upper strata, we find the former inadmissible and the latter fairly plausible. Thus in a cultural sense, *the populist democratic establishment created by the rule of AD and COPEI rests on a more solid foundation among those sectors of the society that have changed the least*.

Looking at community from a different perspective, we confirmed the suspected relationship between support for COPEI and religiosity. We found that higher levels of support for the regime also accompanied more intense religiosity. However, we found that ideological tendency lay behind other differences found among the four levels of religiosity. We concluded that the connection between the latter and political behavior is tenuous, and that its impact may be felt indirectly through ideological tendency.

Chapter 5 treated a topic neglected in the disciplinary literature, one which required a very thorough exercise to establish the validity and reliability of the constructs employed. We believe the analysis vindicates our initial assumption that *a majority of Venezuelans can relate to notions of left and right*. Most respondents were on the continuum, their individual locations congruent with their partisan preferences and with other individual orientations of an ideological nature. Adjustments were required to produce an ordinal scale of locations which yielded twelve different ideological positions, later reduced to six ideological tendencies. We felt that treatment of individual ideology as a matter of *tendency*, admittedly a less rigorous conceptualization than the attitude structure approach but no less valid in the final analysis, was justified by the presence of explicitly ideological objects of support and opposition in the Venezuelan political arena. Furthermore, the Chilean coup d'etat of September 1973 heightened the salience of the ideological thinking. It was demonstrated that *the impact of ideological tendency on opinion is not mediated by partisanship* in the more relevant areas. Although ideology and partisanship were shown to be closely related, the latter did not reduce the impact of the former to any significant extent.

There is an ideological aspect to the attitudinal contradictions found in the Venezuelan electorate. This concerns obvious ideological thinking on the part of the right in being less willing to apply the rules of democratic procedure to the left. In other words, *the left cannot be treated with the same set of rules*, they seem to say. By contrast, the high levels of criticism found among followers of leftist ideological tendencies do not seem more conducive to supporting extraconstitutional tactics, at the present time, nor do they appear to reduce the level of political capacity of Venezuelan leftists.

The treatment of partisanship utilized an operational measure that went beyond the usual pattern of nominal identifications with a party label, and included formal membership and feelings about the different parties. It also incorporated the safeguard that an individual characterized as a militant, supporter, or sympathizer of a particular party did not consider that party a closed electoral option. The analysis of partisanship conducted in chapter 6 focused on the verification of additional assumptions concerning probable intergenerational differences in political socialization that could have changed the causal mechanisms behind general and specific aspects of partisanship, namely, the existence of a single causal structure.

Summary and Conclusions

Analysis also included description of the nature and highly complex pattern of overlapping between societal cleavages and loyalties toward the two largest parties and a contrast between *adecos* and *copeyanos*, as well as between pro- and antiestablishment parties.

Replications conducted with the generational cohorts failed to produce many intergenerational differences for the causal mechanisms of political self-image, party sympathy, and actual membership. Thus, despite breakdowns suffered by the democratic regime and the ensuing discontinuities in partisan activity, generational differences seem more relevant sources of contrast when applied to the 1928 generation. This is the more distinct generational cohort.

The connection between societal cleavages and general partisanship comes through political self-image, although this is relatively weak. Self-image and ideological tendency appear to be the more stable sources of party sympathy. Societal cleavages were seen as relevant sources of party membership once the causal effect of self-image was accounted for. Finally, our model of general partisanship aimed to trace the causal flow leading to the strongest indication of partisan behavior, party membership. The model assumes the co-variation between ideological tendency and party sympathy goes from the former to the latter. Ideological tendency, however, does not have *direct* causal impact on membership. Stratification, community size, and the party affiliation of the father have a very similar, albeit modest, impact on party membership.

The treatment of *specific partisanship* focused on the two major parties and on the question of party oppositions. Specific partisanship concerning AD and COPEI was operationalized in terms of a threefold scheme including militants, sympathizers, and potential supporters of the two. Although *adeco* and *copeyano* partisans on first impression seem to come from very similar social groups, the analysis showed that in effect, the two parties elicit opposite reactions from these groups, especially the socioeconomic. More concretely, *copeyanos* appear more middle class, more white collar, and better educated.

The reduced size of the partisan contingents of MAS, MEP, CCN, and other minor parties rendered the type of distinctions utilized with AD and COPEI impossible. Partisanship was operationalized in terms of feelings about these parties as measured by the thermometer technique. The more homogeneous constituencies of these parties and their more specific images permitted better and more accurate results concerning the distribution of sympathy toward them. Factors associated with ideological tendency were highly significant in all three cases. Clearly, there are important

Table VII-I. Societal Cleavages and Political Opinion in Venezuela

	X_1	X_2	X_3	X_4	X_5	X_6	X_7	X_8	X_9	X_{10}	X_{11}	X_{12}	X_{13}	X_{14}
Class image	*	*	*	*	-.14	*	-.12	*	-.09	*	*	*	*	*
Stratification	*	*	*	*	-.23	*	*	.10	*	*	*	*	*	*
Group identification	*	*	*	*	*	*	*	.11	*	.08	*	*	*	*
Region of residence	*	*	*	*	*	*	*	*	*	*	*	*	*	-.10
Community size	*	*	.13	*	*	*	.09	*	*	*	*	.08	*	*
Religiosity	*	*	*	-.04	*	-.11	*	*	*	*	-.10	*	*	*
Gender role	*	.14	*	*	.11	*	*	*	.10	*	*	-.11	-.13	*
Age	*	*	-.14	*	*	*	*	*	-.08	-.09	*	-.08	-.08	-.08
Ideological tendency	*	*	-.17	-.15	-.16	-.12	-.16	.10	*	-.11	-.15	*	*	*
Political self-image	.08	*	.14	.11	*	.12	.19	-.13	.27	.14	*	-.20	-.46	-.38
Party sympathy	-.21	.11	*	-.14	-.21	-.11	*	*	*	-.08	-.10	*	*	.15
Multiple R	.24	.18	.32	.31	.44	.28	.29	.24	.33	.28	.25	.34	.49	.21

Note: All table values are standardized regression coefficients (betas). Asterisks (*) identify cases in which either the beta was not significant (alpha = .01) and/or the proportion of variance of the dependent variable explained was less than 1 per cent. Sample sizes as follows: N = 956 (for X_1, X_2, and X_3), N = 559 (for X_4, X_5, and X_6), N = 897 (for X_7 and X_8), and N = 1,011 (for X_9 through X_{14}).
X_1 is opinion (yes/no) about one-party rule.

X_2 is opinion (yes/no) about desirability of opposition criticism.
X_3 is evaluation (support/criticism) of the institution of elections.
X_4 is evaluation (support/criticism) of regime policies.
X_5 is evaluation (pro/con) of Caldera's policies.
X_6 is opinion about whether government normally does what is right (yes/no).
X_7 is evaluation (favorable/unfavorable) of politician's role.
X_8 is opinion (yes/no) that political parties only care about winning elections.
X_9 is voting (yes/no) under voluntary suffrage.
X_{10} is null voting (yes/no).
X_{11} is participatory mood.
X_{12} is exposure (low/high) to 1973 campaign.
X_{13} is involvement (low/high) in 1973 campaign.
X_{14} is perceived efficacy (low/high) of 1973 campaign.

qualitative differences between these and the causal linkages associated with *adeco* and *copeyano* partisanship. At the risk of gross
oversimplification, one could argue that the principal differences
between the latter are socioeconomic; this is perhaps mildly exaggerated, but the backgrounds of their more partisan loyalists suggest that this may well be the case.

Societal Cleavages and Political Opinion
in Venezuela

Everyone familiar with survey research knows that the best predictor of one attitude is another attitude and that, for the most part,
social circumstances and traits of individuals are poor predictors of
attitudinal preferences. However, explanation of attitudes in terms
of other attitudes leads to an "infinite regress" and to a theoretical
vacuum insofar as the relationship between cleavage structures and
political opinion is concerned. Thus, one should not obviate the
latter.

At different stages of our argument, we have brought two or three
cleavage factors simultaneously into the analysis; this was done with
region and community size, as well as with ideology and religiosity.
At the same time, we compared the causal effect of these cleavage
factors on the crystallization of political self-images and on party
sympathy. Thus, with the exception of partisanship, we have not
compared the relevance of *all* the lines of cleavages examined
throughout our discussion on different aspects of opinion and behavior of the electorate. We will not repeat the discussion on partisanship presented in chapter 6. The evidence is presented in table
VII-1, where we have recorded the results of multiple regressions
of cleavage factors on fourteen different areas of political opinion in
Venezuela.

The first conclusion that the evidence of table VII-1 suggests is
that in Venezuela in general, a person's political self-image is a
more relevant influence on individual political attitudes than the partisan and ideological preferences of that individual and any of his or
her other characteristics. In other words, *political self-image seems
to be the more relevant individual characteristic contributing to the
formation of political attitudes in Venezuela*. Thus, when asked
"what are you in Venezuelan politics?" the most relevant datum
that our respondents gave concerned whether they were partisan,
independents, or apolitical. Consequently, politicization, as measured by political self-image, seems to have greater overall impor-

tance than ideology, partisanship, social circumstances, community context, position in the life cycle (age), and gender role.

Second, party sympathy and ideology seem to be equal or comparable in terms of their causal effects on opinions, although their overlap is far from perfect. The former is more relevant in relation to operational norms of the regime and political institutions. The latter appears somewhat more relevant in the area of policy evaluation, whether of the regime or the administration in power. Their causal effect on these aspects of opinion is even comparable to that of self-image, but the effect of the latter on political participation is incomparably stronger.

Third, of the factors pertaining to individual traits and social circumstances, gender role and generation appear more relevant than those related to community and socioeconomic inequality. The impact of gender role is more dispersed throughout different areas of opinion, and that due to position in the life cycle is more manifest in the area of political participation, where differences due to gender role are also detectable. Fourth, the impact of community-related factors does not follow a systematic pattern, which is not to deny the real differences between communities of different kinds discussed in chapter 4. However, it suggests that the electorate is more homogeneous in this connection than it used to be. Finally, the impact of differences due to socioeconomic inequality is more relevant in terms of policy evaluation and is equal to that of party sympathy and ideological preference, but this is the only area where such an impact merits discussion.

To conclude, our evidence suggests that Venezuelan political opinion responds primarily to the individual's overall orientation to politics, rather than to any other factor. In Venezuela, then, whether one is political or apolitical appears ultimately more relevant than whether one is on the left or the right, *adeco* or *copeyano*, male or female, young or old, urban or rural, and poor or middle class.

Appendix A
The Research Design

Our data were generated by execution of a national survey conducted between October 17 and November 3, 1973, in Venezuela; we interviewed a total of 1,521 adult Venezuelan nationals, drawn from a stratified random sample. A team of some fifty interviewers and ten supervisors conducted the fieldwork. The final instrument— which represented the seventeenth version of our questionnaire—included a total of 113 different items and 145 responses to these items; the average duration of an interview was about 50 minutes; no interviews were terminated before completion. A total of 47.4 per cent of the interviews were verified as follows: 9.2 were checked out through a third party, 24.1 were corroborated with the interviewee, and 14.1 were observed while in progress. The interviewers rated 77.9 per cent of their interviews as "good," while 18.1 were reported as "bad," suggesting some hesitation, reserve, or fatigue on the part of the respondent.

The Preliminary Work

Preparation of the fieldwork began in January 1973, when the operational version of the instrument—which then represented the fifth draft—was discussed in Caracas with Mr. Andrew Templeton and Sr. Nelson Villasmil of DATOS, C.A., a Venezuelan firm specializing in market research and public opinion surveys. Some details of a pilot study were also discussed at that time. This was conducted during the month of June: 250 respondents were interviewed in seven cities and three rural areas, the instrument included 116 items and 161 responses to the items, and the fieldwork was completed in two weeks. This pilot study was valuable from several perspectives, including the classical question involving validity of the instrument and reliability of procedures.

Some crucial considerations stemmed from the very nature of the study: the fact that we were dealing with a very long questionnaire, exclusively concerned with political topics, to be administered during a presidential campaign and including many questions pertaining to the campaign itself; the fact that our Venezuelan associates from DATOS had no previous experience with such a project as ours; and finally, the ominously sensitive fact that the data were to be analyzed by foreign scholars.

Baloyra personally instructed the supervisory staff and the field teams, working with groups of about twelve persons in each training session. Every single question was read and explained, and the sessions were prefaced with general remarks about the nature of the project and a very frank discussion about the operational problems involved. Given the youth of many of the interviewers—most of whom fell between 18 and 22 years of age—they were explicitly encouraged to express any doubts or apprehensions about the study, as well as criticisms and suggestions about the wording of the items. This aspect of the study proved to be highly rewarding, and the training method was continued until the conclusion of the fieldwork. Following these sessions, both the supervisors and the field staff conducted two or three interviews, and a new meeting was held at which they might report their results and add further comments and criticisms; invaluable feedback about the validity of the instrument and the feasibility of the study was produced from these exchanges.

Results of the pilot study were analyzed during July and August in Chapel Hill, and final preparations for the definitive survey began in Caracas in the second half of September. It was clear by that time that the instrument was valid—difficult to administer but capable of giving us the data we sought. The final version of the questionnaire, in Spanish, is presented in Appendix B. The items are translated when reference is made to them in the text.

The Sample

Our research involved two major concerns: first, what is the impact of a presidential campaign on the public, and second, what kinds of political attitudes, beliefs, and opinions characterize the present Venezuelan public? We have dealt with the first topic at great length elsewhere[1] and need not repeat ourselves here. However, given this combination of interests, we wanted to utilize a sample of respondents who had been exposed to the messages and influences of the presidential campaign of 1973. This dictated the elimination of a group of respondents from our sample who for reasons of nationality or ineligibility would not be able to participate in the election. It

Appendix A

Table A-I. Stratification Criteria

	Attribute	Sample estimate	Population parameter[a]	Bias[b]
Sex	Male	49.8	49.97	−.17
	Female	50.2	50.03	+.17
Age	18–24	27.4	28.13	−.73
	25–34	25.2	24.83	+.37
	35–44	19.9	19.58	+.42
	45–54	13.0	13.13	−.13
	55–64	8.6	8.21	+.39
	65+	5.9	6.14	−.24
Size	Metropolitan[c]	46.0	45.6	+.40
	Urban[d]	15.6	13.0	+2.60
	Intermediate[e]	13.9	14.0[g]	−.10
	Rural[f]	24.5	27.5[g]	−2.90
Class	AB	3.2	3.0[h]	+.2
	C	21.6	24.0[h]	−2.4
	D	43.0	39.0[h]	+4.0
	E	32.1	34.0[h]	−1.9

Note: Throughout this volume, cases in which the percentages presented in a table do not add up to 100 per cent are the result of rounding off or truncation procedures. Table values here are percentages.

[a] Unless otherwise specified, these data were obtained from Ministerio de Fomento, Dirección General de Estadística y Censos Nacionales, *IX Censo General de Población (2 de Noviembre de 1971), Venezuela, Resultados Comparativos* (Caracas, 1971).

[b] Bias = (Sample estimate − population parameter).

[c] Larger than 100,000.

[d] From 25,000 to 99,999.

[e] From 5,000 to 24,999.

[f] Smaller than 5,000.

[g] The Venezuelan Census describes "intermediate" between 1,000 and 2,499 inhabitants, and "rural" below 1,000, so these figures were recomputed.

[h] DATOS estimate. See appendix C for the operational criteria utilized by the interviewers to estimate the class status of a respondent.

also implied that while we would not altogether exclude the rural areas, attention would be concentrated on those segments of the public which had a greater probability of exposure to the campaign. Therefore, our sample was slightly biased in favor of the urban areas, to the detriment of more isolated rural areas.

This bias is described in statistical terms in table A-1, which also includes one socioeconomic and two other demographic criteria involved in our stratification procedure. Comparison of the attributes of both sex and age between sample estimates and population parameters is very satisfactory; the rural-urban cleavage of population distribution yields the aforementioned bias in favor of the more urban areas. The final attribute, class status, also shows a somewhat larger bias in favor of what could be loosely construed as the "working class," although both sets of figures are estimates and the effect of this particular bias is more difficult to measure. Nevertheless, the magnitude of sampling bias seems to do minimal violence to the stratification criteria which were based on these four characteristics. It would have been desirable to include one additional criterion of stratification which, in our opinion, was a factor of considerable significance—the economic activity status of the head of household. Due to the fact that we were concerned with voting intention and regime evaluation, we wanted to approximate the true proportion of the unemployed; our assumption was that dissatisfaction would be higher among the unemployed and that they would tend to evaluate the regime more negatively. Lacking recent data on population parameters, and with the government delaying the release of census results pertaining to employment and occupation, we had no way of making sound inferences concerning this important attribute. Both the pilot study and the final survey yielded an unemployment rate of about 8 per cent. We believe that both of these estimates were decidedly low.[2]

In summary, we worked with a progressively stratified random sample of 1,521 respondents; sex, age, community size, and one objective measure of social status were utilized as the stratification criteria. In urban and metropolitan areas, the *barrio* and the *urbanización* were utilized as primary sampling units; in rural areas the community itself was the primary sampling unit. Randomization was utilized to select each and every one of the former from a master list maintained by DATOS. The latter were selected from a list of communities within the range of their size, but some changes were made to maximize geographic variation, in order to include states excluded through the randomized drawings of rural communities.

Appendix A

The Problem of Validity

Traditionally, two major problems confront the scholar involved in survey work: validity and reliability. The first asks whether a particular instrument measures what it is supposed to measure.[3] Reliability questions consistency, the obtaining of similar results from application of the same instrument to comparable populations or to the same population at different intervals in time.[4]

The issue of validity is of utmost importance to cross-cultural research. In our case, it posed an immediate dilemma to be resolved at an early stage in our preliminary preparations: whether to utilize an instrument that had been validated through extensive use in the United States and Western Europe, or to construct an instrument in an ad hoc fashion that would constitute a valid measure of the peculiarities of the Venezuelan case. Since we were not going to emphasize *content* of opinion as much as the direction and intensity of opinion concerning a series of relevant political objects, we chose the former. This did not diminish our awareness of the dangers of misinterpretation of this type of information, as was the case with Almond and Verba's interpretation of the Mexican data of their five-country study.

One very serious criticism of Almond and Verba's seminal study concerns their treatment of the data concerning Mexico as compared to the other four countries in the study. The authors are consistent in ranking Mexico at the very bottom in a series of citizen's attitudes concerning government responsiveness, political cynicism, and similar measures. This is a direct result of their failure to take into account the authoritarian nature of the Mexican regime, and the fact that the Mexican public clearly perceived the corruption and inefficiency of their government.[5] Thus we resolved to go ahead with this kind of instrument, and did not expect that it would or had to produce results which had the same implications in a Venezuelan context that these results have elsewhere.

Ironically, the question of validity is inextricably bound to the argument about the political culture and tradition of Latin America, because we could have gone to the field with an instrument that measured contemporary Venezuelan opinion about a series of liberal-democratic principles which have no salience in the Venezuelan context. Instead we assumed that the political regime is *always* a relevant object of political support and that, given the democratic nature of the Venezuelan regime, it would be appropriate to construct an instrument intended to measure the responses of the Venezuelan public to that type of regime. Moreover, such an instrument would give us the capability to probe the entire set of responses to the regime in all of its institutional aspects—elections, political parties, role of the opposition, role of party politicians, and procedural norms of the regime. This would allow us to make inferences about evaluations of the democratic regime by the Venezuelan public.

Naturally, a knowledge of Venezuelan politics permitted refinement of many of the scales and items utilized so that they would conform to the Venezuelan situation more closely, rather than constituting a series of vacuous and meaningless propositions. Moreover, this encouraged us to explore some specific issues that have attracted the attention of fellow students of Venezuelan politics. In essence, we tried to solve the issue of validity by departing from a core of "valid" items, which were successively refined until we were satisfied that our respondents were both aware of the nature of the questions and able to deal with them meaningfully. We relied heavily on the counsel and criticism of our Venezuelan associates, sharpening the wording of our items until they were satisfied that the average Venezuelan could respond fully.

The Problem of Reliability

Our approach to the problem of reliability focused on two coordinate efforts: first, to centralize the training and supervisory aspects of the project as much as possible and second, to anticipate and identify potential sources of biases. With training centralized, the flow of feedback returned to a single source of decision making in Baloyra, who consulted closely with the field supervisors. This allowed for maximum homogeneity by establishing a structure of authority, and an effective procedure for the consultation and resolution of all doubts concerning the administration of the instrument. Baloyra went to the field with Messrs. Vivas and Roa, supervisors of the Zulia and Andean regions, respectively. Since the Maracaibo area is sufficiently large to warrant a permanent staff and a certain independence from DATOS' main office in Caracas, Baloyra went from Caracas to Maracaibo to train personally the field team that was going to operate in Zulia and Trujillo states under Vivas. From Maracaibo Baloyra went to San Cristóbal to coordinate the efforts of Roa's smaller staff with the additional interviewers sent from Caracas to help him. All other teams operated out of Caracas, going to their assigned regions immediately following their training. In short, the training effect was relatively homogeneous and those interviewers not trained directly by Baloyra were prepared by a senior supervisor following the procedural clarification proposed by Baloyra and the supervisory staff.

Yet if one can reduce interviewer bias, there is still a second source of bias which is much more difficult to anticipate: that of the respondent. In any given population, there may be groups of individuals who respond to the stimuli of the interview situation in an idiosyncratic manner. For reasons of education, culture, personality, and the like, some may respond in a different manner to the interview situation as a whole, or to a series of items in particular. Respondent bias is primarily a result of the predisposition of certain individuals to react to a different set of stimuli than those represented by the instrument and the interview situation. There is also the possibility of inadvertently creating such biases as a result of careless or obscure wording, which may offend or predispose persons who would otherwise answer differently. Interviewers were routinely asked to note the attitude of their respondents in order to control the number of such interviews: any signs of fatigue, boredom, hostility, or incomprehension were carefully recorded for future screening and possible elimination of the interview. Our interviewers were assured that they would be paid for every interview regardless of their comments about respondents' attitude. They were instructed to regard this information as essential to the project and required of all of them. Only 60 of the 1,521 interviews made no reference to respondent's attitude; no attempt was made to induce the interviewer to supply this information because it would have been unreliable. Such cases were fundamentally the responsibility of the supervisor, and nothing could be done to retrieve the information.

We went beyond the normal screening procedure and utilized this information in a more rigorous fashion: these data were coded and punched, together with the rest of the information provided by the instrument, and we treated them as if they constituted another analytic dimension. The initial set of cross-tabulations generated in the analysis involved these data which were utilized to compare "good" versus "bad" interviews along the entire range of items included in the questionnaire. In order better to illustrate our discussion of the results of these cross-tabulations and comparisons, those items of the questionnaire on which we will concentrate here have been divided into two groups: factual items and opinion items.

Appendix A

Table A-2. Potential Sources of Respondent's Bias

Respondent attributes	Value of Cramer's V	Significance (P.<)
Demographic characteristics		
Sex	.08	.005
Age	.06	NS
Region of birth	.09	.05
Region of residence	.10	.005
Marital status	.05	NS
Residential mobility	.04	NS
Size of community	.01	NS
Electoral cohort group	.04	NS
Socioeconomic and cultural characteristics		
Educational level attained	.09	.05
Type of school attended	.03	NS
Type of area where respondent grew up	.06	NS
Religiosity	.03	NS
Opinion about importance of religion	.05	NS
Class status (objective)	.08	.005
Class self-image (subjective)	.08	.05
Income of head of household	.09	.005
Occupation of head of household	.10	.05
Economic activity status of head of household	.04	NS
Employment status of head of household	.06	NS
Job satisfaction of head of household	.04	NS
Group identification	.06	NS
Opinion about actual influence of reference group	.05	NS
Opinion about trend of the influence of reference group	.05	NS
Perception of power of major groups and associations	.05	NS
Score in trust in people scale	.04	NS
Father's occupation	.07	NS
Father's political interest	.04	NS
Father's political involvement	.06	NS
Party affiliation of father	.06	NS
Father's tenure in political office	.03	NS = P > .05

Table A-2. Potential Sources of Respondent's Bias (*Continued*)

Cramer's V is a measure of association between two variables measured nominally. Algebraically, $V = \dfrac{x^2/N}{\text{Min }(r-4),(c-4)}$ 1/2, where r and c stand for the number of rows and columns of the table. Utilization of Cramer's V, which is regarded as a very poor measure of association, was almost mandatory at the time at which we conducted this procedure. The data had not been standardized to reflect ordinal measurement for all variables; since this took place at such an early stage in our analysis, we did not have stronger measures of association that would be comparable in all cases.

Table A-2 presents a summary of the differences between "good" and "bad" respondents in terms of their demographic, socioeconomic, and cultural characteristics. The table records the value of Cramer's V, expressing the relationship between the type of rating given the respondents by the interviewers and the item in question, and the level of statistical significance—the "reliability"—of the value of V obtained. The assumption is, of course, that the interviewers were able to detect and record the respondents' attitude in an accurate fashion and that, more importantly, this procedure provides a reliable measure of respondent bias. The procedure is in a sense a poor man's substitute for a more effective technique but, lacking similar instruments that had been administered to comparable populations, it constituted a genuine attempt to increase reliability.

The results of table A-2 indicated that there were only eight probable sources of respondent bias stemming from the individual background characteristics of respondents: sex, region, level of education, social class, income, and occupation were sources of bias detected in this fashion. Women, people from Zulia and the Plains states, the illiterate and poorly educated, the less affluent, those who identified themselves as lower class or poor, and peasants showed a greater tendency to be poor respondents. The percentage of "bad" interviews among these subgroups was higher than the average for the entire sample.

A more definitive inference may be drawn from the summary data of table A-2: although the differences for these categories are real, they are of limited significance. The highest value for any of the V's obtained is .10. This yields a regression value of .01, which means that less than 2 per cent of the variation in respondent attitude is attributable to occupation, the individual characteristic for which the value was obtained. This is the strongest relationship that was detected so that, in short, the results of the table show that the impact of these potential sources of respondent bias on the administration of the instrument was minimal. Therefore, the 276 respondents who gave us "bad" interviews do not constitute a demographic, socioeconomic, or culturally homogeneous group.

A second aspect of respondent bias queries if these "bad" respondents reacted in a patently different manner to the opinion items included in the instrument. If such was the case, cross-tabulations of respondent attitude by the opinion items should yield a fairly large number of significant relationships. We proceeded to explore this and found that the response patterns to twenty-nine items correlated significantly with respondent's attitude. But, as was the case with individual background characteristics, the impact of the relationships is minimal. In none of the 29 cases is the value of V higher than .15—which represents a regression value of .02, or a maximum of 2 per cent of explained variance for any opinion item.

Nevertheless, for the sake of illustration, the more interesting among these twenty-nine may be discussed further. Four cross-tabulations for which the values of Cramer's V were highest identify those kinds of individuals who could be classified as our worst interviewees. These data indicate that our worst respondents were *mepistas*, independents, those who did not really say why they were not members of any party, those who disliked or considered party politics worthless, those uncertain about which party could govern the country better than the others, and people concerned about housing or the cost of living. Yet the original frequencies associated with the percentages presented in the table indicate that in none of these cases were such "bad" respondents a majority of all the persons included in the category. They did not constitute a majority of the *mepistas*, the independents, or of any of the groups described above.

In summary, the issue of respondent bias was dealt with effectively, considering the dearth of comparable instruments. We realized that the loss of information resulting from the deletion of the 276 interviews far outweighed the limited amount of distortion created by their inclusion. Two related decisions were made: one involved the rejection of any treatment of the "bad" respondents as deviant. In the light of the foregoing analysis, there was not sufficient evidence to perceive them as a group, and much less as one either homogeneous or deviant. As a result, we decided not to control for respondent attitude in view of the relatively small number of individuals who would have been included in the control categories.

A Word on Supervision

We had no idea about the identity or characteristics of the population subgroups which were likely to emerge as important contributors to respondents' bias. We could make intuitive decisions about those groups we wanted the supervisors to concentrate on, but since we were promised a straight 25 per cent rate of supervision by DATOS, we felt that this measure would not be necessary. Moreover, it became apparent that the commitment and enthusiasm of the field supervisors would produce a much higher ratio of supervised interviews. The results of the summer 1973 pretest showed the following rates of supervision: checked without contact, 3.2 per cent; checked through a third party, 18.8 per cent; and checked with interviewee, 30.0 per cent. This came to a flat rate of 52 per cent of the interviews which had had some type of supervision. These percentages were extremely high by any standard, so we attempted to maintain the high level of motivation, with the expectation that the results of the supervision in the definitive study would be comparable.

We cross-tabulated type of supervision by all items included in our instrument and concentrated our attention on those involving individual background characteristics such as sex, age, region and size of community of residence, educational level, class identification, and occupation. We found that, among those groups of individuals who received greater-than-average supervision, people from Zulia and the Andean and Plains states, rural respondents, the illiterate and the poorly educated, those identifying themselves as poor or lower class, the less affluent, and people in the humblest occupations such as peasants, laborers, and peons were subject to a more intensive supervision of their interviews.

In short, we found that those groups that were above average in their proportion of "bad" respondents were almost the same as those more thoroughly supervised. In other words, those subgroups of the sample which would have required greater supervision actually experienced it *without* our intention to do so. This should not and does not constitute a source of false pride, but provides us with assurance that the data would ultimately be reliable because of the seriousness with which our survey was executed. Our analysis is predicated on this assumption, which we believe to have been amply demonstrated.

Appendix B
The Questionnaire

Explanatory Note
The following is an accurate copy of our measuring instrument. Even though some of our colleagues believed that a version in English would be more appropriate we decided to include the Spanish original since *that was the instrument* utilized. Thus, we believe that those who might want to take a look at our questions will find the materials of this appendix useful.

Some words of caution are in order. First, we have included the response frequency of each item. These appear in parentheses immediately following the category to which they apply. In the case of a series of items with the same categories (items 20 through 23, 38 through 43, 64 through 66, 104 and 106) we have presented the item frequencies in tabular form without parentheses. Second, in some cases, notably in items 81 and 82, the format has been changed slightly to reflect drastic coding changes, but the wording of the item has been left intact. Third, there are two items which are out of sequence in our data file. The first is item 58 which, due to an oversight, was not assigned a punching position (column) at the time the questionnaire was printed. The error is identified in this copy. One other case involves the filter question heading item no. 85 (head of household status). In each of these cases the data collected were not lost but simply punched in the third set of data cards, together with the scales and indices. Finally, words or phrases which are italicized in the copy were to be read with a special emphasis by the interviewer.

Appendix B

Appendix B

NOMBRE DEL ENTREVISTADOR: _____

Unidad primaria de muestreo: _____
ciudad o lugar

_____
urbanización o barrio

PRESENTACION:

Muy buenas (tardes, noches) señor (señora, señorita).
Yo pertenezco a la firma DATOS y estamos haciendo una
encuesta para saber la opinión del pueblo venezolano
sobre algunos problemas de actualidad.

¿Tendría ud. la amabilidad de responder a nuestras
preguntas?

Fecha: _____   Hora en que comenzó: _____ $\frac{PM}{AM}$

Hora en que terminó: _____ $\frac{PM}{AM}$

Nombre de la persona entrevistada: _____

Dirección: _____

Zona: _____

Estado: _____

Número de la entrevista: _____   col.1/4

Appendix B

Comencemos con su opinión sobre los gobiernos en general, sobre los gobiernos que ha tenido el país en los últimos quince años

1. Cree Ud. que esos gobiernos han hecho lo correcto, lo que había que
   hacer. . .

   1: casi siempre ? (193)   5: no quiso contestar (4)
   2: con frecuencia ? (189)   6: no sabe (83)
   3: pocas veces ? (626)
   4: casi nunca ? (426)   col.5

2. Cree Ud. que la gente que ha gobernado el país durante los últimos
   quince años son gente capacitada o cree Ud. que ha habido unos cuan-
   tos ahí que no estaban capacitados para gobernar el país?

   1: gente capacitada (880)   4: no quiso contestar (2)
   2: gente no capacitada (404) 5: no sabe (61)
   3: depende (174)   col.6

3. Diría Ud. que los gobiernos de los últimos quince años han empleado
   bien el dinero o que esos gobiernos han malgastado el dinero?

   1: empleado bien el dinero (327) 4: no quiso contestar (7)
   2: malgastado el dinero (859)   5: no sabe (109)
   3: depende (219)   col.7

4. Cree Ud. que la labor desempeñada por esos gobiernos ha sido. . .

   1: beneficiosa para Ud.? (123)   4: no quiso contestar (4)
   2: no lo ha afectado a Ud.? (1123) 5: no sabe (17)
   3: lo ha perjudicado a Ud.? (253)   col.8

5. Cree Ud. que esos gobiernos han servido los intereses de todos los
   ciudadanos o que, por el contrario, esos gobiernos han servido los
   intereses de grupos muy poderosos?

   1: de todos los ciudadanos (233) 4: no quiso contestar (4)
   2: de los dos (209)   5: no sabe (157)
   3: de grupos muy poderosos (917)   col.9

6. Diría Ud. que, en los últimos quince años, ha habido muchos sinvergüenzas en el gobierno, que no ha habido muchos, o que realmente el
   país ha sido gobernado por gente honrada?

   1: gente honrada (190)   4: no quiso contestar (5)
   2: algunos sinvergüenzas (644)   5: no sabe (88)
   3: muchos sinvergüenzas (593)   col.10

7. En resumen, esos gobiernos de los últimos quince años ha sido bene-
   ficiosos para el país o no?

   1: sí (688)   4: no quiso contestar (3)
   2: no (523)   5: no sabe (41)
   3: depende (266)   col.11

Appendix B

Pasemos ahora al tema de los partidos políticos en general. Dígame si Ud. está de acuerdo o no con lo siguiente:

8. Es bueno para el país que sea <u>siempre</u> el mismo partido el que gobierne

   1: si (339)   4: no quiso contestar (5)
   2: no (984)   5: no sabe (28)
   3: depende (165)   col.12

9. Es bueno para el país que los partidos de la oposición, <u>los partidos que no están en el gobierno</u>, critiquen las cosas malas que haga el gobierno

   1: si (1146)   4: no quiso contestar (1)
   2: no (302)   5: no sabe (26)
   3: depende (42)   col.13

10. Los partidos políticos <u>siempre</u> están controlados por un pequeño grupito que sólo se ocupa de sus intereses

    1: si (1130)   4: no quiso contestar (3)
    2: no (182)   5: no sabe (119)
    3: depende (84)   col.14

11. Los partidos políticos <u>sólo</u> se ocupan de ganar las elecciones y <u>nada más</u>

    1: si (1150)   4: no quiso contestar (2)
    2: no (314)   5: no sabe (39)
    3: depende (116)
                                                           col.15

12. Y quién manda en Venezuela?

    0: nadie, no hay autoridad (9)   5: los partidos,los polí-
    1: el Presidente,Caldera (684)   ticos (46)
    2: el Congreso (212)   6: el pueblo, los venezo-
    3: COPEI,el partido del   lanos (66)
       gobierno,los verdes (134)   7: el gobierno (123)
    4: los ricos,los capitalistas,   8: otras respuestas (110)
       los terratenientes (115)   9: no sabe (22)   col.16

13. Y hablando de partidos políticos. . .con cuál de los partidos que existen actualmente en Venezuela simpatiza Ud.?

    0: con ninguno (PASE A LA 15) (530)
    1: con Acción Democrática (339)
    2: con COPEI (408)
    3: con el MAS (96)
    4: con URD (17)
    5: con el MEP (53)
    6: con el PCV (5)
    7: con el FDP (4)
    8: con la Cruzada Cívica Nacionalista (50)
    9: otro (indique cuál):

    _____ (19)   col.17

Appendix B

14. Y es Ud. miembro de ese partido?

    1: SI (pase a la 16) (394)   2: NO (pase a la 15) (655)   col.18

15. Y ha sido Ud. alguna vez miembro de algún partido en Venezuela?

    0: No, de ninguno (477)   1: de Acción Democrática (80)
       (PASE A LA 17)   2: de COPEI   (45)
                               3: de URD   (23)
                               4: del PCV   (5)
                               5: del FDP   (2)
                               6: del FND   (2)
                               7: otro _____   (17)
                               8: de más de uno   (1)
                               9: no quiso contestar   (3)   col.19

16. Y por qué se hizo Ud. miembro de ese partido?

    1: le gusta,le gustaba (117)   5: por una oportunidad de empleo
    2: es,era el mejor (18)   o trabajo (65)
    3: doctrina, posición,   6: un familiar lo convenció (44)
       ideología del partido (130) 7: un amigo lo convenció (20)
    4: labor positiva en el   8: otras razones (49)
       gobierno del país (104)   9: no quiso contestar (1)   col.20

17. Y por qué no ha sido nunca Ud. miembro de un partido?

    1: no le gusta la política (481) 6: no ha tenido,no tiene tiem-
    2: no le interesa la polí-   po,oportunidad (66)
       tica (136)   7: por razones de su trabajo
    3: no entiende la política,   o profesión (16)
       no sabe de política (62)   8: otras razones (137)
    4: no vale la pena (46)   9: no quiso contestar (1)   col.21
    5: la política es sucia (27)

18. En total, desde que Ud. tiene edad para votar, de cuántos partidos
    ha sido Ud. miembro?

    0: de ninguno (983)   2: dos (62)
    1: uno (461)   3: tres o más (15)   col.22

19. En Venezuela se habla mucho de los _independientes_, del _voto indepen-
    diente_. Hoy en día, en la política venezolana, se considera Ud. un
    independiente, un _simpatizante_ de un partido, o una persona que no
    está interesada en la política?

                1: simpatizante   (677)
                2: independiente   (291)
                3: no interesado   (487)
                4: otro: (miem-
                   bro,militante) (62)
                5: rehusó decir   (2)
                6: no sabe   (1)   col.23

Appendix B

Pasemos ahora al tema de las elecciones, a la opinión que Ud. tiene
acerca del voto. Dígame si Ud. está de acuerdo o no con lo siguiente:

	1.SI	2.NO	3.depende	4.rehusó	5.no sabe	
20. El voto es un factor muy importante en la política	1415	82	1	1	22	col.24
21. Para que haya democracia hay que tener elecciones	1367	115	7	1	31	col.25
22. Un candidato electo se o-cupa de los problemas de la gente que lo eligió	733	662	56	-	70	col.26
23. Las elecciones obligan al gobierno a ocuparse de los problemas de la gente	1050	392	21	2	55	col.27

24. Y hablando de elecciones, cuál fue la primera vez que a Ud. le tocó
votar para Presidente en Venezuela?

1:	1947 o antes	(397)	4:	1968	(271)
2:	1958	(355)	5:	ahora en 1973	(331)
3:	1963	(161)			col.28

ENTREVISTADOR: Dependiendo del año que el entrevistado haya indicado,
------------ pregúntele:

25. Por quién votó Ud. en 1947?(Si el entrevistado titubea o dice un nombre que no aparece en la lista, léale. . .)

1:	Rómulo Gallegos	(219)	4: no votó	(18)		
2:	Rafael Caldera	(67)	5: votó nulo	(19)		
3:	Gustavo Machado	(6)	6: rehusó	(2)		
			7: no recuerda		(59)	col.29

26. Por quién votó Ud. en 1958? (Mismo procedimiento)

1:	Rómulo Betancourt	(295)	4: no votó	(46)		
2:	Rafael Caldera	(120)	5: votó nulo	(32)		
3:	Wolfang Larrazábal	(163)	6: rehusó	(23)		
			7: no recuerda		(74)	col.30

27. Por quién votó Ud. en 1963?(Mismo procedimiento)

1:	Raúl Leoni	(348)	7: no votó	(45)		
2:	Rafael Caldera	(191)	8: votó nulo	(44)		
3:	Jóvito Villalba	(68)	9: rehusó	(33)		
4:	Wolfang Larrazábal	(60)				
5:	Arturo Uslar Pietri	(67)	0: no recuerda		(56)	col.31
6:	otros	(7)				

Appendix B

28. Y por quién votó Ud. en 1968? (Mismo procedimiento)

1:	Gonzalo Barrios	(262)	7: no votó	(58)
2:	Rafael Caldera	(411)	8: votó nulo	(82)
3:	Luis Beltrán Prieto	(135)	9: rehusó	(54)
4:	Miguel Burelli Rivas	(134)		
5:	Germán Borregales	(7)	0: no recuerda	(42)
6:	Alejandro Hernández	(7)		col.32

29. Y, si la próxima elección presidencial se celebrase <u>hoy</u>, por quién votaría Ud.? (NO LEA NINGUN NOMBRE)

1:	Carlos Andrés Pérez	(354)	9: Martín García Villasmil	(1)
2:	Lorenzo Fernández	(416)	10: Germán Borregales	(12)
3:	José Vicente Rangel	(101)	11: Flor Chalbaud de Pérez	
4:	Jesús Paz Galarraga	(62)	Jiménez, Marcos Pérez	
5:	Pedro Tinoco	(8)	Jiménez	(39)
6:	Jóvito Villalba	(21)	12: no votaría	(32)
7:	Miguel Burelli Rivas	(4)	13: votaría nulo	(63)
8:	Pedro Segnini	(1)	14: rehusó decir	(123)
			15: no sabe (284)	col.33/34

30. Y cuál de los partidos que existen actualmente en Venezuela gobernaría mejor al país durante los próximos cinco años?

0:	ninguno	(167)
1:	Acción Democrática	(363)
2:	COPEI	(443)
3:	MAS	(112)
4:	MEP	(61)
5:	Nueva Fuerza	(8)
6:	Cruzada Cívica	(62)
7:	URD	(32)
8:	otro:_____	(33)
9:	no sabe	(240)	col.35

31. Supongamos que existiesen nada más que dos partidos en Venezuela, Acción Democrática y COPEI. Por cuál de los dos partidos votaría Ud.?

0: por ninguno de los dos	(224)	
1: no votaría	(23)	
2: votaría nulo	(33)	
3: por AD	(548)	
4: por COPEI	(580)	
5: rehusó decir	(43)	
6: no sabe	(70)	col.36

Appendix B

32. Y existe algún partido en Venezuela por el cual Ud. nunca votaría?

   0: no (PASE A LA 33)   (493)

      si (SONDEE:)→ Y por cuál <u>nunca</u> votaría Ud.?

   1: por AD   (212)   6: Cruzada Cívica, Pé-
   2: por COPEI   (181)   rez Jiménez   (68)
   3: AD y COPEI,ambos (37)   7: URD   (49)
   4: PCV,comunistas (347)   8: otros partidos   (58)
   5: MAS   (92)   9: por ninguno de
                                    los actuales   (21)   col.37

33. En su opinión, hoy en día, los partidos políticos venezolanos. . .

   1: juegan un papel importante en la vida nacional   (1063)
   2: no juegan un papel tan importante   (199)
   3: no tienen importancia en la vida nacional   (149)
   4: depende   (28)
   5: no quiso contestar   (6)
   6: no sabe   (76)   col.38

34. Cree Ud. que, hoy en día, en Venezuela hay. . .

   1: demasiados partidos políticos   (1453)
   2: el número necesario de partidos, o que. . . (42)
   3: no hay suficientes partidos   (9)
   4: no sabe   (15)   col.39

35. Y cuántos partidos debería haber en Venezuela?

   0: ninguno   (43)
   1: uno   (99)
   2: dos   (618)
   3: tres   (352)
   4: cuatro o más   (409)   col.40

36. Mire, y si el voto no fuera obligatorio, Ud. votaría o no?

   1: SI   (726)   4: rehusó decir (1)
   2: depende   (52)   5: no sabe   (4)
   3: NO   (729)   col.41

37. Y votaría Ud. nulo alguna vez?

   0: no (PASE A LA 38)   (1112)

      si, depende (SONDEE) → Y en qué caso votaría Ud. nulo?

   1: si no le gustasen los partidos   5: si no tuviese buena infor-
      o los candidatos (183)   mación y no supiese por
   2: si no estuviese de acuerdo con   quién votar (5)
      los partidos/candidatos (97)   6: siempre   (23)
   3: para protestar contra el   7: de acuerdo con la situa-
      gobierno/el régimen (33)   ción (43)
   4: si estuviese satisfecho con   8: no sabe explicarse (18)
      la labor del gobierno (3)   9: rehusó decir (4)   col.42

Appendix B

Pasemos ahora a hablar sobre los políticos, sobre la gente que se dedica a la política. Dígame, por favor, si Ud. está de acuerdo o no con lo siguiente:

	1:SI	2:NO	3:depende	4:rehusó	5:no sabe	
38. Los políticos siempre engañan a la gente	1234	167	56	7	56	col.43
39. Si no hubiera políticos el gobierno funcionaría mejor	860	537	17	4	102	col.44
40. Los políticos se preocupan de los problemas de la gente como Ud.	407	1013	38	2	59	col.45
41. Los políticos se preocupan por resolver los problemas del país	700	682	89	3	45	col.46
42. Los políticos hablan mucho y no hacen nada	1241	193	50	6	31	col.47
43. Los políticos desempeñan una labor de gran beneficio para la comunidad	631	759	51	3	76	col.48

Pasemos ahora a hablar de los grandes problemas nacionales, de los problemas que Ud. considera que son más importantes en Venezuela en el momento actual y en el futuro próximo, y que Ud. considera que hay que solucionar para asegurar el bienestar del país.

44. Cuáles son, en su opinión, los problemas nacionales más importantes del momento ?(primer problema mencionado)

1: costo de la vida, de la comida (571)
2: escasez de alimentos (82)
3: desempleo, falta de fuentes de trabajo (270)
4: crimen,delincuencia, falta de seguridad personal, las drogas (95)
5: educación;falta de escuelas,indisciplina (147)
6: vivienda;escasez de vivienda,alquileres (62)
7: sequía, agua (7)

8: pobreza,hambre,miseria (52)
9: infancia abandonada (34)
10: madres abandonadas, desorganización familiar (5)
11: atención medica;falta de camas, de hospitales,de medicinas (17)
12: la agricultura (43)
13: petróleo; nacionalización, precios (18)
14: otros: _____ (99)
15: no quiso contestar (10)
16: no sabe (6)

col.49/50

(segundo problema mencionado: idénticas categorías _____)   col.51/52

45. Y cuál de éstos es el problema nacional más importante? _____   col.53/54
(idénticas categorías)

Appendix B

46. Quién o quienes cree Ud. que deben tener la mayor responsabilidad en la solución de ese problema?

    0: nadie, no sabe   (53)
    1: el Presidente de la República   (190)
    2: el gobierno   (754)
    3: una agencia del gobierno   (228)
    4: el Congreso Nacional   (65)
    5: la empresa privada   (23)
    6: una persona determinada   (8)
    7: el pueblo venezolano   (28)
    8: candidatos presidenciales   (53)
    9: otras respuestas   (119)   col.55

47. Cómo evaluaría Ud. la labor del gobierno del Presidente Caldera resolviendo los problemas nacionales durante los últimos cinco años? Evaluaría Ud. esa labor como excelente, buena, regular, mala o muy mala?

    1: excelente   (188)
    2: buena   (375)
    3: regular   (685)
    4: mala   (153)   6: no quiso contestar (2)
    5: muy mala   (105)   7: no sabe   (13)   col.56

48. Cree Ud. que si un partido distinto llegase al poder, al ganar las próximas elecciones, el gobierno de ese partido haría una mejor labor que la del gobierno del Dr. Caldera resolviendo los problemas nacionales?

    1: sí   (504)
    2: depende qué partido   (485)
    3: no   (358)
    4: no quiso contestar (6)
    5: no sabe   (167)   col.57

49. Y cuál es el problema personal que más le preocupa a Ud. actualmente?

    0: ninguno   (368)
    1: el problema económico   (181)
    2: el entrevistado o alguien de su familia
       inmediata está desempleado   (335)
    3: el costo de la vida   (139)
    4: sus estudios   (91)
    5: la educación de un hijo/familiar   (93)
    6: la seguridad personal   (55)
    7: un problema personal/familiar no especificado (4)
    8: su salud/la salud de un familiar   (50)
    9: todos los demás   (205)   col.58

50. Y quién o quienes pueden ayudarlo a Ud. a resolver ese problema?

    0: nadie, no sabe   (419)   5: un candidato presidencial (41)
    1: el mismo   (101)   6: un pariente   (71)
    2: el gobierno   (584)   7: una persona determinada   (32)
    3: el Presidente   (43)   8: un empresario   (40)
    4: un nuevo gobierno (67)   9: otras respuestas   (123)   col.59

Appendix B

También queremos saber cuánta atención le ha prestado Ud. a la campaña presidencial de este año. . .

51. Ha leído Ud. cosas sobre la campaña en los periódicos y revistas?

    1: no (PASE A LA 52)   (658)

      si (SONDEE:) → Y ha leído Ud. . .

                2: un poco,   (590)
                3: bastante, o (193)
                4: mucho sobre la campaña? (80)   col.60

52. Ha escuchado Ud. algún discurso de alguno de los candidatos por la radio o la televisión?

    1: no (PASE A LA 53)   (550)

      si (SONDEE:) → Y ha escuchado Ud. . .
                2: algunos discursos, o   (699)
                3: muchos discursos?   (271)   col.61

53. Ha visto Ud. alguno de los programas que los candidatos tienen por televisión?

    1: no (PASE A LA 54)   (676)

      si (SONDEE:) → Y ha visto Ud. . .
                2: algunos de esos programas, (605)
                3: bastantes de esos programas (141)
                4: o muchos de esos programas? (99)   col.62

54. Y ha asistido Ud. a algun mitín político de los candidatos o de los partidos?

    1: no (PASE A LA 55)   (1005)

      si (SONDEE:) → Y ha asistido Ud. a los mitines de. . .
                2: un solo partido, o   (280)
                3: de varios partidos   (236)   col.63

55. Ha visto Ud. de cerca o ha conocido Ud. en persona a alguno de los candidatos?
              1: no (PASE A LA 56)   (628)

    2: Carlos Andrés Pérez (264)   6: Pedro Tinoco (2)
    3: Lorenzo Fernández   (269)   7: Jóvito Villalba (47)
    4: José Vicente Rangel (110)   8: otros_____ (58)
    5: Jesús Paz Galarraga (72)   9: varios de ellos (70)   col.64

    (SONDEE:) - Y qué impresión le produjo el candidato?
    0: ninguna (128)   2: regular (32)   4: rehusó decir (4)
    1: mala   (59)   3: buena (688)   5: no sabe   (1)   col.65

218

Appendix B

56. Ha tratado Ud. de convencer a algún familiar o amigo para que vote por su candidato o partido?

    1: no (1117)   sí (SONDEE:) Y han sido esos. . .
      (PASE A LA 57)   2: algunos parientes/amigos, o   (233)
                    3: muchos parientes/amigos?   (166)   col.66

57. Y ha habido alguien que haya tratado de convencerlo a Ud. a votar por uno de los candidatos presidenciales?

    1: no   (786)   2: sí   (731)   col.67

58. Ha hecho Ud. algún tipo de trabajo voluntario por su partido o su candidato favorito?

    1: no   (1181)   2: sí   (336)   * * *

59. Ha estado Ud. muy interesado, algo interesado o nada interesado en esta campaña presidencial?

    1: nada interesado (708)   4: rehusó decir (3)
    2: algo interesado (526)   5: no sabe   (4)
    3: muy interesado (280)   col.68

60. Cree Ud. que el resultado de esta elección presidencial es importante para el país?

    1: no   (56)   4: rehusó decir (2)
    2: sí   (1394)   5: no sabe   (33)
    3: depende (36)   col.69

61. Le importa a Ud. mucho qué partido va a ganar esta elección presidencial?

    1: no   (468)   3: rehusó decir (12)
    2: sí   (1002)   4: no sabe   (36)   col.70

62. Y cuál de las campañas de los candidatos presidenciales le ha gustado más a Ud.?

    0: ninguna   (398)   5: Pedro Tinoco   (5)
    1: Carlos Andrés Pérez (399)   6: Jóvito Villalba   (19)
    2: Lorenzo Fernández (524)   7: Miguel Burelli Rivas (5)
    3: José Vicente Rangel (94)   8: Pedro Segnini   (4)
    4: Jesús Paz Galarraga (55)   9: otros   (18)   col.71

63. Para terminar este aspecto, cree Ud. que esta campaña presidencial lo la ayudado a Ud. a escoger su candidato presidencial en esta elección?

    1: no   (871)   2: sí   (645)   col.72

* * * Due to an oversight the punching position of item 58 is out of sequence in the data file.

Appendix B

Pasemos ahora a un tópico un poco distinto. Yo tengo aquí una lista de figuras políticas venezolanas. Y yo quisiera que Ud. me dijera si siente mucha simpatía, bastante simpatía, alguna simpatía, no mucha simpatía o ninguna simpatía por estas personas. Empezamos con los cuatro Presidentes más recientes que ha tenido el país...

64. Comencemos por el actual Presidente, Dr. Rafael Caldera; cuanta simpatía siente Ud. por el Dr. Caldera: mucha, bastante, alguna, no mucha o ninguna simpatía?

	1 ninguna	2 no mucha	3 alguna	4 bastante	5 mucha	6 rehusó	7 no sabe	
Rafael Caldera	417	171	367	185	365	7	8	col.73
Raúl Leoni	378	143	415	271	291	6	11	col.74
Rómulo Betancourt	830	156	226	128	147	6	27	col.75
Marcos Pérez Jiménez	892	149	217	101	107	7	48	col.76

65. Pasemos ahora a los candidatos presidenciales de la contienda actual. Cuánta simpatía tiene Ud. por...

	1 ninguna	2 no mucha	3 alguna	4 bastante	5 mucha	6 rehusó	7 no sabe	
Carlos Andrés Pérez	781	125	228	116	249	8	14	col.77
Lorenzo Fernández	613	157	288	137	307	8	11	col.78
José Vicente Rangel	882	150	260	78	100	8	43	col.79
Jesús Paz Galarraga	1050	113	202	40	70	8	37	col. 5 (CARD 2)
Pedro Tinoco	1219	96	121	23	12	8	42	col. 6
Jóvito Villalba	1223	98	126	24	25	8	16	col. 7

66. Pudiésemos repetir la pregunta con respecto a los partidos nacionales principales. Cuánta simpatía siente Ud. por...

	1 ninguna	2 no mucha	3 alguna	4 bastante	5 mucha	6 rehusó	7 no sabe	
AD	796	112	205	121	261	12	9	col. 8
COPEI	660	142	263	125	310	11	9	col. 9
URD	1198	124	123	23	30	10	13	col.10
MEP	1134	121	157	28	49	9	22	col.11
MAS	1019	119	197	60	86	9	31	col.12
FDP	1173	95	153	36	27	10	24	col.13
CCN	1137	87	155	45	65	10	22	col.14
PCV	1244	80	115	17	25	9	21	col.15

Appendix B

ASPECTO DEMOGRAFICO:

67. (ENTREVISTADOR: Anote el sexo de la persona entrevistada:)

    1: masculino (752)   2: femenino (762)   col.16

68. Dónde nació Ud.? Venezuela: Y en qué estado nació Ud.?
Venezuela: (estados y territorios)

Estados:				
1: Anzoátegui	(70)	13: Monagas	(70)	
2: Aragua	(59)	14: Nueva Esparta	(37)	
3: Apure	(33)	15: Portuguesa	(39)	
4: Barinas	(31)	16: Sucre	(120)	
5: Bolívar	(37)	17: Táchira	(86)	
6: Carabobo	(60)	18: Trujillo	(82)	
7: Cojedes	(9)	19: Yaracuy	(44)	
8: Falcón	(85)	20: Zulia	(171)	
9: Guárico	(55)	21: Distrito Federal	(146)	
10: Lara	(102)	22: Amazonas	-	
11: Mérida	(68)	23: Delta Amacuro	(6)	
12: Miranda	(74)	24: EN EL EXTRANJERO	(36)	col.17/18

69. Qué edad tiene Ud.?

1: 18-24	(417)	6: 45-49	(121)
2: 25-29	(222)	7: 50-54	(79)
3: 30-34	(169)	8: 55-59	(74)
4: 35-39	(157)	9: 60 y más	(144)
5: 40-44	(136)		col.19

70. Es Ud. soltero, casado, divorciado o viudo?

    1: soltero (nunca se ha casado)   (436)
    2: unido y vive con compañera(o)   (173)
    3: casado y vive con cónyugue   (775)
    4: separado   (26)
    5: divorciado   (35)
    6: viudo   (76)   col.20

71. Qué tiempo hace que Ud. vive en esta casa?

    1: menos de un año   (231)
    2: entre uno y cuatro años   (401)
    3: entre cinco y nueve años   (310)
    4: diez años o más   (577)   col.21

ASPECTO CULTURAL:

72. Hasta qué grado llegó Ud. en el colegio?

    0: no fue al colegio (PASE A LA 74)   (220)

1: primaria (algo)	(398)	6: Instituto Pedagógico	(37)
2: primaria completa	(346)	7: universidad (algo)	(82)
3: secundaria (algo)	(283)	8: grado universitario	(14)
4: secundaria completa	(103)	9: otro	(-)
5: escuela técnica o comercial	(38)		col.22

Appendix B

73. Y fue Ud. a la escuela pública o a un colegio privado?

```
1: escuela pública, liceo              (1037)
2: colegio privado laico                 (60)
3: escuela pública y colegio laico       (26)
4: escuela pública y colegio religioso   (56)
5: colegios privados:laico y religioso    (8)
6: colegio religioso                     (110)
7: otro                                   (1)        col.23
```

74. Y dónde creció Ud.? Es decir, dónde vivió Ud. entre los 7 y los 18 años? Fue en una ciudad, en un pueblo del interior, en el campo o dónde?

```
1: en una ciudad                        (656)
2: en un pueblo del interior            (664)
3: en el campo, en una finca            (194)
4: otro (anote cuál) _____          (4)        col.24
```

75. Y a qué se dedicaba su papá cuando Ud. estaba creciendo? (ENTREVISTADOR: Si la persona entrevistada no conoció a su padre, marque este espacio _____ y pase a la pregunta 80)

```
1: propietarios, gerentes, directores de empresas  (24)
2: profesionales, comerciantes, detallistas       (262)
3: hacendados,ganaderos,dueños de finca o hato      (91)
4: técnicos, trabajadores por su cuenta             (33)
5: empleados,vendedores,dependientes,trabajadores
   de servicios                                    (165)
6: obreros industriales,operarios,artesanos        (179)
7: agricultores,campesinos,pescadores              (487)
8: peones,obreros no calificados,jornaleros         (76)
9: todos los demás                                  (41)        col.25
```

76. Diría Ud. que su papá estaba muy interesado, algo interesado, o nada interesado en la política?

```
1: muy interesado                       (186)
2: algo interesado                      (223)
3: nada interesado                      (715)

4: otras respuestas: ". . .no había política,
   no había partidos. . ."               (97)
5: no quiso contestar                     (-)
6: no recuerda                          (127)        col.26
```

77. Discutía él de política en la casa, o hablaba él de política con alguien de la familia o con sus amigos?

```
1: no (PASE A LA 78)                    (1014)
   sí (SONDEE:)  Discutía o hablaba él de política. . .
2: con muy poca frecuencia,             (167)
3: con bastante frecuencia, o            (89)
4: con mucha frecuencia?                 (55)        col.27
```

222

Appendix B

78. Simpatizó él o fue miembro de algún partido o movimiento político?

    1: no   (PASE A LA 79)   (835)
       sí   (SONDEE:) Cuál?
    2: Gomecista, Partido Democrático Venezolano, Medinista,
       Agrupaciones Cívicas Bolivarianas, Lopecista   (11)
    3: Acción Democrática, ORVE, PDN   (250)
    4: COPEI   (131)
    5: Partido Comunista   (3)
    6: Partido Liberal, Cipriano Castro   (3)
    7: Unión Republicana Democrática   (38)
    8: Pérez Jiménez   (24)
    9: otros   (25)   col.28

79. Y ocupó él alguna vez un cargo del gobierno?

    1: no   (PASE A LA 80)   (1128)
       sí   (SONDEE:) Y qué cargo fue ése?
    2: policía, miembro de las Fuerzas Armadas   (70)
    3: cargo municipal   (60)
    4: cargo administrativo estadual (incluye gobernador) (4)
    5: cargo electivo estadual   (5)
    6: cargo judicial (a cualquier nivel)   (13)
    7: empleo en algún ministerio   (55)
    8: todos los demás   (13)
    9: no recuerda   (3)   col.29

ASPECTO RELIGIOSO:

80. Cuál es su religión?   ninguna (SONDEE:)   (59)

    Católicos, protestan-   81. Diría Ud. que es ateo o que, sim-
    tes, etc. . .   plemente, la religión no le interesa?

81. Con qué frecuencia a-   1: ateo   (8)
    siste Ud. a las cere-   2: no le interesa   (51)   col.30/31
    monias de su religión?

    3: católico devoto (diariamente, varias veces por semana) (23)
    4: católico práctico (los domingos, varias veces al mes) (516)
    5: católico nominal (una vez al mes o menos)   (882)
    6: protestante devoto(diariamente, varias veces por semana) (8)
    7: protestante práctico (una vez por semana, varias al mes)(14)
    8: protestante nominal (una vez al mes o menos)   (8)
    9: religioso, otro   (7)   col.30/31

82. Diría Ud. que la religión es. . .

    1: algo de muy poca importancia,   (206)
    2: algo importante, o   (807)
    3: algo indispensable en la vida?   (501)   col.32

Appendix B

ASPECTO SOCIOECONOMICO:

83. Hoy en día se habla y se escribe mucho sobre las clases sociales,
a qué clase social pertenece Ud.?

1: clase alta	(16)	5: clase pobre, humilde	(374)	
2: clase media	(871)	6: otras respuestas	(35)	
3: clase obrera, clase				
trabajadora	(61)	7: rehusó decir	(4)	
4: clase baja	(94)	8: no sabe	(62)	col.33

84. En esta tarjeta aparecen anotadas unas cuantas cantidades que co-
rresponden a la entrada mensual que una persona puede percibir en
Venezuela. (ENTREVISTADOR: Déle a la persona entrevistada la tarjeta No. 1. Si la persona no sabe leer, léale las cantidades y
marque aquí _____).
Podría Ud. decirme la letra de la cantidad aproximada que el Jefe
de Familia recibe como entrada mensual?

A.	menos de 100 bolívares al mes	1:	(125)
B.	de 100 a 500 bolívares al mes	2:	(464)
C.	de 500 a 1,000 bolívares al mes	3:	(399)
D.	de 1,000 a 2,000 bolívares al mes	4:	(281)
E.	de 2,000 a 3,000 bolívares al mes	5:	(103)
F.	de 3,000 a 4,000 bolívares al mes	6:	(40)
G.	de 4,000 a 5,000 bolívares al mes	7:	(22)
H.	más de 5,000 bolívares al mes	8:	(25)
	rehusó decir	9:	(60) col.34

85. Es Ud. el jefe de esta familia? Es decir, es Ud.la persona que
mantiene económicamente a la familia?
1: si (614)   2: no (907)   * * *
Y a qué se dedica Ud.?   A qué se dedica esa persona?

1: directores,propietarios,mayoristas,almacenistas,contratistas,
   gerentes y administradores de grandes empresas no agrícolas (28)
2: rentistas,apoderados,pequeños comerciantes,detallistas (145)
3: profesionales,profesores universitarios,oficiales de alta graduación,pilotos,publicitarios (75)
4: hacendados,ganaderos,avicultores,empresarios agrícolas (35)
5: maestros,periodistas,enfermeros,trabajadores sociales,comisio-
   nistas,agentes viajeros,concesionarios (96)
6: técnicos:peritos,laboratoristas,agrimensores,dibujantes (59)
7: trabajadores por su cuenta (no agrícolas), chofer por puesto (19)
8: empleados de oficina (153)
9: obreros calificados,capataces,caporales (40)
10: dependientes de comercio y trabajadores de servicio (265)
11: artesanos,operadores, maquinistas (234)
12: trabajadores del servicio doméstico (51)
13: agricultores,trabajadores agrícolas,campesinos (107)
14: obreros no calificados,peones,jornaleros (107)
15: ama de casa (10)
16: militar (enlistado,baja graduación),policía (19)
17: retirado (34)
18: todos los demás (6)
19: no bien especificados (37)   col.35/36

* * * Punched out of sequence

Appendix B

86. Y está Ud. trabajando
    en la actualidad?

86. Y esa persona está trabajando
    en la actualidad?

    1: si (PASE A LA 87) (1331)
    no (SONDEE:) Y está Ud./esa
    persona buscando trabajo?
    2: si (PASE A LA 88) (108)
    3: no (PASE A LA 89) (80)   col.37

87. Y trabaja Ud. por su
    cuenta o para alguien?

87. Y esa persona trabaja por su
    cuenta o para alguien?

    1: por su cuenta   (499)
    2: ambas cosas   (28)
    3: para alguien   (818)   col.38

88. Y está Ud. satisfecho
    con su trabajo?

88. Y esa persona está satisfecha
    con su trabajo?

    1: si   (1078)
    2: no   (248)
    3: rehusó decir   (4)
    4: no sabe   (22)   col.39

89. Cree Ud. que, durante este último gobierno del Dr. Caldera, la si-
    tuación económica de su familia. . .

    1: ha mejorado   (269)
    2: se ha mantenido igual(742), o
    3: ha empeorado?   (505)
    4: no sabe   (5)   col.40

90. Y cree Ud. que la situación económica de su familia va a mejorar
    durante el próximo gobierno?

    1: no (PASE A LA 91) (331)
    si, depende (SONDEE:)
    Mejoraría porque el partido que gobierna
    gobernaría aún mejor o porque un partido
    distinto gobernaría mejor?

    2: mismo partido   (416)
    3: distinto partido (586)
    4: depende   (18)
    5: cualquiera,da igual (19)
    6: rehusó decir   (3)
    7: no sabe   (141)   col.41

Appendix B

91. Pasemos ahora a hablar de la gente como Ud.,del tipo de gente con
    la que Ud. se siente bien. Yo tengo aquí una lista de algunos gru-
    pos de personas (ENTREVISTADOR: Déle al entrevistado la tarjeta
    No. 2.Si la persona no sabe leer, léale Ud. los grupos y marque
    este espacio_____).

    Yo quisiera que Ud. me dijese a cuál de estos grupos pertenece Ud.
    Cuál de éstos es, pues, su grupo?
                1: los trabajadores, los obreros   (329)
                2: los campesinos   (113)
                3: los estudiantes   (186)
                4: las amas de casa   (318)
                5: la gente de clase media   (217)
                6: la gente común y corriente   (257)
                7: los profesionales   (59)
                8: los empresarios,la gente de negocios (24)
                9: otros   (17)   col.42

92. Cuánta influencia cree Ud. que (GRUPO FAVORITO) tiene en la vida
    política venezolana? Cree Ud. que. . .
                1: mucha influencia   (414)
                2: bastante influencia   (312)
                3: poca influencia   (528)
                4: ninguna influencia   (195)
                5: no sabe   (72)   col.43

93. Cree Ud. que, en el momento actual, la influencia de (GRUPO FAVO-
    RITO) está. . .
                1: aumentando   (570)
                2: manteniéndose igual,   (503)
                3: o disminuyendo?   (373)
                4: no sabe   (75)   col.44

94. Cree Ud. que la labor del gobierno del Presidente Caldera ha sido
    beneficiosa para (GRUPO FAVORITO). . .
                1: no   (PASE A LA 95)   (735)
                   si   (SONDEE:) Y ha sido. . .
                2: algo beneficiosa,   (438)
                3: bastante beneficiosa, o   (197)
                4: muy beneficiosa?   (82)
                5: no quiso contestar   (2)
                6: no sabe   (66)   col.45

95. Y cualquier gobierno que pudiera llegar al poder respetaría los
    intereses de (GRUPO FAVORITO). . .
                1: aún más,   (499)
                2: igualmente, o   (501)
                3: menos que el actual gobierno   (104)
                4: depende   (12)
                5: no quiso contestar   (7)
                6: no sabe   (397)   col.46

Appendix B

96. Existen grupos, como los mencionados anteriormente, que están muy bien organizados y que con cierta regularidad intervienen o pueden intervenir en la vida política del país. Podría Ud. decirme cuál, de esta lista adicional de grupos, considera Ud. que es el grupo más poderoso en la vida política venezolana? (ENTREVISTADOR: Déle al entrevistado la tarjeta No.3. Marque aquí si Ud. la lee ____).
1: la Iglesia Católica (128)   6: las Fuerzas Armadas (366)
2: la C.T.V. (143)   7: las compañías petroleras (237)
3: la F.C.V. (277)   8: los estudiantes (132)
4: FEDECAMARAS (277)   9: los colegios profesionales (41)
5: FEDEAGRO (23)   0: no sabe, rehusó (114)   col.47

IDEOLOGIA:
97. Pasemos ahora a un tópico un poco distinto:al de los golpes militares. Piensa Ud. que,en general,hay ocasiones en que se justifican los golpes militares o no?
1: no   (482)   4: rehusó decir   (9)
2: depende (150)   5: no sabe   (114)
3: si   (766)   col.48

98. Recientemente el Presidente de la República de Chile,Dr.Salvador Allende,fue derrocado por un golpe militar.Está Ud. enterado de este suceso? 1: no (PASE A LA 99) (209) si (SONDEE:) Cómo evaluaría Ud. el golpe que derrocó al Presidente Allende? Cree Ud. que ésta fue una medida necesaria o innecesaria por parte de las Fuerzas Armadas chilenas?   2: necesaria (337)   5: rehusó (3)
                      3: depende (70)   6: no sabe (257)
                      4: innecesaria (645)   col.49

99. Tomando como ejemplo el caso de Venezuela,en noviembre de 1948 fue derrocado el Presidente Rómulo Gallegos, de Acción Democrática,por un golpe militar.Recuerda o conoce Ud.este suceso? 1: no (715) si (SONDEE:) Cree Ud. que ese golpe militar. . .   (PASE A LA 100)
2: estuvo justificado   (116)
3: depende   (30)   5: rehusó decir   (4)
4: no estuvo justificado (457)   6: no sabe   (196)   col.50

100. Y qué piensa Ud. del golpe militar del 23 de Enero de 1958 que derrocó al General Pérez Jiménez? Cree Ud. que ese golpe fue necesario?
1: si (299)   3: no (285)   5: no sabe (237)
2: depende (64)   4: rehusó (5)   col.51

101. Para terminar este aspecto dígame,por favor,cuál de las siguientes frases expresa mejor su pensamiento acerca del papel que deben jugar las Fuerzas Armadas en la vida nacional. Es decir,con cuál de estas frases está Ud.más de acuerdo? (ENTREVISTADOR: Déle la tarjeta No. 4). Las Fuerzas Armadas. . .
1: siempre deben respetar al gobierno constitucional   (466)
2: deben actuar en política solamente cuando piensen que
   no se está cumpliendo la constitución   (280)
3: deben respaldar la voluntad popular cuando el régimen
   no corresponda a las aspiraciones del pueblo   (532)
4: deben intervenir en política siempre que lo juzguen necesario (180)
5: no quiso contestar   (6)
6: no sabe   (49)   col.52

227

Appendix B

102. Como ya estamos llegando al final quiero preguntarle algo. Por ahí
se habla mucho sobre los sistemas económicos. Se habla del capitalismo, del socialismo y del comunismo. Cuál de estos sistemas e-
conómicos le gusta más a Ud.?   0: ninguno   (455)
1: capitalismo   (324)   4: rehusó   (17)
2: socialismo   (615)   5: no sabe   (82)
3: comunismo   (28)   col.53

103. Se habla también, en el terreno político,de que fulano o mengano
están a la derecha, al centro, o a la izquierda en la vida política
venezolana. Dónde está Ud. en la vida política venezolana. . .
1: a la izquierda,   (312)   4: rehusó decir (3)
2: al centro, o   (334)   5: no sabe   (165)
3: a la derecha?   (465)   0: ninguna parte (242)   col.54

104. Y, en la vida política venezolana, dónde están algunos de los candidatos presidenciales? Dónde está, por ejemplo, Carlos Andrés Pérez: a la izquierda, al centro o a la derecha? (ENTREVISTADOR: marque el espacio que convenga)

	0 nin- guna	1 iz- quierda	2 centro	3 de- recha	4 rehusó	5 no sabe	
Carlos Andrés Pérez	15	318	197	683	14	294	col.55
Lorenzo Fernández	11	196	176	864	12	262	col.56
José Vicente Rangel	16	937	110	92	14	352	col.57
Jesús Paz Galarraga	24	878	104	81	14	420	col.58
Pedro Tinoco	27	417	206	349	15	507	col.59
Jóvito Villalba	91	474	242	243	17	454	col.60
Miguel Burelli	64	424	249	277	17	490	col.61
Pérez Jiménez	77	406	277	288	14	459	col.62

105. Hace un rato hablamos de los problemas nacionales. Dichos problemas se refieren a tres grandes grupos de políticas que puede se-
guir el gobierno. Dichas políticas son: acelerar el desarrollo e-
conómico, mantener la democracia y redistribuir la riqueza. Sí Ud.
fuera Presidente de la República, a cuál de éstas tres políticas
le daría Ud. mayor importancia?
1: acelerar el desarrollo   (879)
2: mantener la democracia   (217)   4: rehusó decir (6)
3: redistribuir riqueza   (341)   5: no sabe   (75)   col.63

106. Para que la economía venezolana pueda avanzar con rapidez en los
próximos años quizás se necesiten hacer algunos sacrificios. De
la siguiente lista que yo le voy a leer, dígame por favor, cuáles
sacrificios deben exígersele a Ud. y cuáles no.

	1 sí	2 no	3 rehusó	4 no sabe	
A: Renunciar a aumentos de salarios o ingresos	330	1121	13	57	col.64
B: pagar más impuestos	268	1197	18	36	col.65
C: destinar una parte de su salario a plan de ahorro	1246	226	11	38	col.66
D: gastar menos dinero en diversiones y lujo	1256	227	11	27	col.67

Appendix B

CONFIANZA EN LOS DEMAS:
107. Por regla general, cree Ud. que se puede confiar en la gente o
que hay que andar por ahí con el ojo pelado?
1: se puede confiar (93)
2: hay que pelar el ojo (1381)   4: rehusó decir (3)
3: depende (42)   5: no sabe   (1)   col.68

108. Diría Ud. que la mayoría de las veces,la gente trata de ayudarlo
a uno o que, por regla general,cada uno anda en lo suyo y nada más?
1: tratan de ayudar   (159)
2: cada uno en lo suyo (1252)   4: rehusó decir (1)
3: depende   (97)   5: no sabe   (12)   col.69

109. Diría Ud. que si uno se descuida la gente se aprovecha de uno o
que los demás tratan de ser honestos con uno?
1: se aprovechan   (1284)
2: tratan de ser honestos (95)   4: rehusó decir (2)
3: depende   (124)   5: no sabe   (15)   col.70

EFICACIA POLITICA:
110. Cree Ud. que la gente del gobierno se preocupa de lo que piensa
la gente como Ud. o no?
1: sí se preocupan   (307)   3: rehusó decir (2)
2: no se preocupan   (1118)   4: no sabe   (93)   col.71

111. Cree Ud. que la gente como Ud. tiene poder para influenciar lo
que hace el gobierno o no?
1: sí tiene   (414)   3: rehusó decir (5)
2: no tiene   (1002)   4: no sabe   (99)   col.72

112. Cree Ud. que a veces la política es tan complicada que la gente
como Ud. no sabe lo que está pasando?
1: sí lo cree   (1070)   3: rehusó decir (-)
2: no lo cree   (396)   4: no sabe   (55)   col.73

113. Cree Ud. que votando es de la única manera que Ud. puede influenciar lo que hace el gobierno?
1: sí, es la única   (984)   3: rehusó decir (7)
2: no, no es la única (453)   4: no sabe   (77)   col.74

- ESTO COMPLETA NUESTRA ENTREVISTA

- MUCHISIMAS GRACIAS

Appendix B

PAGINA DEL SUPERVISOR

Perfil de la persona entrevistada:

Clase social:	1:	A,B	(49)	
	2:	C	(329)	
	3:	D	(654)	
	4:	E	(488)	col.75

Sexo:	1:	hombre	(752)	
	2:	mujer	(759)	col.76

Grupo de edad:	1:	18-24	(416)	
	2:	25-34	(383)	
	3:	35-44	(303)	
	4:	45-54	(198)	
	5:	55-64	(131)	
	6:	65 +	(89)	col.77

Comentarios del entrevistador:

	0:	ninguno	(60)	
	1:	persona recelosa y/o poco interesada	(276)	
	2:	persona contestó y colaboró bien	(1185)	col.78

Chequeo de la entrevista:

	0:	ninguno	(667)	
	1:	intentado,sin contacto	(133)	
	2:	a través de una tercera persona	(140)	
	3:	con la persona entrevistada	(366)	
	4:	durante la entrevista	(214)	col.79

CONSTANCIA

Hago constar que la presente entrevista fue hecha personalmente en la dirección y con la persona indicada en la clasificación. Las anotaciones en el cuestionario son una transcripción fiel de las respuestas de la persona entrevistada. Las preguntas fueron hechas según las especificaciones dadas por el supervisor del estudio.

_____   _____
FIRMA DEL ENCUESTADOR   FIRMA DEL SUPERVISOR

230

Appendix C
Estimation of Social Class Status

We followed the approach utilized by DATOS, which conforms to standard usage in market research, for two basic reasons: first, it is a fairly complete criterion, incorporating many different aspects which may be "objectively" appraised by individuals familiar with Venezuelan culture and society. We find Butler and Stokes (1971: chapter 4) utilizing a modified market research criterion in their own study *combined* with class self-images. We also utilized this combination in this study. Second, given the debate about the specific parameters of social class in Latin America, and given the lack of more satisfactory criteria, this approach represented a viable solution to the problem of "objective" measures of social class. The following paragraphs are translated and abridged from an internal document of DATOS, which is part of their training protocol, and was the document consulted by our interviewers to estimate the social class of their respondents in the fulfillment of their quotas. (Italics are those of the original text.)

> In countries of retarded development, *the income of the head of household* may be utilized as the main indicator (of social class) . . . although in the case of Caracas, with a more rapidly changing society . . . this is insufficient. . . . There are other elements that may indicate social class and must be taken into consideration, especially when the person is interviewed at home. . . . How articulate is the person? . . . What model and year of car does he or she own? . . . What is the look of the dwelling? . . . What kind of furniture is there? Are there any curtains in the house? What is the condition of the walls? These factors are less significant than occupation and place of residence but they may help you decide a borderline case . . .
>
> The importance of the *occupation* lies, within certain limits, in the salary received by the person. The importance of the *place of residence* depends on rent, which may vary enormously. . . . Let us examine the question of occupation in greater detail, in terms of the occupations which are typical of each class:

Appendix C

Class A. The very rich. These are persons of great professional success—lawyers, physicians, architects, etc., in industry, commerce, and the construction industry. They are managers and proprietors of large enterprises and first-rate technicians, high government officials, and officers of the Armed Forces. Also in this group are the successful speculators and the rentiers. We find them in great *quintas* (villas) in places like Country Club, Altamira, Los Chorros, El Paraíso, and other suburban areas. They have domestic servants; luxury cars, probably three or more; luxurious furniture; their rent is above Bs. 1,500 in cases where they do not own the dwelling.

Class B. These are people in a good position, secure, and very affluent, but they lack the grandiose success of their class A counterparts. They include those managers, proprietors, and technicians who are second-rate and the government and armed forces officials of somewhat less importance. Included here are many people in banking, insurance, finance, and the smaller rentiers. They can be distinguished from class A because they may own luxurious vehicles but only one, and the others are used or less expensive. They live in smaller and less expensive quintas, or in high-rise apartments in the aforementioned areas plus the following: San Bernardino, Las Acacias, Los Palos Grandes, etc. They have house servants but not as many, their furniture is also very good but less luxurious, and their rents are smaller.

Class C. The middle class, with some luxury, and affluent. These are dependent people, but they enjoy some responsibility. These are the managers of small enterprises, small merchants, employees of the large firms, salaried workers in government, industry, and commerce. Always with limited initiative, who are not leaders of their craft. They live in small quintas, or in apartments where we also find class B and class D. They may have one servant. Often they own a car, appliances; their furniture is not luxurious; they may be able to afford rents as high as Bs. 1,000 because more than one person in the family has income. They dwell in new as well as old sections of towns such as San José, San Juan, Santa Rosalía, Vista Alegre, Los Caobos, Bello Monte, Bello Campo, etc.

Class D. The working class. They may be distinguished from class C in that their responsibilities are very limited. If, for example, the person is a mason, he will be less skilled; if an employee in a department store, the salary will be smaller. If employed in an office, it will be as a messenger or office boy; if in the construction industry, he will be employed as a laborer but not as an electrician nor as a skilled worker of any sort. These are the street vendors, sanitation workers, factory operatives, etc. They live in government housing (Banco Obrero), small homes in the *cerros* (*barriadas*), or in *ranchos* (makeshift). We find them in homes in El Manicomio, in *ranchos* throughout the inner city, if a single male in the *pensión*. They are also the servants of class A.

Class E. The poor. The distinction between class D and class E is the most difficult to make. Class D types normally have employment; class E, due to instability, old age, illness, or other factors have no security whatsoever. If employed they can be found as messengers, janitors, street vendors. Normally, they are beggars.

In closing, it should be stressed that this approach utilized by DATOS incorporates two factors that have long been recognized as blurring the systems of stratification in Latin America. One is that class is a consequence of the relationship to the means of production as it is, as a result, of the relationship to the articles of consumption. Thus the indication of differences between the patterns of consumption of class A and class B.

Incidentally, we had to lump these two classes together in order to facilitate statistical manipulation due to their relative smallness. It should also be mentioned that the connotation of "working class" attached to the operational definition of class D goes beyond the distinction of blue versus white collar. There are blue-collar types in class C, yet the important point is that a class D person does undesirable work. The second point worth mentioning is related to the problem of ecological fallacies embedded in stratification techniques. For instance, DATOS has subdivided every major Venezuelan city, and a section of the city may be selected at random. Yet they had the personnel capable of selecting the more desirable sampling point from that, still large, area. On the other hand, the greater mixture of different neighborhood and dwelling types that is typical of the Venezuelan cities—as it is of the rest of Latin America—makes it more difficult to select typical neighborhoods, so it is necessary to go to more subtle and finer discriminations.

Appendix D
Note on the Use of Regression Analysis

Having what amounts to a nonexpert familiarity with regression and path-analytic techniques, we have confined these to model-building attempts which involved four or more variables and could not be approached with other, equally powerful, multivariate techniques. In other words, we have avoided regression as much as possible but have not hesitated to use it when necessary. We are aware that, among others, McKelvey and Zavonia have shown that the assumptions of normally distributed error term with constant variance and zero mean are not met by categorical data.[1] They offer the alternative of *probit analysis* which rests on less demanding assumptions. Even though we have not followed their recommendation, we refrain from treating any of our models as BLUE (best, linear, unbiased) estimators.

Verba and Nie were faced with a similar situation and they defended their usage of regression analysis in a very extended note.[2] The contention is that, if the data meet ordinal assumptions, and all of our variables do, and if some of the variables are indices and scales, very frequently the case in our own study, then regression analysis produces fairly reliable results.

Finally, our utilization of regression analysis is based on the SPSS version of the stepwise multiple regression technique,[3] and informed and guided by the discussions of Duncan,[4] Kim and Kohout,[5] and Van de Geer[6] on path-analytic techniques.

Appendix E
Note on Inference Making
from Multiple-Range
(one-way analysis of variance) Tests

Multiple range comparisons test a group of means in order to determine how many different clusters of means can be formed on the basis of real differences between them. Normally, considerable caution is exercised concerning the status of means that fall into more than one homogeneous set. Usually very little is said about them. Notice the language of Li talking about Duncan's (new) multiple range test showing one treatment mean (B) that lies in the intersection of two different homogeneous sets (A and C): "The position of B is *not clearly* determined. It may belong to the same group as A or the same group as . . . C. Indeed it *may be a group by itself*. Only further experimental evidence, that is, an increased n, will clarify the situation. . . ."[1] The redoubtable Snedecor offers very little help on this point.[2]

The basic problem here is, at least in our experience, that overlapping of treatment means is a very common result of this test. Not only that, but it may involve more than two sets. Following a purely statistical criterion, one would be confined to making inferences about nonoverlapping means, which may be but two out of six or seven being compared.

Following set theory we have treated intersections created by one or more homogeneous sets of means as separate subsets in their own right. In short, we consider means in these intersections to be different. One could formulate a corollary of Mill's "Canon of Agreement" (if two or more instances of the phenomenon under investigation have only one circumstance in common, the circumstance alone in which all the instances agree is the cause [or effect] of the given phenomenon), to the extent that "if a set of objects (homogeneous sets of means) is different from another set, but the two have one area in common (intersection), the objects (means) located in that area (sharing the property unique to the area) are, by definition, different from the objects in each of the original sets."

Appendix F
Scales and Indices

Guttman scales:
1. Criticism of the policies of the democratic regimes: negative responses to items 7, 3, 5, 6 (c.r. = .90) (c.s. = .67)
2. Criticism of the institution of elections: nonsupportive responses to items 20, 21, 23, 22 (c.r. = .94) (c.s. = .73)
3. Criticism of politicians: responses other than favorable to items 41, 43, 40, 42 (c.r. = .89) (c.s. = .70)
4. Individual involvement in the 1973 campaign: nonparticipatory responses to items 56, 59, 58, 54 (c.r. = .92) (c.s. = .60)
5. Individual exposure to the 1973 campaign: moderate or high levels of exposure as measured by items 51, 53, 52 (c.r. = .93) (c.s. = .78)
6. Perceived efficacy of the 1973 campaign: favorable responses to items 63, 61, 62, 60 (c.r. = .90) (c.s. = .64)
7. Evaluation of the Caldera administration: favorable responses to items 94, 89, 64, 8 (c.r. = .91) (c.s. = .65)

Note: The items included in each scale are listed in the order in which they were scaled. The magnitudes of the coefficient of reproducibility (c.r.), measuring cumulativeness, and the coefficient of scalability (c.s.), measuring dimensionality, are identified for each scale.

Indices derived by standardization:
1. Index of socioeconomic status: items 72, 84, 85.
2. Index of satisfaction with the policies of the Caldera administration: items 8, 89, 94.
3. Index of political capacity: items 92, 93, 111, 113.

Note: All of these indices are four-point (1, 4) scales, which were derived from the linear combinations of the standardized (Z) scores of the items.

Categorical scales:
1. Stratification: based on the index of socioeconomic status and the indicator of class status described in appendix C.

2. Ideological position, ideological tendency: see the discussion in chapter 5.

3. Political mood: based on the combination of the index of political capacity and the scale of criticism of the policies of the regime.

4. Political agility: total number of "do not know" responses to the attitudinal and/or political information items, divided by 92 × 100. The resulting scores were transformed into dichotomous measurement reflecting whether the individual was below or above the sample mean of nonresponses.

5. Overall attitude about military coups: a cumulative scale involving more than one dimension, including items 99, 101, 98, 97 (c.r. = .90) (c.s. = .47)

Appendix G
Note on the Use
of Multidimensional Scaling

Even though multidimensional scaling (MDSCAL) is a relatively new technique in political science, we utilized the technique to develop the configuration presented in figure 13. Two reasons dictated that usage. First, we had considerable expertise at hand, in the person of our colleague, George Rabinowitz, as well as the staffs of the Institute for Research in Social Science and the Thurstone Psychometric Laboratory, both at UNC. Thus, we had the opportunity to apply a sophisticated technique oriented by expert advice. Secondly, the fact that a particular technique may not be very familiar to a wide audience is really no reason to abstain from its utilization. On the contrary, if the technique is germane to the problem at hand, its novelty should not represent an obstacle.

The procedure utilized to generate the configuration of figure 13 involves a nonmetric multidimensional scaling analysis of a line-of-sight correlation matrix. Raw data for the exercise came from the responses to the thermometer items concerning former presidents (item 64), the more relevant presidential candidates in the 1973 race (item 65), and the national political parties (item 66). We had a set of 1,342 complete responses to these three items. The thermometer scores were transformed into a measure more analogous to perceived interobject distance. An algorithm developed by Rabinowitz was utilized for this purpose.[1]

The iterative method utilized by the algorithm has the following steps:

1 for each pair of objects, sort *differences* from largest to smallest, and *sums* from smallest to largest;
2 for each pair, the single smallest sum and the single largest difference are added;
3 pairs are ranked on the basis of the values obtained; values and rankings are saved;
4 for each pair, the next smallest sum is added to the next largest difference; the resulting value is added to the previous value obtained for each pair;
5 pairs are ranked again; the new values and ranks are saved;

238

6 beginning in the third iteration, it is possible to compute the values of four different functions for each additional iteration:

   1 the value of Spearman's *rho* correlation between the current and last set of rankings obtained; after the first few iterations this value should stay close to 1;

   2 the value of *DISCRIM*, the total number of distinct ranking positions obtained, divided by the total number of pairs; our limited experience with this routine suggests that DISCRIM will jump to a value above .50 after the first few iterations, and increase in value depending on number of objects and their relative similarity;

   3 the value of *DENSE*, which is simply the ratio of the sample size minus the number of observations currently used per pair, divided by sample size minus one; unless something is terribly wrong, this value should stay very close to 1.0;

   4 and the value of *ADEQU* which is the product of the values of the preceding three, seems to be most sensitive to the fluctuations in the value of DISCRIM. ADEQU is the test statistic utilized as criterion by the algorithm in order to stop the iterative procedure. ADEQU measures the adequacy of the solution.

7 if the value of ADEQU is greater than any previous ADEQU obtained, both the raw values (distance or similarity values between objects, obtained in the manner described in 1 through 5, above) matrix and the rank matrix are saved. These matrices are the raw data for the next step. In reality, only the raw values matrix is necessary.

In our case, the algorithm terminated after 78 iterations. The magnitudes of the four functions (rho, DISCRIM, DENSE, and ADEQU) were .99, .74, .94, and .70, respectively, at that point. The *dissimilarity* matrix of raw values had 153 elements (our 18 objects × 17 ÷ 2), with a range from a minimum of 1.08 (for the pair of COPEI and its presidential candidate, Lorenzo Fernández, the most similar pair) to a maximum of 3.69 (for the most dissimilar pair including leftist MEP and rightist CCN). Inspection of the dissimilarity values for the elements of the matrix suggested that, in general, those pairs of objects that we expected to be far apart had been assigned high values, while those whom anyone familiar with Venezuelan politics could expect to be close together, had been assigned low values in the matrix. It should be remembered that the whole purpose of the iterative process is to have the distance between pairs decrease monotonically as pairs are perceived to be more similar.

One assumption of the line-of-sight technique is that individuals will be able to perceive some contrast, some distance between the

Appendix G

Table G-1. Stress Values for Different Dimensionalities

---

a. Fixed Start with Four Dimensions

iterations	dimensions	Stress (II)
40	4	.155
19	3	.280
19	2	.455
16	1	.630

b. Random Starts, First Series

iterations	dimensions	Stress (II)
50	3	.232*
25	2	.434
16	1	.587

c. Random Starts, Second Series

iterations	dimensions	Stress (II)
36	3	.247
30	2	.384
16	1	.674

---

*Selected as optimal

objects. The fact that we included parties and their candidates in the exercise made the assumption more tenable. The next step of the procedure compares the line-of-sight values of our dissimilarity matrix with a set of *target* values (also called *disparities* or *target distances* in the literature). Pairs (or points) are moved around on a (Shepard) graph: if actual distance for a pair is greater than the target value, the points will be moved closer together; if the points are closer than they should be, they will be moved farther apart. Target values can be calculated in two different ways and neither seems to make much difference, according to Rabinowitz.[2] The important point is that one is trying to "fit" the distances to the target values. The graph utilized in the scaling process is always two-dimensional. The (POLYCON) program utilized plotted our dissimilarity values on the Y axis, while it assigned the X axis to the actual (d) and estimated ($\hat{d}$) distances, that is, the actual and anticipated values of the scaling space.

Criteria are needed to determine when to stop moving the points around (that is, rearranging the elements of the matrix) and how to decide on the optimal dimensionality. Following the monotonicity requirement, the analyst seeks an optimal configuration for a desired dimensionality. A natural measure of how close a solution is to satisfying monotonicity would be the average or mean squared differences between the actual and the target distances. This test statistic is called *Stress*, which is a measure of "badness of fit" and has a range of zero to one.[3] Several computational formulas are available; the one utilized here (Stress II) would place the magnitude of the value found for our three-dimensional solution (Stress = .23) in a range of "fair." Whether on sound theoretical bases or intuitive grounds, the analyst is free to anticipate a preferred dimensionality. In our case we believed that three dimensions would best represent Venezuelan political space but, following the advice of Rabinowitz, attempted several different approaches including random starts and a four-dimensional start. The results of these checks on the optimal dimensionality are presented in table G-1. Even though the lowest value of Stress was obtained for the four-dimensional solution (at .16) we felt more comfortable with three dimensions.

Table G-2. Input Points for the Three-dimensional Solution

Point #	X	Y	Z
1 Rafael Caldera	.125	.033	−.093
2 Raúl Leoni	.068	.249	−.080
3 Rómulo Betancourt	.210	.896	−.386
4 Marcos Pérez Jiménez	.787	.024	−.207
5 Carlos Andrés Pérez	.147	.842	−.103
6 Lorenzo Fernández	.257	−.177	−.079
7 José Vicente Rangel	−.320	−.105	−.866
8 Jesús Paz Galarraga	−.959	.176	−.345
9 Pedro Tinoco	.072	−.885	.965
10 Jóvito Villalba	.141	.361	1.296
11 Acción Democrática	.134	.771	−.058
12 COPEI	.270	−.193	−.074
13 URD	.011	.065	1.303
14 MEP	−1.150	.131	−.178
15 MAS	−.384	−.090	−1.021
16 FDP	.479	−1.261	.037
17 Cruzada Cívica	1.154	−.023	−.024
18 PCV	−1.041	−.815	−.086

Appendix G

The POLYCON-derived three-dimensional solution produced the data for the third and final step in the process. The matrix of 18 rows and 3 columns (presented in table G-2) indicating the locations of the 18 objects in the three-dimensional space was subject to the final manipulation, that is, the plotting of planar projections of a three-dimensional block model. This program produced the final configuration which served as a basis for figure 13. The only difference between the Calcomp plotter diagram produced by the blocks program and figure 13 stems from the fact that the poles of the left-right dimension were reversed on the former, which would have undoubtedly produced considerable confusion if presented in that form. The regular perspective for that Calcomp plotter diagram set the focal point and the eye point at −10, 10, and 4.

Notes to Chapter 1

Political Attitudes in Venezuela: Problems and Prospects

1 Our usage of the terms "sociologism" and "critical Marxism" is borrowed from José Nun's brilliant essay, "Notes on Political Science and Latin America," in Manuel Diegues and Bryce Wood (eds.), *Social Science in Latin America: Papers* (New York: Columbia University Press, 1967), pp. 67–120.

2 Probably the best description is Celso Furtado's *Economic Development of Latin America: A Survey from Colonial Times to the Cuban Revolution* (Cambridge: Cambridge University Press, 1970).

3 See Fernando Henrique Cardoso and Enso Faletto, *Dependencia y desarrollo en América Latina* (México: Ediciones Siglo XXI, 1969), and Theotonio dos Santos, *La crisis del desarrollismo y la nueva dependencia* (Lima: Moncloa, 1969).

4 See the lead article by Ronald H. Chilcote, "Dependency: A Critical Synthesis of the Literature," in *Latin American Perspectives*, 1, 1 (Spring 1974): 4–29, and the rest of the articles in that issue. See also Susan J. Bodenheimer, "Dependency and Imperialism: The Roots of Latin American Underdevelopment," *Politics and Society*, 1, 3 (May 1971): 327–57, for an early statement by a North American scholar following this orientation.

5 One of the best recent assessments is Cardoso's "The Consumption of Dependency Theory in the United States," *Latin American Research Review*, 12, 3 (1977): 7–25.

6 See Glen C. Dealy, "Prolegomena on the Spanish American Political Tradition," *Hispanic American Historical Review*, 48, 1 (February 1968): 37–58.

7 See Howard J. Wiarda, "Corporatism and Development in the Iberic-Latin World: Persistent Strains and New Variations," *Review of Politics*, 36, 1 (January 1974): 3–33. A similar point of view has been expressed by Jacques Lambert, *Latin America: Social Structure and Political Institutions*, translated by Helen Katel (Berkeley and Los Angeles: University of California Press, 1969), pp. 52–58, and chapter 5, pp. 98–105.

8 Glen C. Dealy, "The Tradition of Monistic Democracy in Latin America," *Journal of the History of Ideas*, 35, 4 (October–December 1974): 625–46.
9 Howard J. Wiarda, "Toward a Framework for the Study of Political Change in the Iberic-Latin Tradition: The Corporative Model," *World Politics*, 25, 1 (January 1973): 206–35.
10 Such is the argument of Ronald C. Newton, "Natural Corporatism and the Passing of Populism in Spanish America," *Review of Politics*, 36, 1 (January 1974): 34–51.
11 With respect to corporatism, Philippe C. Schmitter has argued that it is preferable to divorce the concept of corporatism from ideological, cultural, or authoritarian connotations, on the grounds that corporatism is "an observable general system of representation which is 'compatible' with several different regime-types." See his "Still the Century of Corporatism?" *Review of Politics*, 36, 1 (January 1974): p. 92. In short, the type of overlap between authoritarianism, monism, and corporatism which is considered to be typical of Latin America by these authors should be made more specific.
12 This is a crucial point which must be clarified. A group of historians have tried to address themselves to this question, with their observations recorded in the following articles: Woodrow Borah, "Colonial Institutions and Contemporary Latin America: A. Political and Economic Life"; Charles Gibson, "B. Social and Cultural Life"; and Robert A. Potash, "C. A Commentary on Two Papers," all in *Hispanic American Historical Review*, 43, 3 (August 1963): 371–94. Gibson provided one of the more interesting contributions with a paradigm of the possible types of institutional continuity and change covering three different periods: the colonial, the national, and the contemporary. This paradigm could be incorporated into the arguments of the cultural revisionists.
13 Lewis J. Edinger and Donald D. Searing have challenged the notion that social background is a useful predictor of elites' attitudes. See their "Social Background in Elite Analysis: A Methodological Inquiry," *American Political Science Review*, 61, 2 (June 1967): 428–45. Furthermore, survey research has established that there is a wide gap between the elite and the mass public in terms of attitudes and belief systems, so the utilization of the concept of political culture that this group of authors has espoused is at best questionable. Finally, content analysis of documentary sources must be complemented by policy analysis in order to establish the degree of commitment to

abstract principles and ideas, and this is a very difficult analytical task.

14 Robert A. Dahl, *Polyarchy: Participation and Opposition*, second printing (New Haven and London: Yale University Press, 1972), pp. 181–82.

15 For a recent and notable example, see Louis K. Harris and Víctor Alba, *The Political Culture and Behavior of Latin America* (Kent, Ohio: Kent State University Press, 1974). The point is not that these types of works should not be published, but that they contribute little to clarify controversial points or present new evidence.

16 See Daniel H. Levine, "Issues in the Study of Culture and Politics: A View from Latin America," *Publius*, 4, 2 (Spring 1974): 77–78.

17 See Devine, *The Political Culture of the United States: The Influence of Member Values on Regime Maintenance* (Boston: Little, Brown and Co., 1972).

18 We refer to the joint MIT-CENDES study directed by Frank Bonilla and José A. Silva Michelena. See note 15, chapter 2; note 28, chapter 4.

19 See Lucian W. Pye, "Culture and Political Science: Problems in the Evaluation of the Concept of Political Culture," *Social Science Quarterly*, 53, 2 (September 1972): 285–96.

20 The items and scales include: trust in people (SRC: 1964, 1966), personal competence (SRC: 1958, 1960, 1964), attitudes toward democratic principles (Prothro and Grigg, 1960), conservatism scale (McCloskey, 1958; Campbell et al., 1960; Matthews and Prothro, 1966), ideological self-image (Comparative State Election Project, 1968), political interest (SRC: 1952, 1956, 1960, 1964), attitudes toward politics in general (Agger et al., 1964; McCloskey, 1964; Litt, 1963), attitudes toward government in general (SRC: 1958, 1964, 1966; McCloskey, 1964), attitudes toward political parties (SRC: 1964; McCloskey, 1964; AIPO, 1959), attitudes toward elections (SRC: 1964; Agger et al., 1964), citizen duty scale (Campbell et al., 1954), attitudes toward politicians (Agger et al., 1964; McCloskey, 1964; Litt, 1963), party identification (AIPO, standard; ORCO, 1961; Comparative State Election Project, 1968), party loyalty (AIPO: Minnesota study, 1960; RCOM, 1960), thermometer scale (Converse and Dupeux–SOFFRES, 1962; Weisberg and Rusk, 1970), party evaluation (AIPO, standard; ORCO, 1963), issue orientation (AIPO, standard; Comparative State Election Project, 1968), mass media exposure (SRC: 1952, 1956, 1960,

1964), campaign exposure (Comparative State Election Project, 1968), political involvement (Campbell et al., 1960), electoral participation (Campbell et al., 1954), past voting behavior (Comparative State Election Project, 1968), party affiliation (AIPO, standard), and voting intention (Comparative State Election Project, 1968). Many of these items and scales did not survive translation of the instrument, and others were deleted after the pretest. The rest were thoroughly reworded until they proved to be satisfactory. David Kovenock provided us with a copy of the instrument utilized in the Comparative State Election Project. The format of the remaining items described above were taken directly from Robinson et al. (1968). Thanks to the generosity of Professor Philip Converse we were able to consult his SOFFRES instrument—cited above—as well as the instruments (forms I and II) utilized by the SRC in its 1972 pre- and postelection studies. We borrowed liberally from the general information items concerning demographic and socioeconomic characteristics of these instruments, and they survived the wear and tear of the revisions of our own instrument. Complete references for these studies may be found in John P. Robinson et al., *Measures of Political Attitudes* (Ann Arbor: Survey Research Center, 1969).

21 Sidney Verba and Norman H. Nie, *Participation in America: Political Democracy and Social Equality* (New York: Harper and Row, 1972), p. 13.

22 See Enrique A. Baloyra and John D. Martz, "Classical Participation in Venezuela: Campaigning and Voting in 1973," paper delivered at the Seminar on the Faces of Participation in Latin America: A New Look at Citizen Action in Society, University of Texas at San Antonio, November 12–13, 1976.

23 *Participation in America*, p. 14.

24 Baloyra and Martz, "Classical Participation in Venezuela," pp. 17–27.

25 Angus Campbell et al., *The American Voter* (New York: John Wiley and Sons, 1960).

26 This point of view has been argued cogently and persuasively by Philip E. Converse, "The Nature of Belief Systems in Mass Publics," in David Apter (ed.), *Ideology and Discontent* (New York: Free Press, 1964), pp. 206–61.

27 For a discussion of contradictory views being held simultaneously by the public see Lloyd A. Free and Hadley Cantril, *The Political Beliefs of Americans: A Study of Public Opinion* (New Brunswick, N.J.: Rutgers University Press, 1968).

28 The literature is very extensive in this area. A few of the more relevant works are Bernard Berelson et al., *Voting* (Chicago: University of Chicago Press, 1945), chapter 13; David Butler and Donald Stokes, *Political Change in Britain* (New York: St. Martin's Press, 1971), chapter 12; Campbell et al., *The American Voter*, pp. 105–8; V. O. Key, Jr., *Public Opinion and American Democracy*, reprint (New York: Alfred A. Knopf, 1967), chapter 2; Herbert McClosky et al., "Issue Conflict and Issue Consensus among Party Leaders and Followers," *American Political Science Review*, 54, 2 (June 1960): 406–27; and James W. Prothro and Charles M. Grigg, "Fundamental Principles of Democracy, Bases of Agreement and Disagreement," *Journal of Politics*, 22, 2 (May 1960): 276–94. For a recent critique and discussion of new evidence see David G. Lawrence, "Procedural Norms and Tolerance: A Reassessment," *American Political Science Review*, 70, 1 (March 1976): 80–113.

29 This usually revolves around the interpretation of election results: the "restoring election of 1960," the McCarthy vote in the 1968 New Hampshire primary, and the "special case" of the 1964 presidential election. For contrasting views, see Gerald Pomper, "From Confusion to Clarity: Issues and American Voters, 1956–1968," *American Political Science Review*, 66, 2 (June 1972): 415–28, and Philip E. Converse et al., "Continuity and Change in American Politics: Parties and Issues in the 1968 Election," *American Political Science Review*, 63, 4 (December 1969): 1083–1105.

30 The contrasting positions have perhaps been best summarized by Michael J. Shapiro in "Rational Political Man: A Synthesis of Economic and Social Perspectives," *American Political Science Review*, 63, 4 (December 1969): 1106–19.

31 See Norman H. Nie's criticism of Converse's position in Nie and Kristi Andersen, "Mass Belief Systems Revisited: Political Change and Attitude Structure," *Journal of Politics*, 36, 3 (August 1974): 540–91. For a rebuttal, see Philip E. Converse, "Public Opinion and Voting Behavior," chapter 2 in Fred I. Greenstein and Nelson W. Polsby (eds.), *Handbook of Political Science, Vol. 4: Non-governmental Politics* (Reading, Mass.: Addison-Wesley, 1975).

32 As quoted by Joseph A. Kahl in *Modernization, Exploitation and Dependency in Latin America* (New Brunswick, N.J.: Transaction Books, 1976), p. 105.

33 For review and commentary, see Alejandro Portes and John

Walton, *Urban Latin America: The Political Condition from Above and Below* (Austin and London: University of Texas Press, 1976). For more specific treatment and results which challenge the conventional wisdom regarding urban migrants, see Wayne A. Cornelius, *Politics and the Migrant Poor in Mexico City* (Stanford, California: Stanford University Press, 1975).

34 For a general discussion and critique of the validity of concepts like the "*encogido syndrome*," the "image of the limited good," and "amoral familism," see Gerritt Huizer, *The Revolutionary Potential of Peasants in Latin America* (Lexington, Mass.: D. C. Heath and Co., 1972). For recent country studies which seem to corroborate Huizer's views, see John S. Gitlitz, "Hacienda, Comunidad, and Peasant Protest in Northern Peru," unpublished doctoral dissertation (University of North Carolina, Chapel Hill, 1975). See also the suggestive and very sophisticated treatment of peasant participation in Costa Rican politics by John A. Booth and Mitchell A. Seligson, "Peasant Political Participation: An Analysis Using Two Costa Rican Samples," paper delivered at the Seminar on the Faces of Participation in Latin America, University of Texas at San Antonio, November 12–13, 1976, and Seligson's test of the standard socioeconomic model in "Trust, Efficacy and Modes of Political Participation," paper delivered at the Annual Meeting of the Southwestern Political Science Association, Dallas, Texas, March 1977.

35 Peter L. Berger, *Pyramids of Sacrifice: Political Ethics and Social Change* (Garden City, N.Y.: Anchor Books, 1976), pp. 60 and 134.

36 Theodore Roszak, *Where the Wasteland Ends: Politics and Transcendence in Postindustrial Society* (Garden City, N.Y.: Anchor Books, 1973), p. 237.

37 Converse, "Public Opinion," p. 87.

Notes to Chapter 2

The Social Context of Political Opinion

1 The brand of cultural revisionism envisaged in our first chapter has not made serious inroads among Venezuelanists, yet two Venezuelan authors have had a long-standing association with this approach. Laureano Vallenilla Lanz (*padre*) could be considered an intellectual forerunner of cultural revisionism. His *Cesarismo democrático: Estudio sobre las bases sociológicas de la constitución efectiva de Venezuela* (Caracas: Garrido, 1960; first published El Cojo, 1919) constitutes a classic discussion of the leading assumptions of this approach. The historian Guillermo Morón is another figure who could be so identified; his *Democracia y educación* (Caracas: Italgráfica, 1973) is a recent work in which he dwells on assumptions drawn from this intellectual reservoir.

2 Recently, attempts have been made to update and reformulate development theory as applied to Latin America; see Robert L. Ayres, "Development Policy and the Possibility of a 'Livable' Future for Latin America," *American Political Science Review*, 69, 2 (June 1975): 507–25.

3 See Héctor Malavé Mata, *Formación del anti-desarrollo histórico de Venezuela* (La Habana: Casa de las Américas, 1974) for a discussion of the "development of underdevelopment" in Venezuela.

4 On the number of classes, see Richard N. Adams, "Political Power and Social Structures," in Claudio Véliz (ed.), *The Politics of Conformity in Latin America* (New York: Oxford University Press, 1967), pp. 15–42, where he argues forcefully for a dichotomous classification of Latin American class structure. William S. Stokes, by contrast, produced very complex criteria which conceptualized many different strata in *Latin American Politics* (New York: Thomas Y. Crowell Co., 1959), chapter 1. Usage of the term "feudal," together with the advent of the "dual society thesis," complicated the discussion to unmanageable limits. A leading exponent of the dual society thesis was Jacques Lambert, *Latin America: Social Structure and Political*

Institutions, translated by Helen Katel (Berkeley and Los Angeles: University of California Press, 1969).

5 See Frederick B. Pike, "Aspects of Class Relations in Chile, 1850–1960," *Hispanic American Historical Review*, 42, 1 (February 1963): 14–33; Frank Safford, "Bases of Political Alignment in Early Republican Spanish America," in Richard Graham and Peter H. Smith, *New Approaches to Latin American History* (Austin and London: University of Texas Press, 1974), pp. 71–111; and Milton I. Vanger, "Politics and Class in Twentieth Century Latin America," *Hispanic American Historical Review*, 49, 1 (February 1969): 80–93.

6 See Ronald C. Newton, "On 'Functional Groups,' 'Fragmentation,' and 'Pluralism' in Spanish American Political Society," *Hispanic American Historical Review*, 50, 1 (February 1970): 1–29.

7 In 1948 the Office of Social Sciences of the Pan American Union set out to gather materials on the Latin American middle classes. After an initial period during which existing studies and data sources were compiled, the Office commissioned a group of Latin American scholars to study the subject in their own countries. The report of this study, considered a rare and very valuable bibliographic item today, appeared in a six-volume set. See Unión Panamericana, Departamento de Asuntos Culturales, *Materiales para el estudio de la clase media en la América Latina*, six vols. (Washington: Publicaciones de la Oficina de Ciencias Sociales, 1950–1951). More recent discussions on the middle class can be found in Charles Wagley, *The Latin American Tradition* (New York: Columbia University Press, 1968); John J. Johnson, *Political Change in Latin America: The Emergence of the Middle Sectors* (Stanford: Stanford University Press, 1958); and John P. Gillin, "The Middle Segments and Their Values," in John D. Martz (ed.), *The Dynamics of Change in Latin American Politics*, 2d ed. (Englewood Cliffs: Prentice-Hall, 1971), pp. 86–100.

8 Obviously, the linkages cannot be described for situations in which parties do not exist and/or are not allowed to operate. Argentina was a case in which the study of the relationship had produced relatively satisfactory results. See Alberto Ciria, *Partidos y poder en la Argentina moderna, 1930–1946* (Buenos Aires: Jorge Alverez, 1964); Torcuato di Tella, *El sistema político argentino y la clase obrera* (Buenos Aires: Eudeba, 1964); Peter H. Smith, "Social Mobilization, Political Participation and the Rise of Juan Perón," *Political Science Quarterly*,

34, 1 (March 1969): 30–49; and Peter G. Snow, *Argentine Radicalism* (Iowa City: University of Iowa Press, 1965).

9 *Class and Class Conflict in Industrial Society* (Stanford, Cal.: Stanford University Press, 1972; first published 1959).

10 *The Industrial Society: Three Essays on Ideology and Development* (New York: Clarion Books, 1968; first published 1967).

11 *The State in Capitalist Society* (New York: Basic Books, 1969).

12 *One Dimensional Man* (Boston: Beacon Press, 1964).

13 Vanger's critique of the reformist interpretation of the political behavior of the Latin American middle classes is well taken, "Politics and Class in Twentieth Century Latin America," pp. 83–84. However, the reductionist explanation that he offers as an alternative is far too ambitious. José Nun's reinterpretation of the relationship between the middle classes and the military proved much more satisfactory and long-lasting. See his much-celebrated "A Latin American Phenomenon: The Middle Class Military Coup," in James Petras and Maurice Zeitlin (eds.), *Latin America: Reform or Revolution?* (New York: Fawcett, 1968), pp. 145–85.

14 See the essays in "Imperialism and the Working Class," in *Latin American Perspectives*, 3, 1 (Winter 1976).

15 José A. Silva Michelena, *The Politics of Change in Venezuela, Vol. III: The Illusion of Democracy in Dependent Nations* (Cambridge and London: M.I.T. Press, 1971), p. 83.

16 Our usage of the concepts of "conflict groups" and "quasi groups" conforms to Dahrendorf's. He borrowed the latter from Morris Ginsberg, who defined them as "aggregates or portions of the community which have no recognizable structure, but whose members have certain interests or modes of behavior in common, which may at any time lead them to form themselves into definitive groups," Ginsberg, *Sociology* (London: n.p. 1953), p. 40, cited by Dahrendorf, *Class and Class Conflict*, p. 180. Quasi groups are thus a result of the societal cleavages.

Although he never really defines "conflict groups" and admits that the concept may be too vague (p. 203), Dahrendorf tends to treat conflict groups as a category of interest groups, which are the real agents of conflict (p. 180), are inextricably bound to authority relations (pp. 172–73), and are formed from quasi groups when the latent interests of the latter become manifest as a result of a variety of factors (pp. 174–79). Our treatment of conflict groups is related to societal cleavages which have been politicized and organized, whether in coalition with other groups or by themselves. Much of the analysis of the first section of this volume is simply an attempt to examine the attitudinal differences between relevant quasi groups in Venezuela.

17 The notion of cleavage, which is widely utilized in political sociology, has received close attention from a group of scholars associated with the Committee on Political Sociology of the International Sociological Association. Much of this work is based on aggregate data but is nevertheless useful and intellectually stimulating. See Erik Allardt and Yrjo Littunen (eds.), *Cleavages, Ideologies and Party Systems* (Helsinki: Westermack Society, 1964); Seymour Martin Lipset and Stein Rokkan (eds.), "Cleavage Structures, Party Systems and Voter Alignments: An Introduction," in *Party Systems and Voter Alignments: Cross-National Perspectives* (New York: Free Press, 1967), pp. 1–64; and Erik Allardt and Stein Rokkan (eds.), *Mass Politics: Studies in Political Sociology* (New York and London: Free Press, 1970).

A concise and useful definition of cleavage is offered by Giuseppe Di Palma: it is "simply the difference in objective social and economic positions." See "Conclusion," in Di Palma (ed.) *Mass Politics in Industrial Societies: A Reader in Comparative Politics* (Chicago: Markham, 1972), p. 394. Quite correctly, Di Palma argues that cleavages are characteristic of every society, yet they are not always politicized, nor are they necessarily accompanied by distinctive attitudes and beliefs.

18 *The Psychology of Social Classes: A Study of Class Consciousness* (Princeton, N.J.: Princeton University Press, 1949). Centers could not have stated the aims of his study in more appropriate and universal terms. He wrote: ". . . [the] important questions which this research attempts to answer are such as. . . . Does class consciousness exist in our society, and if so, in what fashion is it manifest? What strata of the population does it primarily divide? With what attitudes and beliefs is it correlated? By what frustrations, antagonisms, and grievances is it accompanied? Upon what criteria is it based? By what subjective and objective conditions is it determined?" ibid., p. 29.

19 *The State in Capitalist Society*, p. 20.

20 C. Richard Bath and Dilmus D. James, "Dependency Analysis of Latin America," *Latin American Research Review*, 11, 3 (1976): 34. To further illustrate problems of reconciliation, consider the nature of the differences between John J. Johnson's treatment of the middle sectors, *Political Change in Latin America*, and André Gunder Frank's in *Lumpenbourgeoisie*,

> Lumpendevelopment: Dependence, Class, and Politics in Latin America (New York: Monthly Review Press, 1972).

21 David Butler and Donald Stokes, Political Change in Britain (New York: St. Martin's Press, 1971), especially chapters 4, 6, and 7.

22 Peter Blau and Otis Dudley Duncan, The American Occupational Structure (New York: John Wiley and Sons, 1967), chapter 4, and the development of a model of occupational mobility on pp. 165–77.

23 For an extended discussion of this question, see Elton F. Jackson and Richard F. Curtis, "Conceptualization and Measurement in the Study of Social Stratification," in Hubert M. Blalock, Jr., and Ann B. Blalock (eds.), Methodology in Social Research (New York: McGraw-Hill, 1968), pp. 112–49.

24 The Politics of Change in Venezuela, p. 86.

25 It should be emphasized that this measure of class status was conceptualized and operationalized for market research and not for social science research. Nevertheless, we will utilize the index in order to examine different aspects of the Venezuelan social structure.

26 In our summer of 1973 pretest, we utilized a closed question of class identification, giving respondents a choice between upper class, middle class, working class, and lower class. More respondents identified with the working class but indicated the middle class as the group with which they most identified. Since it was difficult to utilize the open and closed questions simultaneously we opted for the former, assuming that the labels produced by the respondents would be more meaningful to them than any closed categories suggested to them by our interviewers.

27 The Psychology of Social Classes, pp. 27 and 78.

28 This seems to be the implication of Guillermo O'Donnell's discussion in Modernization and Bureaucratic Authoritarianism, Studies in South American Politics, Politics of Modernization Series, 9 (Berkeley: Institute of International Studies, 1973), pp. 56–70. See also Ronald C. Newton, "Natural Corporatism and the Passing of Populism in Spanish America," Review of Politics, 36, 1 (January 1974): 34–51.

29 Current interpretations of the Cuban Revolution include this element as an important component of that process. See James O'Connor, The Origins of Socialism in Cuba (Ithaca and London: Cornell University Press, 1970) and Edward Boorstein,

The Economic Transformation of Cuba (New York: Monthly Review Press, 1968). Concerning the Venezuelan *trienio* of 1945–1948, the legitimacy of the new *adeco* regime is offered as a leading explanation for the military coup. Yet most authors concur that this alleged legitimacy was being more severely contested by some sectors of the middle class, led by COPEI and other opposition parties. On the other hand, the *adeco* regime was trying to gear most of its policies to benefit the poor. Thus, although it would be exaggerated to say that class conflict was explicit at that time, it played a role which was overshadowed by the controversy surrounding the education issue and other questions that created concern among the middle class. For a description of the atmosphere surrounding the 1948 coup see Glen L. Kolb, *Democracy and Dictatorship in Venezuela, 1945–1958* (New London: Connecticut College, 1974), chapter 4. An excellent discussion of the controversy about the education issue may be found in Daniel H. Levine, *Conflict and Political Change in Venezuela* (Princeton: Princeton University Press, 1973). Martz, *Acción Democrática: Evolution of a Modern Political Party in Venezuela* (Princeton: Princeton University Press, 1966) provides description and commentary about AD's goals and strategy at that time, pp. 81–89.

30 Concerning the Venezuelan poor, see Talton F. Ray, *The Politics of the Barrios of Venezuela* (Berkeley and Los Angeles: University of California Press, 1969); Lisa R. Peattie, *The View from the Barrio* (Ann Arbor: University of Michigan Press, 1968); and Carlos Acedo Mendoza, *Desarrollo comunal y promoción popular: Marginalidad e integración* (Caracas: Fondo Editorial Común, 1968). Scholarly discussions about the Venezuelan middle class are relatively hard to come by, although we consider most of the groups included in the CONVEN sample to be representative of that middle class.

31 We have borrowed these descriptions from Jeannette Abouhamad's *Los hombres de Venezuela: Sus necesidades, sus aspiraciones* (Caracas: Universidad Central de Venezuela, 1970), pp. 240–41, 264, 282, and 301. The translation is ours, but we followed her usage in introducing the different types of respondents. For the complete description of these profiles, see pp. 225–315.

32 *The Politics of Change in Venezuela*, p. 84.

33 See Manuel Pernaut, S.J., *Diez años de desarrollo económico y social en Venezuela* (Caracas: Artegrafía, C.A. for Ediciones del Cuatricentenario de Caracas, 1966), p. 98. Pernaut iden-

tified the different income strata as identical with the class structure of the country.

34 Ibid., p. 63.

35 Ibid., p. 68.

36 Comité de Obras Económicas, *Estudio sobre barrios de Caracas* (Caracas: Artegrafía, C.A. for Ediciones del Cuatricentenario de Caracas, 1968), pp. 63 and 142.

37 *The Politics of the Barrios of Venezuela*, pp. 57–58. Ray's usage of the terms "aspiring class" and "general class" represents a different approach than ours because these terms were not derived from interview techniques or similar procedures. It would probably have been more appropriate for Ray to refer to these as strata rather than classes or subclasses. Nevertheless his characterization of the two seems accurate and relevant, and although *rancho* dwellers do not perceive themselves as "general class" or "aspiring class," there is a cleavage separating two groups which bear the characteristics described by Ray. On the other hand, Ray could have employed these labels in order to differentiate the two groups by survey techniques and conduct his discussion in terms of the two classes if the labels had proven relevant to the respondents.

38 Centro de Estudios del Desarrollo, *Muestras de campesinos tradicionales, campesinos en asentamientos del I.A.N. y obreros agrícolas*, Estudio de conflicto y consenso: Serie de resultados parciales, 6 (Caracas: Editorial Arte for Universidad Central de Venezuela, 1967).

39 We computed these figures from Dirección General de Estadística y Censos Nacionales, División de Muestreo, "Encuesta de Hogares por Muestreo," *Documento REH-13, Julio 1971, Empleo, desempleo y Analfabetismo* (Caracas: Ministerio de Fomento, 1972), pp. 58, 62.

40 *The Psychology of Social Classes*, p. 27.

41 Ibid., pp. 13 and 15, emphasis in original.

42 The four scale values represent intervals of Z values at least one standard deviation lower than average, less than one standard deviation lower than average, less than one standard deviation above average, and at least one standard deviation above average.

43 Inspection of the field tally sheets of our interviewers assigned to the Prados del Este section of Caracas shows that classes A and B proved extremely difficult to interview. The sheets report strings of 20 and 30 consecutive refusals; in many cases, the interviewers reported that maids and butlers refused even to ask

their employers if they were willing to be interviewed for fear of being reprimanded. This led us to believe that those individuals from classes A and B whom we managed to interview are not very representative of their own class and that, although their interviews could be utilized in other respects, it would be risky to include them in our analysis of stratification as representative of the top strata. A final comment: the distribution of the two classes is such that they are concentrated in Caracas and very few other metropolitan areas; therefore, we could not substitute with classes A and B from smaller urban areas because they did not have this type of respondent.

44 One such difference refers to the rural-urban cleavage, which seemed to overlap with the boundary of the two lowest levels of socioeconomic status. It is important to preserve this distinction, at least in terms of this measure, since class identification and the index of class status make no such distinction.

45 We recognize that use of the index in combination with the three variables utilized in its construction is somewhat tautological. However, it is important to show the types of clusters created by different combinations of the categories of income, education, and occupation.

46 See Dirección General de Estadística, "Encuesta de Hogares," p. 11.

47 We are aware of ongoing controversies concerning the utilization of regression analysis with nonmetric data. We have attempted to explain our approach to the use of regression analysis in appendix D.

48 All the beta coefficients identified here are significant at the .01 level.

49 The regression equation being

$$\text{class image} = .96 + .15 \text{ socioeconomic status} + .16 \text{ class status.}$$

50 See table A-2, appendix A, for more specific detail concerning our sample bias for occupational categories.

51 The typical question on group identification goes like this: "Here is a list of some groups. I want you to tell me which of these groups you feel particularly *close* to—people who are most like you in their ideas and interests and feelings about things."

52 See, for example, Robert A. Dahl, *Polyarchy: Participation and Opposition*.

53 For a comprehensive discussion of cleavage structures and their

interaction, see Lipset and Rokkan, "Cleavage Structures, Party Systems and Voter Alignments."

54 The exact wording appears in appendix B, item 91.

55 Sidney Verba and Norman H. Nie, *Participation in America*, p. 157.

56 See their treatment of blacks and their patterns of participation which are affected by group consciousness related to race, ibid., chapters 10 and 14.

57 Paths are expressed as standardized beta weights. Straight arrows are paths, curves with arrows are unanalyzed correlations, curves without arrows are noncausal covariations, and absence of any lines shows the absence of statistically significant relationships. Whenever additional comments are necessary to explain divergence from standard practice these appear in the text. For a discussion of path analytic methodology by one of its more prominent advocates, see Otis Dudley Duncan, *Introduction to Structural Equation Models* (New York: Academic Press, 1975).

58 Disturbance terms measure the proportion of unexplained variance of a dependent variable.

59 *Los hombres de Venezuela*.

60 By "rural" we mean communities of less than 5,000 inhabitants.

61 See appendix A for a discussion of the magnitude and implications of this sampling bias.

62 For a description of the procedure and available options and assumptions, see Jerome C. R. Li, *Statistical Inference, I*, 2d ed. rev. (Ann Arbor, Mich.: Edwards Brothers, 1965), chapter 15.

63 The literature is unclear on the problem of inference making from results of this type of analysis. For a discussion and description of how we have dealt with this problem, see appendix E.

64 See *Class and Politics in the United States* (New York: John Wiley and Sons, 1972).

65 Walter Dupouy, "La clase media en Venezuela," in Unión Panamericana, *Materiales para el estudio de la clase media*, vol. 5, pp. 68–102.

Notes to Chapter 3

The Social Context
of Political Experience

1 Richard F. Hamilton, *Class and Class Politics in the United States* (New York: John Wiley and Sons, 1972), p. 170.
2 By "paradigmatic thinking" we mean the type of formulation concerned with overarching or *grand* theory. For a brief discussion see David E. Apter, *Introduction to Political Analysis* (Cambridge, Mass.: Winthrop Publishers, 1977), pp. 536–38.
3 Seymour Martin Lipset, *Political Man* (Garden City, N.Y.: Doubleday, 1960), chapter 4.
4 See John J. Johnson, *Political Change in Latin America: The Emergence of the Middle Sectors* (Stanford: Stanford University Press, 1958).
5 For a comprehensive discussion, see Richard F. Hamilton, *Affluence and the French Worker in the Fourth Republic* (Princeton, N.J.: Princeton University Press, 1967).
6 See John H. Goldthorpe et al., "The Affluent Worker in the Class Structure," *Cambridge Studies in Sociology*, 3 (Cambridge: Cambridge University Press, 1971). See also David Butler and Donald Stokes, *Political Change in Britain* (New York: St. Martin's Press, 1971), especially chapters 4, 6, and 7.
7 See José Nun's much-celebrated article, "A Latin American Phenomenon: The Middle Class Military Coup," in James Petras and Maurice Zeitlin (eds.), *Latin America, Reform or Revolution?* (Greenwich, Conn.: Fawcett, 1968), pp. 145–85.
8 For a review and critique see Hamilton, *Class and Class Politics*, chapter 11.
9 See note 28, chapter 1.
10 Glen Caudill Dealy, "The Tradition of Monistic Democracy in Latin America," *Journal of the History of Ideas*, 35, 4 (October–December 1974): 625–46.
11 For similar treatment, see Wayne A. Cornelius, *Politics and the Migrant Poor in Mexico City* (Stanford: Stanford University Press, 1975), pp. 54–63.
12 We find Linz' attempt to define subtypes of authoritarian re-

gimes in terms of the groups which are excluded from direct participation useful and applicable to democratic regimes, although in the sense of groups and individuals who find themselves particularly incapable of influencing the outcome of public policy. See Juan Linz, "Notes toward a Typology of Authoritarian Regimes," delivered at the annual meeting of the American Political Science Association, Washington, D.C., 1972.

13 David Easton, *The Political System: An Inquiry into the State of Political Science* (New York: Alfred A. Knopf, 1953), pp. 126–32.

14 See John D. Martz and Enrique A. Baloyra, *Electoral Mobilization and Public Opinion: The Venezuelan Campaign of 1973* (Chapel Hill: University of North Carolina Press, 1976), pp. 160–63.

15 David Eugene Blank, *Politics in Venezuela* (Boston: Little, Brown and Co., 1973), p. 129.

16 Ronald C. Newton, "Natural Corporatism and the Passing of Populism in Spanish America," *Review of Politics*, 36, 1 (January 1974): 37.

17 Ibid.

18 For the most elegant summary of this type of interpretation, see Philip E. Converse, "Public Opinion and Voting Behavior," chapter 2 in Fred I. Greenstein and Nelson W. Polsby (eds.), *Handbook of Political Science, vol. IV: Non-governmental Politics* (Reading, Mass.: Addison-Wesley, 1975).

19 This procedure seems more valid in Venezuela when compared to the standard practice of measuring this variable by the respondent's ability to name elected public officials. In Venezuela, this becomes very difficult, since electors vote straight party tickets for all legislative seats, federal, state, and municipal. For example, in the elections of 1973, constituents from Miranda state elected a total of 82 different persons with their small ballot, including senators, deputies, municipal councilmembers, and their alternates. We cannot conceive that anyone would be capable of naming all 82, regardless of level of political interest.

20 The statistical procedure utilized was a two-way analysis of variance.

21 As suggested by Dealy, "The Tradition of Monistic Democracy."

22 According to Lipset, *Political Man*, and others.

23 Involving support for democratic institutions, tolerance of unpopular views, and support for the actual applicability of democratic rules of procedure.
24 See Converse, "Public Opinion and Voting Behavior."
25 See Oficina de Estudios Económicos (OESE), ¿Sociedad en
Crisis? (Caracas: Gráficas Armitano, C.A. for Fondo Editorial
Común, 1973), pp. 269–324. It should be mentioned, however,
that the marginals come to think of the government as the
moving power of all national activity, ibid., p. 309, an attitude
not shared by the upper strata.
26 As suggested by the following data:

	Inflation	Unemployment
Poor	42%	25%
Middle class	36%	18%
Manual strata	44%	25%
White-collar strata	36%	17%

27 We borrowed this question from the protocol of the CENDES-
MIT study of conflict and consensus among Venezuelan elites.
28 Theodore Lowi, The End of Liberalism: Ideology, Policy, and
the Crises of Public Authority (New York: W. W. Norton and
Co., 1969). On this point, see Humberto Njaim, "Marco Conceptual," Ricardo Combellas, "La actuación de Fedecámaras y
la C.T.V. ante la Reforma Tributaria," and Andrés Stambouli,
"La actuación de Fedecámaras y la C.T.V. ante el Pacto Subre-
gional Andino," in Politeia, 2 (1973): 285–348. See also Robert
P. Clark, "Fedecámaras en el proceso de la formulación de
política en Venezuela," Comisión de Administración Pública,
Estudios de Casos, 6 (Caracas: Centro de Investigaciones Ad-
ministrativas y Sociales, 1966).
29 See The End of Ideology (Glencoe, Ill.: Free Press, 1960).
30 William Bluhm, Ideology and Attitudes: Modern Political Cul-
ture (Englewood Cliffs, N.J.: Prentice-Hall, 1974); David I.
Finlay et al., "The Concept of Left and Right in Cross-National
Research," Comparative Political Studies, 7, 2 (December
(1974): 209–21; Clifford C. Geertz, "Ideology as a Cultural Sys-
tem," in David E. Apter (ed.), Ideology and Discontent (New
York: Free Press, 1964), pp. 47–76; J. Laponce, "Note on the
Use of the Left-Right Dimension," Comparative Political
Studies, 2, 4 (January 1970): 481–502; Robert D. Putnam,
"Studying Elite Political Culture: The Case of Ideology,"
American Political Science Review, 65, 3 (September 1971):

651–81; and Giovanni Sartori, "Politics, Ideology and Belief Systems," *American Political Science Review*, 62, 2 (June 1969): 398–411.

31 Philip E. Converse, "The Nature of Belief Systems in Mass Publics," in Apter, *Ideology and Discontent*, pp. 206–61. Also Norman H. Nie and Kristi Andersen, "Mass Belief Systems Revisited: Political Change and Attitude Structure," *Journal of Politics*, 36, 3 (August 1974): 540–91; Robert D. Putnam, *The Beliefs of Politicians* (New Haven and London: Yale University Press, 1973); Milton Rokeach, *Beliefs, Attitudes and Values* (San Francisco: Jossey Bass, 1969); and Harry L. Wilker and Lester W. Milbrath, "Political Belief Systems and Political Behavior," *Social Science Quarterly*, 51, 3 (December 1970): 477–93.

32 Don A. Dillman and James A. Christenson, "Toward the Assessment of Public Values," *Public Opinion Quarterly*, 38, 2 (Summer 1974): 206–21; Robert Inglehart, "The Silent Revolution in Europe: Intergenerational Change in Post-Industrial Societies," *American Political Science Review*, 65, 4 (December 1971): 991–1017; Milton Rokeach, *The Nature of Human Values* (New York: Free Press, 1973) and "Change and Stability in American Value Systems, 1968–1971," *Public Opinion Quarterly*, 38, 2 (Summer 1974): 222–38; and Donald D. Searing, "Measuring Values in Elite Research," paper presented at the Annual Meeting of the American Political Science Association, Chicago, 1974.

33 "Note on the Use of the Left-Right Dimension," *Comparative Political Studies*, 2, 4 (January 1970): 481–502.

34 OESE, *¿Qué piensan los marginados? La actitud del pobre ante el país y el mundo* (Caracas: Gráfica Americana, C.A., n.d.), p. 43.

35 Computed from José A. Silva Michelena, *The Illusion of Democracy in Dependent Nations* (Cambridge, Mass.: MIT Press, 1971), table 5.8, and pp. 140–41.

36 When our small and predominantly urban pretest sample of 250 respondents was asked about differences between the left and the right in Venezuela, the majority of those who articulated a distinction (about 48 per cent) argued that it entailed differences between rich and poor (19 per cent) or between democratic and revolutionary politics (10 per cent). Others (6 per cent) perceived the matter as a confrontation between government and opposition, which makes some sense because, after all, in Venezuela the left has always been in the opposition. Finally, there

were those who adduced that the right governed better (7 per cent) or that, in the final analysis, there was no difference between left and right politicians in Venezuela.

37 OESE, *¿Qué piensan los marginados?*, p. 45.

38 Ibid.

39 For an attempt to sustain this interpretation, see Howard J. Wiarda, "Corporatism and Development in the Iberic-Latin World: Persistent Strains and New Variations," *Review of Politics*, 36, 1 (January 1974): 3–33.

40 Verba and Nie define participation in terms of acts that aim to influence the government: *Participation in America: Political Democracy and Social Equality*, p. 2.

41 See Enrique A. Baloyra and John D. Martz, "Classical Participation in Venezuela: Campaigning and Voting in 1973," paper delivered at the Seminar on the Faces of Participation in Latin America: A New Look at Citizen Action in Society, University of Texas at San Antonio, November 12–13, 1976.

42 See Enrique A. Baloyra and John D. Martz, "Dimensions of Campaign Participation: Venezuela, 1973," in John A. Booth and Mitchell A. Seligson (eds.), *Citizen and State in Latin America: Participation in Politics* (New York: Holmes and Meier, 1978), pp. 61–84.

43 *Participation in America*, pp. 13–14.

44 By "strongly articulated parties" we mean parties with complex organizational structures, such as branches and functional ancillary organizations, and high internal discipline. See Maurice Duverger, *Political Parties* (New York: John Wiley and Sons, 1963).

45 *Participation in America*, p. 127.

46 *The Voter Decides* (Evanston, Ill.: Row Peterson, 1954).

47 See John Fraser, "The Mistrustful-Efficacious Hypothesis and Political Participation," *Journal of Politics*, 32, 2 (May 1970): 444.

48 For a somewhat divergent interpretation based on ecological data, see Lester M. Salamon and Stephen Van Evera, "Fear, Apathy, and Discrimination: A Test of Three Explanations of Political Participation," *American Political Science Review*, 67, 4 (December 1973): 1288–1306, as well as the critical comments of Sam Kernell and the rejoinder by the authors in the same issue.

49 Our own definition.

50 The differentiation of four different modes of political participa-

tion is, undoubtedly, one of the major contributions of the Verba
and Nie volume. Our own work suggests that the campaign
mode is itself multidimensional, and not unidimensional as conceived thus far. Consequently, we are aware of the complexity
of participatory phenomena and unwilling to hypothesize about
these two modes without evidence at hand.
51 *Power and Discontent* (Homewood, Ill.: Dorsey Press, 1968).
52 Ibid., p. 48. This is a reformulated version of similar typologies
based on the trust-efficacy hypothesis. For a very careful interpretation along more conventional lines, see Mitchell A. Seligson, "Trust, Efficacy and Modes of Political Participation,"
paper delivered at the Annual Meeting of the Southwestern
Political Science Association, Dallas, Texas, March 1977.
53 *Politics and the Migrant Poor in Mexico City*, p. 107, and the
sources cited therein. See also the essays in the forthcoming
volume by John A. Booth and Mitchell A. Seligson (eds.),
Political Participation and the Poor in Latin America (New
York: Holmes and Meier).
54 Even Verba and Nie, who otherwise deviate considerably from
the conventional wisdom and its operational practices, accept
the notion of "civic mindedness" without much criticism. They
treat it as "the degree to which the respondent considers himself
to be a contributor to the welfare of the community," *Participation in America*, p. 85.
55 Ronald H. McDonald, *Party Systems and Elections in Latin
America* (Chicago: Markham, 1971), pp. 25–26.
56 Commenting on the Venezuelan case, David Eugene Blank has
argued that "there is no way of determining whether a blank or
nullified ballot is the result of error or intent," *Politics in Venezuela*, p. 92. Our data seem to confirm Blank's contention.
Blank also points out that (unlike 1973) there is no record of
there being any organized campaign in the elections of 1958,
1963, and 1968 to have voters cast blank ballots, ibid., p. 93.
57 By "rational theories of voting" we mean those which treat the
voting act as a rational decision, similar to a choice between
competing alternatives in a market situation. See Anthony
Downs, *An Economic Theory of Democracy* (New York: Harper
and Brothers, 1957) and V. O. Key, *The Responsible Electorate*
(Cambridge, Mass.: Harvard University Press, 1966) for two
classical formulations of this theory. Further refinement has
come from the work of a group at the University of Rochester.
For an initial statement see William H. Riker and Peter C. Or-

deshook, "A Theory of the Calculus of Voting," *American Political Science Review*, 62, 1 (March 1968): 25–42.

58 Juan Luna, *Voto nulo: Una línea revolucionaria*, vol. 1 (Caracas: Editorial Proceso, 1973), p. 81.

59 Baloyra and Martz, "Classical Participation in Venezuela."

60 Baloyra and Martz, "Dimensions of Campaign Participation."

61 "Dilemmas in the Study of Latin American Political Parties," *Journal of Politics*, 26, 3 (August 1964): 509–32.

62 The analysis showed that both are significant and that they do not interact.

63 See Blank, *Politics in Venezuela*, pp. 128–29. A similar emphasis, although based on much more rigorous observation and operationalization, is found in John Duncan Powell, *The Political Mobilization of the Venezuelan Peasant* (Cambridge, Mass.: Harvard University Press, 1971).

64 See the essay by the late Otto Kirchheimer, "The Transformation of the Western European Party Systems," in Joseph LaPalombara and Myron Weiner (eds.), *Political Parties and Political Development* (Princeton, N.J.: Princeton University Press, 1966), pp. 177–200.

65 See Donald E. Stokes, "Spatial Models of Party Competition," chapter 9 of Angus Campbell et al. (eds.), *Elections and the Political Order* (New York: John Wiley and Sons, 1966), pp. 161–79.

66 See Juan Carlos Rey, "El sistema de partidos venezolano," *Politeia*, 1 (1972): 175–230.

67 A description of the technique and an example of its application may be found in Herbert F. Weisberg and Jerrold G. Rusk, "Dimensions of Candidate Evaluation," *American Political Science Review*, 64, 4 (December 1970): 1167–85. Given the inexperience of some of our interviewers and the low educational level of many of our respondents, we substituted for the "temperature readings" of the "feeling thermometer" a Likert-type scale distinguishing between "great sympathy," "much sympathy," "some sympathy," "not much sympathy," and "no sympathy whatsoever."

Notes to Chapter 4

Cultural Diversity
and Political Cleavages, I:
The Community Context

1 *Polyarchy: Participation and Opposition*, p. 106.
2 See Kenneth R. McRae (ed.), *Consociational Democracy:*
   Political Accommodation in Segmented Societies (Toronto:
   McClelland and Stewart, 1974), pp. 2–27.
3 This is analogous to looking for deviations from the standard
   socioeconomic model, although the baseline here is cultural differences, not social inequality.
4 Val Lorwin, "Segmented Pluralism: Ideological Cleavages and
   Political Cohesion in the Smaller European Democracies,"
   Comparative Politics, 3, 2 (January 1971): 141.
5 Attempts have been made to measure the extent of segmentation
   of some of the societies which are more affected by it. See Lorwin, "Segmented Pluralism," pp. 148–59. Douglas Rae and
   Michael Taylor offer an operational measure of fragmentation in
   The Analysis of Political Cleavages (New Haven and London:
   Yale University Press, 1970), pp. 23–29.
6 The idea of *zuilen* has had long standing in Dutch political
   thinking. However, in recent times, it was originally emphasized by J. P. Kruijt in *Verzuiling* (Zaandijk: Heijnis, 1959),
   an argument later amplified and popularized by Arend Lijphart
   in *The Politics of Accommodation: Pluralism and Democracy in*
   the Netherlands (Berkeley and Los Angeles: University of
   California Press, 1968).
7 Jeffrey Obler and Jurg Steiner, *The "Burden" of Con-*
   sociationalism: A Review Essay of Austria, Belgium, The
   Netherlands, and Switzerland, Comparative Political Series, 6
   (Beverly Hills, Cal.: Sage Publications, 1977), pp. 1–64.
8 See Val Lorwin, "Linguistic Pluralism and National Tension in
   Modern Belgium," *Canadian Journal of History*, 1, 1 (March
   1970): 1–23; and James A. Dunn, Jr., "Consociational Experiences," *Comparative Political Studies*, 5, 1 (April 1972): 3–40.
9 See Jurg Steiner, *Amicable Agreement versus Majority Rule:*

Conflict Resolution in Switzerland (Chapel Hill: University of North Carolina Press, 1972).

10 Rodney P. Stiefbold, "Political Change in a Stalemated Society: Segmented Pluralism and Consociational Democracy in Austria," in Norman J. Vig and Rodney P. Stiefbold (eds.), *Politics in Advanced Nations: Modernization, Development, and Contemporary Change* (Englewood Cliffs, N.J.: Prentice-Hall, 1974), pp. 425–77.

11 See J. P. Kruijt, "The Influence of Denominationalism on Social Life and Organizational Patterns," *Archives de Sociologie des Religions* 4, 8 (July–December 1959): 105–11, reprinted in McRae, *Consociational Democracy*, pp. 128–36.

12 For an example concerning the Austrian case, see Alfred Diamant, *Austrian Catholics and the First Republic: Democracy, Capitalism, and the Social Order, 1918–1934* (Princeton, N.J.: Princeton University Press, 1960).

13 Seymour Martin Lipset and Stein Rokkan, "Cleavage Structures, Party Systems and Voter Alignments: An Introduction," in Lipset and Rokkan (eds.), *Party Systems and Voter Alignments: Cross National Perspectives* (New York: Free Press, 1967), pp. 6 and 13, italics in original.

14 Ibid., p. 3.

15 See Ronald C. Newton, "On 'Functional Groups,' 'Fragmentation,' and 'Pluralism' in Spanish American Political Society," *Hispanic American Historical Review*, 50, 1 (1970): 1–29.

16 For a discussion of caudillism in Venezuela, see Ramón Díaz Sánchez, *Guzmán: Elipse de una ambición de poder* (Caracas: Ediciones Hortus, 1953); Robert L. Gilmore, *Caudillism and Militarism in Venezuela: 1830–1910* (Athens: Ohio University Press, 1964); Virgilio Tosta (ed.), *El Caudillismo según once autores venezolanos: Contribución al estudio del pensamiento sociológico nacional* (Caracas: Tipografía Garrido, 1954); George S. Wise, *Caudillo: A Portrait of Antonio Guzmán Blanco* (New York: Columbia University Press, 1951); and probably the most famous essay on the topic, Laureano Vallenilla Lanz, *Cesarismo democrático: Estudio sobre las bases sociológicas de la constitución efectiva de Venezuela* (Caracas: El Cojo, 1919).

17 "Bases of Political Alignment in Early Republican Spanish America," in Richard Graham and Peter H. Smith (eds.), *New Approaches to Latin American History* (Austin and London: University of Texas Press, 1974), p. 82.

18 The national period corresponds to the years between 1830 and

1880–90, although the close of the period varies with the country. See Charles C. Griffin, *The National Period in the History of the New World: An Outline and Commentary* (Mexico: Instituto Panamericano de Geografía e Historia, 1961). An alternative or "new" type of periodization refers to the period between 1790 and 1850–60 as the "neocolonial" period. The main assumption behind this is that independence did not bring about major socioeconomic changes and, therefore, one should not consider the independence a major historical watershed in Latin America.

19 Regarding *patronato* and the general question of church and state in Venezuela, the following accurately summarizes nineteenth-century conditions:

. . . the constituent congress, by resolution, on October 14, 1830, declared that the right of patronage belonged to the nation and incorporated the *Ley de Patronato* of 1824. . . . In the course of its national history Venezuela has enacted twenty-six constitutions but it has never . . . altered the essential features of the Law. . . . Restrictions on Church influence began earlier and were carried further in Venezuela than elsewhere in Latin America. Anticlericalism, based in liberal philosophy and political design rather than Church's behavior in the war of emancipation (which left much to be desired), was strong in the small minority which exercised leadership. Unchecked anticlericalism resulted in legislation that restricted the Church more than in any other country of the continent.

See J. Lloyd Mecham, *Church and State in Latin America: A History of Politico-Ecclesiastical Relations*, revised edition (Chapel Hill: University of North Carolina Press, 1966; first published, 1934), p. 99.

20 For the antecedents of the agrarian question and its impact on the War to Death see Germán Carrera Damas, "Estudio preliminar," in his compilation *Materiales para el estudio de la cuestión agraria en Venezuela: (1800–1830), vol. I* (Caracas: Imprenta Universitaria, 1964), pp. vii–clxiv. For a discussion of the agrarian question in the politics of the national period see Luis Troconis Guerrero, *La cuestión agraria en la historia nacional*, Biblioteca de Autores y Temas Tachirenses, vol. 29 (Caracas: n.p. 1962).

21 José Santiago Rodíguez, *Contribución al estudio de la Guerra Federal en Venezuela* (Caracas: Ediciones Conmemorativas del Primer Centenario de la Revolución Federal, 1960), 2 vols. Several different authors have argued that the social question

was also a factor in the war and that this was, to a certain extent, a war of the poor against the rich. See Mariano Picón, "La aventura venezolana," in Presidencia de la República, *150 años de vida republicana, 1811–1961* (Caracas: Ediciones de la Presidencia de la República, 1963), pp. 40–42.

22 See John Lombardi, *The Decline and Abolition of Negro Slavery in Venezuela: 1820–1854* (Westport, Conn.: Greenwood, 1971). See also Miguel Acosta Saignes' classic *Vida de los esclavos negros en Venezuela* (Caracas: Librería Politécnica, 1967).

23 See Lombardi's discussion of the "model agricultural export economy of Venezuela," its credit and capital formation mechanisms, the development of the crisis of coffee, and the interest conflict between planters and moneylenders, *The Decline and Abolition of Negro Slavery*, chapter 5. Challenging some standard notions of class conflict and class formation in nineteenth-century Hispanic America, Safford underlines the irony that this conflict polarized conservative moneylenders, who were the capitalist "vanguard" of the time, and liberal but paternalistic planters who joined with artisans to support the Liberal party, although this alliance was not long-lasting, "Bases of Political Alignment," pp. 76, 82–88, 92–94.

24 *The Analysis of Political Cleavages*, p. 1, where they define *cleavages* as "the criteria that divide the members of the society into groups" and allude to *ascriptive* or "trait" cleavages, *attitudinal* or opinion cleavages, and *behavioral* or "act" cleavages.

25 See Daniel H. Levine's description and analysis of the educational crises of 1946–48 and 1966–67. Although Levine was aware of the literature of segmented pluralism and drew some comparisons between the Venezuelan and the consociational regimes, he did not undertake a full-fledged attempt to treat the conflict as a result of pillarization. However, he acknowledged that one major difference between the two crises was the fact that Catholic organizations had been created during the fifties to represent the interests of Catholics who were sending their children to private schools. The ability of these leaders and the leaders of the major national political parties to isolate their membership from the negotiations and confrontations proved to be decisive for the resolution of the conflict. See *Conflict and Political Change in Venezuela* (Princeton, N.J.: Princeton University Press, 1973). It is also instructive that although the church hierarchy and the lay leaders of AVEC and FAPREC

utilized the argument that they represented majority opinion, they acted very much like a minority throughout the two crises, and the intensity of their protest and the strategies which they utilized are relatively similar to those utilized by Catholic Mexicans in their confrontation with the P.R.I. government over the same issue.

26 According to Mecham, in 1873 Antonio Guzmán Blanco . . . inaugurated one of the most complete and devastating attacks ever directed against the Catholic Church in Latin America. The initial act deprived the clergy of control over the civil registry. . . . It was hoped that this would diminish clerical influence over domestic relations. . . . At the same time the civil rite of marriage was declared to be the only legal form. . . . Monastic and church property was confiscated for the benefit of the government. The customary ecclesiastical revenues were abolished and appropriations for the Church were suspended. Public education was declared to be lay, gratuitous, and obligatory. . . . The dictator had been successful in destroying what influence the Church had managed to retain. The clergy became servile to a government that treated them with indignity. The Church was never able to recover its lost prestige.
Church and State in Latin America, pp. 107–8. Mecham also details how Guzmán tried to attract Protestant sects to fill this vacuum but was unsuccessful. These are some of the reasons pointing to the historical institutional weakness of the church in Venezuela. The church was weak and dependent, both economically and politically.

27 José A. Silva Michelena argues that regionalism actually helped the formation of the Venezuelan state because it not only led to the secession from the Gran Colombia superstate, but also because Venezuelans were extremely disoriented about their national loyalties, having gone in thirty years from colony of Spain to a province of Gran Colombia and finally to an independent republic. Silva Michelena contends that, perhaps, "the most natural reaction in this situation was to strengthen local loyalties as the only road to salvation before a sense of national identity could be obtained. . . ." See *The Politics of Change in Venezuela, Vol. III: The Illusion of Democracy in Dependent Nations* (Cambridge, Mass. and London: M.I.T. Press, 1971), p. 46. In this sense, regionalism helped to integrate the country from below.

28 Jorge Ahumada, "Hypothesis for Diagnosing Social Change: The Venezuelan Case," in Frank Bonilla and José A. Silva

Michelena (eds.), *The Politics of Change in Venezuela, Vol. I: A Strategy for Research in Social Policy* (Cambridge, Mass. and London: M.I.T. Press, 1967), pp. 5–6. It should be pointed out that the late Ahumada wrote this piece before the "dual society" hypothesis was challenged by Stavenhagen and others. Silva's substitution of *cultural heterogeneity* for Ahumada's *cultural dualism* responds to the criticism of the dual society thesis, a criticism that Ahumada would have incorporated.

29 For a discussion of the impact of regionalism in Venezuelan politics conceived in the traditional sense, see Charles C. Griffin "Regionalism's Role in Venezuelan Politics," *Inter-American Quarterly*, 3, 4 (October 1941): 21–35. It should be mentioned that Griffin utilized ethnic, economic, and sociocultural criteria to differentiate the regions.

30 We ran four separate analyses based on data from the censuses of 1941, 1950, 1961, and 1971; the latter has not been fully reported, and consequently we could not utilize the same variables in the four different replications. In all instances we found that the most parsimonious explanation to be derived from our factor-analytic solutions were typologies based on three factors: the urban-rural, a factor based on migration which we called "drift," and a third having to do with cultural heterogeneity. Our intention was to determine the degree to which the same states would tend to fall into the clusters recorded by the different factor-analytic solutions.

31 See Richard Simeon and David J. Elkins, "Regional Political Cultures in Canada," *Canadian Journal of Political Science*, 7, 3 (September 1974): 397–437.

32 Ibid., pp. 397–99.

33 See David Myers' treatment of these center-periphery relations in "Urban Voting, Structural Cleavages, and Party System Evolution, The Case of Venezuela," *Comparative Politics*, 1 (October 1975): 119–51. Incidentally, Myers' typology of the Venezuelan regions is very similar to ours, ibid., p. 126.

34 Oficina Central de Coordinación y Planificación, *Documentos de la regionalización del desarrollo* (Caracas: Imprenta Nacional, 1969), pp. 9–10.

35 DATOS, C.A., *Indice económico 1973* (Caracas: n.p., 1973).

36 *Acción Democrática: Evolution of a Modern Political Party in Venezuela* (Princeton, N.J.: Princeton University Press, 1966), appendix B, "Regional Electoral Data," pp. 403–12.

37 Simeon and Elkins, "Regional Political Cultures in Canada," utilized this approach in their analysis of Canadian regionalism.

Their sample was sufficiently large to allow them to treat the Canadian provinces separately. In our case not only was the sample smaller but the number of states was twice as large. From a methodological standpoint, a good way to verify the results of our analysis would be to draw a much larger sample and to see if, in terms of differences and similarities between the states, the type of configuration that emerges resembles our typology of the regions.

38 See Myers, "Urban Voting, Structural Cleavages, and Party System Evolution," pp. 124–27 for a brief discussion of the role of center-periphery distinctions in the formation and development of partisan loyalties.

39 See Juan Linz and Armando de Miguel, "Within-Nation Differences and Comparisons: The Eight Spains," in Richard L. Merritt and Stein Rokkan (eds.), *Comparing Nations* (New Haven and London: Yale University Press, 1966), pp. 267–319.

40 Ibid., pp. 275–76.

41 After a series of attempts, this effort produced the following classification: (1) the metropolitan Center, (2) other metropolitan, (3) all urban areas, (4) rural areas of the Center and West, (5) rural areas of Zulia and the East, (6) Andes, and (7) Plains. The intermediate and rural areas were combined. The major assumption behind this effort was that if urbanization is the one element most responsible for reducing regional differences, the metropolitan and urban areas would be less subject to the influence of regional factors. We settled on the aforementioned classification on the grounds that it yielded optimal results by comparison with the alternatives; by "optimal" we mean that it produced a higher number of significant correlation coefficients and stronger values for them. The position of the Andes and the Plains were the most difficult to determine, given the high levels of participation and partisanship of these two areas.

42 See Bonilla and Silva Michelena, *The Politics of Change in Venezuela*.

43 "Regional Political Cultures in Canada."

44 For discussion and illustration, see Norman H. Nie et al., *SPSS, Statistical Package for the Social Sciences*, second edition (New York: McGraw-Hill, 1975), pp. 383–97.

45 Enrique A. Baloyra and John D. Martz, "Culture, Regionalism, and Political Opinion in Venezuela," *Canadian Journal of Political Science* 10, 3 (September 1977): 527–72.

46 Ibid. Table 5 in that article presents a more complete set of results.

47 It should be mentioned that party membership is measured dichotomously as yes/no, which implies increasing frequency of *nonmembers* when the coefficient is positive.

48 The particular model of analysis of variance utilized for these tests conceives the categories of region and community size as *fixed* (that is, *not* the result of a random drawing), while the unequal cell frequencies make the model a factorial design of unequal sample sizes. The ten items analyzed show that the main effect of urbanization and regionalism is always significant, but that the interaction between the two is limited to support for the institution of elections and party militancy. In these cases, the interaction effects are significant and interaction between the two factors makes their separate effect difficult to interpret (normally when interaction is found the other tests are not performed, but computer programs now make all of the results available simultaneously).

49 See Baloyra and Martz, "Culture, Regionalism, and Political Opinion in Venezuela," table 6 for the complete set of results.

50 For two classic formulations, see Daniel Lerner, *The Passing of Traditional Society: Modernizing the Middle East* (New York: Free Press, 1958), and Karl W. Deutsch, "Social Mobilization and Political Development," *American Political Science Review*, 55, 3 (September 1961): 493–514. One of the more successful attempts to "soften" the more problematic assumptions of the Deutsch-Lerner paradigm is Norman H. Nie, G. Bingham Powell, Jr., and Kenneth Prewitt, "Social Structure and Political Participation: Developmental Relationships, Part I," *American Political Science Review*, 63, 2 (June 1969): 361–78, and "Part II," *American Political Science Review*, 63, 3 (September 1969): 808–32.

51 "Parochial" is borrowed from Gabriel A. Almond and Sidney Verba, *The Civic Culture, Political Attitudes and Democracy in Five Nations* (Boston: Little, Brown and Co., 1965). This usage is intended to dramatize the contrast between the conclusions of that study and our own findings.

52 David Eugene Blank, *Politics in Venezuela*, pp. 140–42.

53 John D. Martz and Peter B. Harkins, "Urban Electoral Behavior in Latin America, The Case of Metropolitan Caracas, 1958–1968," *Comparative Politics*, 4 (July 1973): 523–50.

54 Santiago Alejandro Bonomo, *Sociología electoral en Venezuela: Un estudio sobre Caracas*, Biblioteca de Psicología Social y Sociología, vol. 61 (Buenos Aires: Editorial Paidos, 1973).

55 Myers, "Urban Voting, Structural Cleavages, and Party System Evolution," pp. 145–46.
56 *Politics in Venezuela*, p. 142.
57 Probably the most outstanding example is J. Lloyd Meacham, *Church and State in Latin America*, revised edition (Chapel Hill: University of North Carolina Press, 1966; first published, 1934).
58 See Luigi R. Einaudi et al., "Latin American Institutional Development: The Changing Catholic Church," *Memorandum RM-6136-DOS* (Santa Monica: Rand Corporation, October 1969), and Luigi R. Einaudi and Alfred C. Stepan III, "Latin American Institutional Development: Changing Military Perspectives in Peru and Brazil," *Memorandum R-586-DOS* (Santa Monica: Rand Corporation, April 1971).
59 Brian H. Smith, S.J., "Religion and Social Change," *Latin American Research Review*, 10, 2 (Summer 1975): 25.
60 For more ample detail, see Mary Watters, *A History of the Church in Venezuela* (Chapel Hill: University of North Carolina Press, 1933).
61 See Levine, *Conflict and Political Change in Venezuela*, chapters 4 and 5, for a description.
62 We refer to the Declaration serving as the concluding statement to the General Conference of Latin American Bishops held in Medellín, Colombia in August and September of 1968 and attended by Pope Paul VI. The general thrust and spirit of the document was one of solidarity with the oppressed, denunciation of the institutionalized forms of social inequality (structural violence), and commitment to change. Progressive Latin American Catholics have invoked this document to legitimize their politics of collaboration with the left. For the initial version of the Declaration, see *¡Ahora!* no. 249 (August 19, 1968): 30–32, 50–57, 76. A number of sources have preserved the final version. One of these is Segunda Conferencia General del Episcopado Latinoamericano, *Documentos finales*, second edition (Buenos Aires: Ediciones Paulinas, 1970).
63 One of the most recent attempts to give the Catholic laity an institutional charter came in the form of one of the Constitutions of the Second Vatican Council. The Constitution *Gaudium et spes*, the *pastoral* Constitution voted by Vatican II, tried to return to the laity a position eroded by centuries of neglect.
64 An early attempt, long before Vatican II, which has resisted the test of time and relevance was Yves Congar, *Jalons pour une théologie du laïcat*, Unam Sanctam No. 23 (Paris: Editions du

Cerf, 1953). Congar, one of the major European theologians of his time, although probably less well known in the United States than Karl Rahner or Teilhard de Chardin, provided much of the spadework for *Gaudium et spes*, the first version of which, not accidentally, was written in French.

65 See the data presented in chapter 6 of Enrique A. Baloyra and John D. Martz, "Political Attitudes in Venezuela, A Report to the National Science Foundation," manuscript (Chapel Hill, N.C., 1976), especially table VI-3.

66 See Glenn L. Kolb, *Democracy and Dictatorship in Venezuela, 1945–1958* (New London: Connecticut College, 1974).

67 One of the more cogent discussions of this viewpoint is Howard J. Wiarda, "Toward a Framework for the Study of Political Change in the Iberic-Latin Tradition: The Corporative Model," *World Politics*, 25, 1 (January 1973): 206–35.

68 "Colonial Institutions and Contemporary Latin America, B. Social and Cultural Life," *Hispanic American Historical Review*, 43 (1963), reprinted in Lewis Hanke (ed.), *Readings in Latin American History, Vol. II: Since 1810* (New York: Crowell, 1966), pp. 26–34.

69 Philippe C. Schmitter, "Still the Century of Corporatism?" *Review of Politics*, 36, 1 (January 1974): 85–131.

70 For political capacity, the analysis of variance results was as follows:

Source of variation	Sums of squares	d.f.	Mean squares	F	P
Main effects	7.37	5	1.48	1.89	.09
Religion	2.86	3	.95	1.22	.30
Ideology	4.52	2	2.26	2.90	.05
Interaction	12.24	6	2.04	2.62	.02
Explained	19.61	11	1.78	2.29	.01
Residual	849.62	1091	.78	—	—
Total	869.23	1102	.79	—	—

Multiple R = .09

Interpretation here is straightforward despite interaction, since the multiple correlation coefficient is very low. Thus, the combined impact produced by the interactive effect is slight.
The results for sympathy toward MAS were more robust.

Source of variation	Sums of squares	d.f.	Mean squares	F	P
Main effects	221.28	5	44.26	32.68	.001
Religion	49.91	3	16.64	12.87	.001
Ideology	171.36	2	85.68	63.27	.001
Two-way interaction	20.85	6	3.48	2.57	.02
Explained	242.13	11	22.01	16.25	.001
Residual	1438.20	1062	1.35	—	—
Total	1680.33	1073	1.57	—	—

Multiple R = .36

In this case it can be seen that even though ideology has a much stronger impact (beta −.32) than religion (beta −.12), both are significant as well as their interaction.

Notes to Chapter 5

Cultural Diversity
and Political Cleavages, II:
The Ideological Connection

1 For the contrasting perspectives on the contemporary importance of ideology, see Daniel Bell, *The End of Ideology* (New York: Free Press, 1960), and Joseph LaPalombara, "Decline of Ideology: A Dissent and an Interpretation," *American Political Science Review*, 60, 1 (March 1966): 5–16. For a more complete inventory, see Chaim I. Waxman (ed.), *The End of Ideology Debate* (New York: Funk and Wagnalls, 1968).

    Concerning the phenomenology of ideology, see Giovanni Sartori, "Politics, Ideology, and Belief Systems," *American Political Science Review*, 63, 2 (June 1969): 398–411. We cannot begin to describe the extension of the literature in the problem of the definition of ideology. David W. Minar produced a fairly complete catalogue of definitions in "Ideology and Political Behavior," *Midwest Journal of Political Science*, 5, 4 (November 1961): 317–331. See also the bibliography in David E. Apter (ed.), *Ideology and Discontent* (New York: David McKay, 1969), pp. 329–34.

2 For an example of this type of conceptualization, see Clifford Geertz, "Ideology as a Cultural System," in Apter, *Ideology and Discontent*, pp. 47–92.

3 For illustration, see Minar, "Ideology and Political Behavior."

4 Notably Milton Rokeach, *The Open and Closed Mind* (New York: Basic Books, 1960).

5 William T. Bluhm, *Ideologies and Political Attitudes: Modern Political Culture* (Englewood Cliffs, N.J.: Prentice-Hall, 1974), p. 5.

6 More cogently expressed by Philip E. Converse in "The Nature of Belief Systems in Mass Publics," in Apter, *Ideology and Discontent*, pp. 206–61.

7 David J. Finlay et al., "The Concept of Left and Right in Cross-National Research," *Comparative Political Studies*, 7, 2 (July 1974): 209–21.

8 J. A. Laponce, "Note on the Use of the Left-Right Dimension,"
   Comparative Political Studies, 6, 4 (January 1970): 481–502.
9 Oficina de Estudios Económicos, *¿Qué piensan los marginados?* (Caracas: Gráfica Americana, C.A., n.d.), p. 43.
10 Computed from José A. Silva Michelena, *The Politics of
   Change in Venezuela, Vol. III: The Illusion of Democracy in
   Dependent Nations* (Cambridge, Mass.: M.I.T. Press, 1971),
   table 5.8 and pp. 140–41.
11 The two different sets of questions included a "leftist" and a
   "rightist" battery of Likert-type (complete agreement, agree-
   ment, indifferent, opposed, and definitely opposed) items.
   The leftist battery included:
   The state should immediately nationalize the oil firms.
   Foreign companies should become the property of the Ven-
   ezuelan state.
   The state should be the owner of all industries.
   The state should control the price of land and the value of
   dwellings.
   The rightist set of questions included:
   The state should give less money for agrarian reform.
   The state should not regulate wages.
   Venezuela should only trade with Western (nonsocialist) coun-
   tries.
   Agrarian reform should be carried out only on state lands.
   The influence of political parties in unions should be eliminated.
   The administration of all industries including those of the state
   should remain in private hands.
   The mean value of the responses given by every individual to
   the rightist and leftist set of questions were computed separately, and the two sets of means were compared to form the
   types, ibid., p. 141. We thought about including some or all of
   these items in our questionnaire, but two considerations militated against such inclusion. First, there seemed to be a consensus of opinion about the nationalization of the oil and iron industries when we went to the field in the autumn of 1973. Only 23
   of our respondents (or 1.5 per cent of the sample) mentioned oil
   as a problem of national importance at the time of our survey.
   So at least two of the four questions included in the batteries
   referred to what had become *valence* issues or issues reflecting
   desiderata of broad majorities. The other such issue, the question of agrarian reform, was not attracting as much interest in
   1973 as it did in the early sixties (3.4 per cent of our respondents

mentioned agriculture as the most important problem among those of national scope).

Given the fact that we could not faithfully replicate the CENDES-MIT approach, we decided to measure the left-right continuum in more direct fashion. The second consideration was that given the differences in the nature of the sampling plans of the CENDES-MIT study and our own, we could not realistically expect to replicate their findings. The best we could do was use those items of their instrument that had been shown to be capable of measuring important distinctions between the respondents. Given our limitations of space and the attention we wanted to give to campaign participation, we did not have much choice.

12 Enrique A. Baloyra and John D. Martz, "Political Attitudes in Venezuela, A Report to the National Science Foundation," manuscript (Chapel Hill, N.C., 1976), p. 178.

13 Anthony Downs assumed that the "content" of the left-right dimension was ideological and that, in the North American case, the space of the dimension was occupied by the distribution of opinion about government intervention in the economy; see *An Economic Theory of Democracy* (New York: Harper and Brothers, 1957). In short, Downs' assumption is that self-placement on the continuum and choice of economic system are relatively congruent. Donald Stokes has taken issue with this interpretation through the last decade on the grounds that (1) political conflict is generally multidimensional, (2) the spaces on which parties compete can be of highly variable structure, (3) parties may not be able to adopt different stands on some of the more relevant and desirable goals demanded by the public, and (4) party leaders and followers do not necessarily utilize the same frame of reference; see "Spatial Models of Party Competition," in Angus Campbell et al., *Elections and the Political Order* (New York: John Wiley and Sons, 1966), chapter 9. This controversy is relevant to our discussion, because we will combine self-placement on the ideological continuum with what could be construed as "opinion about the right amount of government intervention in the economy" (choice between communism, socialism, and capitalism as optimal economic systems for Venezuela). We are not following Downs to the letter on this, although we believe his interpretation to be extremely useful. Instead, our position is closer to that of Barnes, who contended that it was possible to conceptualize the space of the left-right continuum as "open"; see Samuel H. Barnes, "Left,

Right, and the Italian Voter," *Comparative Political Studies*, 4, 2 (July 1971): 157–75.

14 In his secondary analysis of data about the North American electorate, Converse concludes that only 17 per cent of the public recognized the "key ideological" distinctions between "liberal" and "conservative" labels; 37 per cent could perceive the distinctions between "liberal" and "conservative" labels; 37 per cent could perceive the distinctions vaguely, while the remaining 46 per cent "demonstrates considerable uncertainty and guesswork in assigning meaning to the terms," "The Nature of Belief Systems in Mass Publics," p. 223. A dissenting interpretation is offered by Norman H. Nie and Kristi Andersen in "Mass Belief Systems Revisited: Political Change and Attitude Structure," *Journal of Politics*, 36, 3 (August 1974): 540–91.

15 We ran a set of exploratory, preliminary comparisons between the different groups of respondents who had been able to make a choice of any pairs of labels. These comparisons indicated to us the tremendous similarity between the *leftist capitalists* and the *centrist capitalists*.

Given the relatively reduced number of respondents who made pairs of choices, selecting one alternative from each continuum (723 all told), we were anxious to increase the number of individuals whom we could fit into a particular ideological category. At first, we thought that ideological groups based on two labels would turn out to be more consistent than those based on a single label (a single selection from either continuum). This was not the case and, as a matter of fact, the position and preference of some of the single-label groups were as consistent, if not more so, than the position of the double-label groups.

After all, someone who selects the label *socialist* or *leftist* may not see much value in adding the other as a qualifier. So we do not assume in the analysis that, for instance, a *leftist socialist* is more consistent than a *socialist* or a *leftist* in adopting a leftist position on most issues.

In forming aggregates with these possible combinations of choices we made two decisions that could be construed as arbitrary. First, we deleted all nonleftist communists (center and rightist communists) from any further consideration on the grounds that the only admissible choices in this respect were either *communists* (without any choice of self-placement) or *leftist communists*. The second decision was to combine *leftist capitalists* and *centrist capitalists* into a single category (*leftists and centrist capitalists*). The reason for this combination

stemmed from similarities that we found between the two
groups through a series of comparisons.

16 Philip E. Converse and Roy Pierce, "Basic Cleavages in French
Politics and the Disorders of May and June, 1968," paper delivered at the Seventh World Congress of Sociology, Varna, Bul-
garia, September 1970, p. 5, emphasis added.

17 Our usage of constraint conforms to Converse's (functional
interdependence)—see "The Nature of Belief Systems in Mass
Publics," p. 207.

18 Samuel H. Barnes, "Ideology and the Organization of
Conflict," *Journal of Politics*, 28 (August 1966): 513–30, reprinted in Norman J. Vig and Rodney P. Steifbold (eds.), *Politics in Advanced Nations* (Englewood Cliffs, N.J.: Prentice-
Hall, 1974), pp. 409–24.

19 David Butler and Donald Stokes, *Political Change in Britain*,
college edition (New York: St. Martin's Press, 1971), p. 209.

20 See note 14. See also Angus Campbell et al., *The American
Voter* (New York: John Wiley and Sons, 1960). For the French
case, see Philip E. Converse and Georges Dupeux, "Politicization of the Electorate in France and the United States," in Angus
Campbell et al., *Elections and the Political Order*, pp. 269–91.
For Italy, see Samuel H. Barnes, "Participation, Education,
and Political Competence: Evidence from a Sample of Italian
Socialists," *American Political Science Review*, 60, 2 (June
1966): 348–54.

21 David Eugene Blank, *Politics in Venezuela*, p. 165. Blank's
interpretation is especially ambiguous. On the one hand he
points out that both the AD and COPEI have functioned primarily as electoral machines (pp. 172–73), but he argues that
COPEI has moved to the left and AD to the right (p. 138), and
COPEI's internal ideological diversity has threatened party
unity (p. 170). Thus, he does not produce a clear picture of the
influence of ideology on the party system as such, the different
parties, their elites, or the connection between party identification and ideology at the level of the mass public.

22 Daniel H. Levine, *Conflict and Political Change in Venezuela*
(Princeton, N.J.: Princeton University Press, 1973), p. 59.
Levine argues that three distinct ideological tendencies can be
observed in contemporary Venezuela: (1) the "New National
Ideal," a Venezuelan version of bureaucratic authoritarianism
promoted by General Pérez Jiménez and a host of right-wing
politicians; (2) the "establishment reformism" of the dominant
parties; and (3) "revolutionary leftist ideology," ibid., pp.

58–59. Although not entirely confirmed by our findings, Levine's scheme has considerable value.

23 Humberto Njaim et al., *El sistema político venezolano* (Caracas: Instituto de Estudios Políticos, 1975), pp. 20–22.

24 Juan Carlos Rey, "El sistema de partidos venezolano," *Politeia*, 1 (1973): 175–230.

25 For a discussion of our use of these techniques, see appendix G.

26 See appendix G for a discussion concerning the validity of the three-dimensional solution.

27 James W. Prothro and Patricio E. Chaparro, "Public Opinion and the Movement of Chilean Government to the Left, 1952–72," *Journal of Politics*, 36, 1 (February 1974): 2–43.

28 "Politics, Ideology, and Belief Systems," p. 403.

29 "Basic Cleavages in French Politics," pp. 3–5.

30 "Politics, Ideology, and Belief Systems," pp. 408 and 411.

31 See "Issue Conflict and Issue Consensus among Party Leaders and Followers," *American Political Science Review*, 54, 2 (June 1960): 406–27.

32 From Willard A. Mullins, "Sartori's Concept of Ideology: A Dissent and Alternative," in Allen R. Wilcox (ed.), *Public Opinion and Political Attitudes* (New York: John Wiley and Sons, 1974), pp. 223–37.

33 See "Studying Elite Political Culture: The Case of 'Ideology,'" *American Political Science Review*, 65, 3 (September 1971): 651–81.

34 "Sartori's Concept of Ideology," pp. 236–37.

35 Robert E. Lane, *Political Ideology: Why the American Common Man Believes What He Does* (New York: Free Press, 1962), p. 16.

36 Defended very persuasively by Philip Converse in "Public Opinion and Voting Behavior," chapter 2 in Fred I. Greenstein and Nelson W. Polsby (eds.), *Handbook of Political Science, Vol. IV: Non-governmental Politics* (Reading, Mass.: Addison-Wesley, 1975), especially pp. 86–89.

37 Illustrated by the work of Lane, *Political Ideology*, among others.

38 See Federico G. Gil et al., *Chile 1970–1973: Lecciones de una experiencia* (Madrid: Editorial Tecnos, 1977), especially parts 1 and 2.

39 See Philippe C. Schmitter, "La Europa Latina y las 'lecciones' de Chile," in Gil, *Chile 1970–1973*, pp. 343–58.

40 We have analyzed these in some detail in John D. Martz and Enrique A. Baloyra, *Electoral Mobilization and Public Opin-*

ion: The Venezuelan Campaign of 1973 (Chapel Hill: University of North Carolina Press, 1976), pp. 198–201.

41 See Schmitter, "La Europa Latina." See also Alan J. Stern, "Una alternativa al ejercicio del poder nacional: el Partido Comunista Italiano y el Compromiso Histórico," in Gil, *Chile 1970–1973*, pp. 439–46.

42 *The Eighteenth Brumaire of Louis Bonaparte*, fourth printing (New York: International Publishers, 1968), chapter 7.

43 For an interpretation of the coup from a leftist point of view, see Domingo Alberto Rangel, *Los andinos en el poder: Balance de una hegemonía, 1899–1945* (Mérida: Talleres Gráficos Universitarios, 1965), pp. 303–29.

44 See Domingo Alberto Rangel, *La revolución de las fantasías* (Caracas: Ediciones Ofidi, 1966), chapters 7, 8, and 9.

45 "Sartori's Concept of Ideology," p. 237.

46 See Teodoro Petkoff, *¿Socialismo para Venezuela?* (Caracas: Editorial Fuentes, 1972).

47 For an illustration, see J. R. Núñez Tenorio, *El carácter de la revolución venezolana* (Caracas: Editorial Crítica Marxista, 1969).

48 The article forbids the death penalty in Venezuela.

49 Such was the argument of José Vicente Rangel, who in November 1966 accused the *adeco* administration of covering up the death of Alberto Lovera, a communist leader, who had been tortured to death by police investigators. See his *Expediente negro* (Caracas: Editorial Domingo Fuentes, 1969).

50 Analyzing the results of the election of 1973, Américo Martín, a leader of the Movimiento de Izquierda Revolucionaria (MIR) wrote: "The *copeyano* alternative was grounded on the hope of the continuity of the system, but on the attempt to avoid the most acute confrontations. COPEI offered itself as a compromise solution: the only [party] capable of maintaining order while securing the compliance of the Left. . . ." "1973, ¿Victoria o derrota?" in Federico Alvarez et al., *La izquierda venezolana y las elecciones del 73, (Un análisis político y polémico)* (Caracas: Síntesis Dos Mil, 1974), p. 150.

51 The PCV and MIR were illegal at the time of the 1963 election; MIR's status had not changed by the time of the 1968 contest. Legalization of MIR was one of the aspects of the pacification program of COPEI.

52 For the standard critique, see Guillermo García Ponce, *Teoría política y realidad nacional* (Caracas: Editorial La Muralla,

1967), pp. 61–66. A more complex and sophisticated treatment is found in Domingo Alberto Rangel, *Los mercaderes del voto: Estudio de un sistema* (Valencia: Ediplan, C.A., 1973), especially chapter 7.

53 See the series of essays preceding the 1973 election by José Vicente Rangel, *Tiempo de Verdades* (Caracas: Ediciones Centauro, 1973). Rangel, of course, was not a disinterested observer, but his arguments reflect the deep concern of the Venezuelan left with the question of unity, as well as the fact that the establishment parties overwhelmed all other participants with their machines and economic resources.

54 See the essays in Alvarez, *La izquierda venezolana*.

55 Lane, *Political Ideology*, p. 177.

56 *A Framework for Political Analysis* (Englewood Cliffs, N.J.: Prentice-Hall, 1965).

57 Gabriel A. Almond and Sidney Verba, *The Civic Culture, Political Attitudes and Democracy in Five Nations* (Boston: Little, Brown and Co., 1965).

58 Ibid., p. 196.

59 *Power and Discontent* (Homewood, Ill.: Dorsey Press, 1968).

60 Mitchell A. Seligson, "Trust, Efficacy and Modes of Political Participation," revised version of a paper delivered at the Annual Meeting of the Southwestern Political Science Association, Dallas, Texas, March 1977, pp. 3–14.

61 Richard Simeon and David J. Elkins, "Regional Political Cultures in Canada," *Canadian Journal of Political Science*, 7, 3 (September 1974), p. 409.

62 See Seligson, "Trust, Efficacy and Modes of Political Participation."

63 Compare the Kendall coefficients of figures 10 and 18 and table III-3.

64 We are aware that one of the problems with operational measures combining trust and efficacy is that, when the four categories are put on a single dimension, this will reflect one of the two. That is, the results that one may obtain utilizing the measure will parallel those for the one measure which divides the dimension into two ranges. For example, in our case the highest value is for critics, the lowest for supporters. Intermediate values are for discontents (3) and deferents (2). Thus, the dimension tends to emphasize the evaluative aspect, although going through different levels of capacity.

65 We have presented a more complete set of results in this table

than in others to facilitate evaluation of the pattern of differences by the reader. However, we follow the same rationale discussed in appendix E.

66 This refers to instances in which the categories of one or more variables are too numerous, resulting in too many empty cells when these are cross-tabulated with others. The fact that we can measure individual ideology in terms of three, six, or twelve categories allows us to use that particular measure which best fits the situation.

67 "Sartori's Concept of Ideology."

68 See Downs, *An Economic Theory of Democracy*, pp. 114–41.

69 See Finlay et al., "The Concept of Left and Right in Cross-National Research."

70 Converse and Dupeux, "Politicization of the Electorate in France and the United States."

71 One of the more interesting exercises is J. A. Laponce, "In Search of the Stable Elements of the Left-Right Landscape," *Comparative Politics*, 4, 4 (July 1972): 455–502. For an example with Venezuelan respondents, see notes 10 and 11, above.

72 "Politicization of the Electorate in France and the United States," p. 11, emphasis added.

73 See chapter 3.

74 In a previous effort we tested the stability of the constraining impact of ideology, controlling for religiosity, region, size of community of residence, stratification, generation, gender role, and group identification. We did not find a single instance in which the relationship between ideological tendency and a vast array of attitudinal factors was reduced or proved nonsignificant by the introduction of controls. See Baloyra and Martz, "Political Attitudes in Venezuela," table V-1, p. 173.

75 "Left, Right, and the Italian Voter," pp. 158–59.

76 Stokes, "Spatial Models of Party Competition," pp. 170–74. See also note 13.

77 See note 74.

78 "Politicization of the Electorate in France and the United States," p. 8.

Notes to Chapter 6

Partisanship in Venezuelan Politics

1 For discussion and commentary, see Robert J. Alexander, *The Venezuelan Democratic Revolution* (New Brunswick, N.J.: Rutgers University Press, 1964); Glen L. Kolb, *Democracy and Dictatorship in Venezuela, 1945–1958* (New London: Connecticut College, 1974); and Manuel Vicente Magallanes, *Los partidos políticos en la evolución histórica de Venezuela* (Caracas: Editorial Mediterráneo, 1973).
2 See Federico Alvarez et al., *La izquierda venezolana y las elecciones del 73*; Juan Carlos Rey, "El sistema de partidos venezolano," *Politeia*, 1 (1972): 174–230.
3 See Robert J. Alexander, *The Communist Party of Venezuela* (Stanford, Calif.: Hoover Institute Press, 1969); Rubén Carpio Castillo, *Acción Democrática, 1941–1971: Bosquejo histórico de un partido* (Caracas: Ediciones República, 1971); Iván Claudio, *Breve historia de URD* (Caracas: n.p., 1968); Manuel Vicente Magallanes, *Cuatro partidos nacionales* (Caracas: Editorial Diana, 1973); John D. Martz, *Acción Democrática: Evolution of a Modern Political Party in Venezuela* (Princeton: Princeton University Press, 1966); José Elías Rivera Oviedo, *Los social cristianos en Venezuela* (Caracas: n.p., 1969); and Juan Bautista Rojas, *Los adecos* (Caracas: Editorial Fuentes, 1973).
4 Daniel H. Levine, *Conflict and Political Change in Venezuela* (Princeton: Princeton University Press, 1973), p. 8, emphasis added.
5 Rey, "El systema de partidos venezolano," p. 206.
6 Humberto Njaim et al., *El sistema político venezolano* (Caracas: Editorial Arte, Instituto de Estudios Políticos, 1975), pp. 17–18.
7 Rey, "El sistema de partidos venezolano," p. 201.
8 Ibid., p. 206.
9 Njaim et al., *El sistema político venezolano*, p. 20.
10 Talton F. Ray, *The Politics of the Barrios of Venezuela* (Berkeley and Los Angeles: University of California Press, 1969), p. 103.

11 John Duncan Powell, *Political Mobilization of the Venezuelan Peasant* (Cambridge, Mass.: Harvard University Press, 1971), p. 121.

12 The concept of party identification was introduced first by George Belknap and Angus Campbell in "Political Party Identification and Attitudes toward Foreign Policy," *Public Opinion Quarterly*, 15 (Winter 1952): 601–23.

13 As defined by Angus Campbell and his associates in *The American Voter*, abridged edition, third printing (New York: John Wiley and Sons, 1964), pp. 67–68, emphasis added.

14 For an illustration of this way of thinking, see David Eugene Blank, *Politics in Venezuela* (Boston: Little, Brown and Co., 1973), pp. 127–28.

15 Ray, *The Politics of the Barrios of Venezuela*, pp. 103–105, and Powell, *Political Mobilization of the Venezuelan Peasant*, allude to this fact in their treatment. In Blank's case, he seems to have generalized from Powell's conclusions about clientelism to the system at large.

16 See David R. Heise, *Causal Analysis* (New York: John Wiley and Sons, 1975), p. 111.

17 See Kolb, *Democracy and Dictatorship in Venezuela, 1945–1958*, chapters 4 and 5.

18 Levine, *Conflict and Political Change in Venezuela*, chapter 3.

19 We refer here to the customary fashion in which party identification questions are phrased by researchers in the United States: "Generally speaking, do you think of yourself as a Republican, a Democrat, an Independent, or what?" Those adopting a party label are asked: "Would you call yourself a strong (Republican, Democrat) or not a very strong (Republican, Democrat)?" Those identifying themselves as Independents are asked: "Do you think of yourself as closer to the Republican or Democratic Party?" Notice that while self-professed partisans are probed about their intensity, the Independents are asked to think in spatial terms.

20 See appendix B, items 13 and 19.

21 Our concept of political self-image is more inclusive than Butler and Stokes' "partisan self-image," which they define as "a generalized partisan inclination . . . [or] lasting sense of being a supporter of a given party." See David Butler and Donald Stokes, *Political Change in Britain*, college edition (New York: St. Martin's Press, 1971), pp. 26–27.

22 See Enrique A. Baloyra and John D. Martz, "Political Attitudes

in Venezuela, A Preliminary Report to the National Science Foundation," manuscript (Chapel Hill, N.C., 1976), p. 284.

23 As follows: 1 = MEP, 2 = MAS, 3 = NONE, 4 = AD, 5 = COPEI, 6 = OTHER.

24 See figure 20.

25 See figure 20(A).

26 See figure 20(B).

27 For an illustration, see Herbert F. Weisberg and Jerrold G. Rusk, "Dimensions of Candidate Evaluation," *American Political Science Review*, 64, 4 (December 1970): 1167–85.

28 This is reported with unquestioned insistence by researchers exploring partisanship and/or voting behavior in the United States. Indicative of what perhaps represents the more sophisticated statement of this line of analysis is Philip E. Converse, "Public Opinion and Voting Behavior," chapter 2 in Fred I. Greenstein and Nelson W. Polsby (eds.), *Handbook of Political Science, Vol. 4: Non-governmental Politics* (Reading, Mass.: Addison-Wesley, 1975), p. 169.

29 See Martz, *Acción Democrática*; also Levine, *Conflict and Political Change in Venezuela*.

30 Since MAS, MEP, and CCN are of very recent vintage, we included the attitudinal component in the regression analyses in order to determine which aspect of the system alienated the supporters of these parties the most.

31 Nominal identifications, electoral polarization between AD and COPEI, and "thermometer feelings" are some of the alternative operational measures which we have explored and found to produce results congruent with those presented here. Our contention is that the latter are based on a more rigorous operational treatment of the concept of partisanship.

32 See John D. Martz and Enrique A. Baloyra, *Electoral Mobilization and Public Opinion: The Venezuelan Campaign of 1973* (Chapel Hill: University of North Carolina Press, 1976), chapter 8.

33 Martz has utilized this categorization in previous work; see *Acción Democrática*, chapter 12, and appendix B, p. 411.

34 From David J. Myers, "Urban Voting, Structural Cleavages, and Party System Evolution," *Comparative Politics*, 8, 1 (October 1975): 119–51.

35 David Eugene Blank, *Politics in Venezuela* (Boston: Little, Brown, and Co., 1973), pp. 155–83.

36 For two recent examples, see the essays in Alvarez et al., *La*

izquierda venezolano; and José Rodríguez Iturbe et al., *Polarización y bipartidismo en las elecciones de 1973* (Caracas: Editorial Arte, 1974).

37 This term was utilized by Juan Carlos Rey in referring to the two centers of the system, without at least one of which no winning coalition can be established. See Rey, "El sistema de partidos venezolano," p. 224.

Notes to Appendixes

Appendix A

1   See John D. Martz and Enrique A. Baloyra, *Electoral Mobilization and Public Opinion: The Venezuelan Campaign of 1973* (Chapel Hill, N.C.: University of North Carolina Press, 1976).
2   For a discussion of unemployment in Venezuela, see Mostafa F. Hassan, *Economic Growth and Employment Problems in Venezuela: An Analysis of an Oil Based Economy* (New York: Praeger, 1975) and also Victor E. Childers, *Human Resources Development: Venezuela* (Bloomington, Indiana: International Development Research Center, 1974), chapter 1.
3   For one of the many adequate discussions in the literature, see A. N. Oppenheim, *Questionnaire Design and Attitude Measurement* (New York: Basic Books, 1966), pp. 69–78.
4   The crux of the question of reliability was well put by Charles H. Backstrom and Gerald D. Hursh, who wrote that "the reliability of survey findings is proportionate to the rigor exercised at each step in assembling and interpreting the data." See *Survey Research*, third printing (Evanston, Illinois: Northwestern University Press, 1963), p. 5.
5   See Gabriel A. Almond and Sidney Verba, *The Civic Culture: Political Attitudes and Democracy in Five Nations*, third printing (Boston: Little, Brown and Co., 1965).

Appendix D

1   Richard D. McKelvey and William Zavonia, "A Statistical Model for the Analysis of Ordinal Level Dependent Variables," mimeo, revised (May 1973).
2   See Sidney Verba and Norman H. Nie, *Participation in America, Political Democracy and Social Equality* (New York: Harper and Row, 1972), appendix G, "Some Methodological Notes on Our Use of Parametric Statistics," pp. 403–409.
3   See Norman H. Nie et al., *SPSS, Statistical Package for the*

Social Sciences, second edition (New York: McGraw-Hill, 1975), chapter 20.
4 Otis Dudley Duncan, Introduction to Structural Equation Models (New York: Academic Press, 1975).
5 Jae-On Kim and Frank J. Kohout, "Special Topics in General Linear Models," in Nie et al., SPSS, chapter 21.
6 John P. Van de Geer, Introduction to Multivariate Analysis for the Social Sciences (San Francisco: W. H. Freeman and Co., 1971).

Appendix E

1 Jerome C. R. Li, Statistical Inference, A Non-Mathematical Exposition of the Theory of Statistics, Vol. 1 (Ann Arbor, Michigan: Edward Brothers, 1965), pp. 272–73 (emphasis added).
2 George W. Snedecor, Statistical Methods Applied to Experiments in Agriculture and Biology, fifth edition, eighth printing (Ames: Iowa State University Press, 1966), in his discussion on pp. 254–56.

Appendix G

1 See George Rabinowitz, "A Method for Recovering a Joint Space from Thermometer Data," mimeo, 1972, for a discussion of the rationale and assumptions. The notions of minimum sum and maximum difference seem to provide the strongest defense for the validity of the algorithm.
2 See his "An Introduction to Nonmetric Multidimensional Scaling," American Journal of Political Science, 19 (May 1975): 343–90.
3 There are two different sets of criteria to evaluate the magnitudes of Stress, depending on whether we are referring to Stress I or II.

Subject Index

Author Index

297